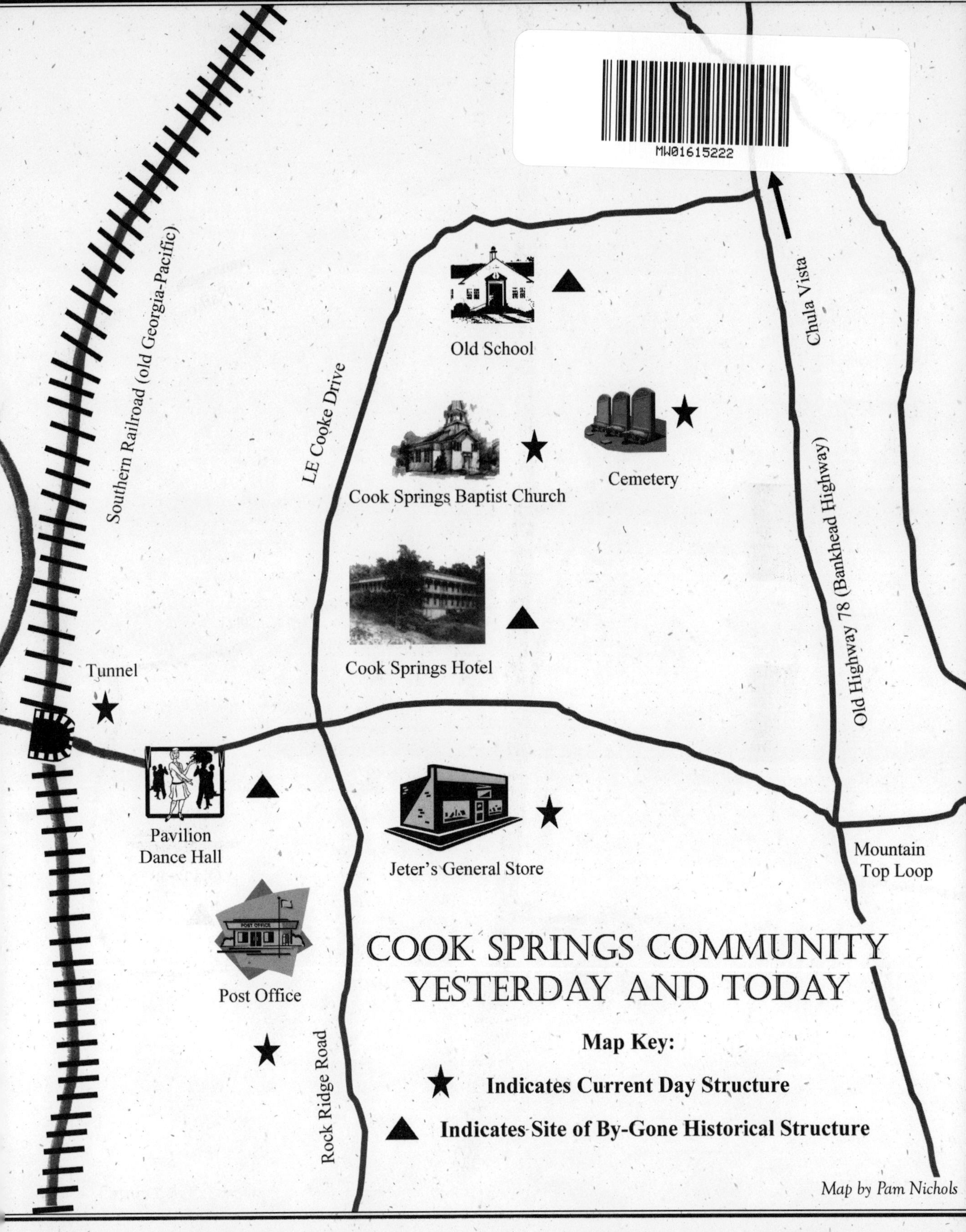

COOK SPRINGS COMMUNITY YESTERDAY AND TODAY

Map Key:

★ **Indicates Current Day Structure**

▲ **Indicates Site of By-Gone Historical Structure**

Map by Pam Nichols

The Village and Its Neighbors

THE VILLAGE AND ITS NEIGHBORS

A History of the Village at Cook Springs and Its Surroundings

ANITA SMITH

Noland Health Services, Inc.
Birmingham, Alabama

Produced for
Noland Health Services, Inc.
600 Corporate Parkway, Suite 100
Birmingham AL 35242

By NewSouth Books
P.O. Box 1588
Montgomery, AL 36102

Cataloging-in-Publication Data
ISBN-13: 978-0-9791343-0-2
ISBN-10: 0-9791343-0-7

Design by Randall Williams
Printed in the United States of America

For information concerning this book, contact:
Executive Director
Village at Cook Springs
415 Cook Springs Road
Cook Springs, Alabama 35052
Telephone: (205) 338-2221
www.villageatcooksprings.com

To Leon C. Hamrick, Sr., M.D.,

who has become a symbol of compassion and quality care

Contents

Foreword

It is with honor and pleasure that I welcome readers to this book that traces the rich history of a delightful senior-living campus known as the Village at Cook Springs.

As board chairman for Noland Health Services, Inc., which operates the Village at Cook Springs, I gladly participate with our administration and the Village's staff in inviting you to join us in celebrating this history.

This is a history that goes back to the 1800s era of a grand mineral-springs resort and hotel that operated in the quaint community of Cook Springs in St. Clair County, one of the oldest counties in Alabama.

On a personal note, I want to share with you why the Village at Cook Springs and the community of Cook Springs in which it is located have touched such strong positive chords with me.

First of all, Cook Springs reminds me of my wonderful childhood. When I visit Cook Springs, I think back to the warmth and love I felt from friends, family and neighbors when I was growing up in the North Georgia community of Ludville, in the foothills of the Blue Ridge Mountains. Just like where I grew up, Cook Springs is cradled in a mountainous, wooded area with almost unbelievable natural beauty. And, just like where I grew up, the people in Cook Springs care about the folks around them and take care of one another. That is true in the community of Cook Springs as a whole. It is true at the Village at Cook Springs.

Secondly, the senior-care mission at the Village at Cook Springs brings home to me insights about senior care that I gained as a physician and surgeon. In practicing medicine in the Birmingham area for a half century, I specialized in general surgery and also did a great deal of family practice. My patients during those 50-plus years included many, many senior citizens. If there is one thing I learned about seniors, it's that so many of them have stamina and determination beyond what we can easily imagine.

I'll give you some examples. Toward the end of my medical practice, I was still seeing a lot of patients in a clinic setting. And I had three very memorable patients to come see me within a short span of time. Now, what's interesting about these three patients in the context of this book about a senior-care institution is that each of these patients was 96 years old. Another thing that's interesting is that all three of these patients walked in to see me under their own power, and all three of them walked out under their own power. At age 96, they were still mobile, still active.

To me, those three patients are in a sense symbolic of the longevity we are seeing in our society, and they are symbolic of how active many of our seniors continue to be in their 80s and 90s and even beyond. The Village at Cook Springs is one of our Noland Health Services institutions that are dedicated to helping seniors be as active as possible as long as possible, and also dedicated to caring for seniors when they no longer can be as active as they once were. I salute that mission, and I am very proud to be a part of that mission.

Thirdly, I can very much identify with Noland Health Services' mission to take care of senior citizens because I am one of those senior citizens. I'm proud to say that I celebrated my 81st birthday in November 2006. For me, it is both a joy and a privilege to be able to share my experiences and philosophies about senior care with these highly capable younger men and women in the management team of Noland Health Services, Inc. Since I've been blessed to live this long, I can look at many aspects of care from the points of view of both a physician and a senior citizen. Since I have those perspectives, it pleases me all the more to introduce this book about the history of the Village at Cook Springs. I feel that I personally understand the needs of seniors, and I'm proud of how the Village and our other Noland Health Services facilities are meeting those needs. Also, I can look at Noland Health Services' programs through the eyes of a family member. My beloved late wife, Bunny, was served by some of Noland Health Services' fine programs and greatly benefited.

On a fourth note, I'm particularly proud to introduce this book because in so doing I feel somewhat like a representative of the late Lloyd Noland, M.D., the famous, caring physician for whom Noland Health Services, Inc., is named. Although I never had the opportunity to meet Dr. Noland, throughout my medical career I have been associated with various healthcare and lifestyle programs that were either founded or inspired by this pioneer in public health and health-delivery systems. It was four years after Dr. Noland died in 1949 when I joined programs he had founded. Dr. Noland would be proud of the Village at Cook Springs and its sister facilities and programs in Noland Health Services, Inc. Those facilities and programs meet the standards of Dr. Lloyd Noland, and Dr. Noland's standards indeed were high.

Finally, I'm very proud to introduce this book of history because I strongly believe in recording and learning from history. As you read this book, you will be reading about several outstanding entities whose destinies intersect. You'll read about the history of the groundbreaking county of St. Clair, the quaint and delightful community of Cook Springs, the magnificent late-1800s and early-1900s mineral-springs resort centered by the Cook's Springs Hotel, and the caring and competent long-term-care institution now known as the Village at Cook Springs.

As you read, I believe that time and again you will encounter individuals and achievements that will fill you with both warmth and admiration.

Reviewing this fine history is truly an inspiration to me. It makes me feel good about the past in Cook Springs, Alabama, and it makes me feel excited about the future. You see, I agree with the historian who said we must learn about our past because our past is a prologue to our future. If that is true, and I believe it is, the pioneering past that is recorded in this book is presenting us with a preview of a bright and promising future in Cook Springs, Alabama.

LEON C. HAMRICK, SR., M.D.
Chairman, Board of Directors
Noland Health Services, Inc.

Birmingham, Alabama, 2007

The Village and Its Neighbors

Section One

~

A Mineral-Springs Hotel Resort

Patsy Lewis Carter, left, at around age 12, waiting at the Cook's Springs Hotel train stop with an unidentified female guest. The photo is from the 1920s, when her father, Preston H. Lewis, managed the hotel. Decades later, she became a resident of the Village at Cook Springs, a retirement community located near the site of the old hotel.

1

Making a Full Circle

*"If Da ddy could see that I'm living back here once again in beautiful Cook
Springs, I think he would say something like, 'Well, Patsy, you've made a
full circle!' "–Patsy Carter, resident, Village at Cook Springs*

On a clear, sunny morning in April 2005, Patsy Lewis Carter sat in
her favorite chair near a large window facing a beautiful countryside
view. The room was filled with sunlight, and also with animated
chatter and laughter. Mrs. Carter was in her own tastefully furnished home
in these serene surroundings. On that morning, 93-year-old Mrs. Carter was
entertaining her guests with memories of her childhood and with stories
about fun-filled activities that made up her current busy life.

In the case of Mrs. Carter, both her childhood and modern-day stories
had the makings of history — a part of the fascinating history of a community
called Cook Springs, in St. Clair County, Alabama.

Mrs. Carter was one of those who could speak of the Cook Springs history in two eras. She could recall it in days gone by, when Cook Springs
was the site of a regal, much-written-about mineral-springs resort featuring
a stately hotel.

Mrs. Carter also could speak with personal knowledge of the modern-
day Cook Springs, which had as one of its features a sprawling senior-living
community known as the Village at Cook Springs.

Patsy Carter could speak of Cook Springs' bygone hotel era because during

A snowy front view of the Cook's Springs Hotel, which opened in the 1880s. Note railroad tracks in foreground.

her childhood years in the 1920s she lived in the hotel — and, she hastened to add with a laugh, *worked* at the hotel. This was during a time when her father was operating the well-known hotel through a lease arrangement with the hotel's founder, LaFayette Cooke.

And, Mrs. Carter could speak of today's life in the Village at Cook Springs, because she was a resident of that senior-living community. A widow, Mrs. Carter had returned after years away from the Cook Springs area, including experience living in various locales with her husband, who was an Army officer and later a teacher.

The senior-living community where Mrs. Carter made her home in her 90s was located less than a half-mile from the popular resort hotel where she had lived as a child. In fact, the wooded acreage on which the senior-living community was located was a part of the large tract of acreage that resort developer LaFayette Cooke had owned dating back into the 1880s.

LaFayette Cooke's success with his hotel and mineral-springs resort,

Back view of the old hotel.

plus the stunning beauty of the woods and the mountains in the area, had attracted Mrs. Carter's father to become the proprietor during a fast-paced period in the nation's history that included the Roaring Twenties.

"If Daddy could see that I'm living back here once again in beautiful Cook Springs, I think he would say something like, 'Well, Patsy, you've made a full circle!'"

2

A Young Girl's Love
for a Special Hotel

"It was my job to get the water and place it in all the hotel rooms for the guests during the summer."—Patsy Carter

As Patsy Carter let her mind travel back to the 1920s, she recalled a lifestyle in a mineral-springs hotel resort that was much like recalling a movie about high society and the good life.

In this case, young Patsy was on both sides of the fence. She was doing some work to make the good life possible for guests who vacationed at the mineral-springs hotel resort at Cook Springs. Also, Patsy was participating in some of that good life.

"Our big season at the hotel was the summertime," said Mrs. Carter. "We had some guests who would come one summer season and then they would come back the next season and the next. Some would stay at the hotel, and others would stay in the little cottages that were nearby. I recall when I was living there at the hotel that some of these same people came to the hotel one summer after another and brought their little families. I was able to watch their little families grow and to play with their children. I so enjoyed that.

"Then there were the dances. Near the hotel was a pavilion building. Downstairs in the pavilion were pumps used to get water from the springs.

20

On the pavilion's second floor was the area where they held the dances. Every Saturday night Daddy had a group of men that came and played musical instruments for the dancing. The people staying at the hotel and cottages would come to the dances, and local people who lived in Cook Springs would come, too.

"And I loved the trains. Oh, I did love the trains. In addition to the passenger trains, we had these freight trains that came through. I would wave at the train-men, and they got to know me. Sometimes they would give me a short train ride, just a short distance out where the train was coming up in front of the hotel. Then I would get off. But Daddy would have killed me if he had known I was doing that!"

Trains, Mineral Springs, and a Luxury Hotel

From the time this hotel was completed in Cook Springs in 1884, the good life at this resort revolved mostly around vacationers who traveled to the mineral-springs resort by train. The hotel was located at the train stop in Cook Springs, with a bridge connecting the hotel entrance to the railroad platform.

It was the building of the railroad through the Cook Springs area in the 1880s that inspired LaFayette Cooke to construct the two-story, 60-room hotel — a hotel that over the years was referred to alternately as the Cook's Springs Hotel, the Cooks Springs Hotel, the Cook Springs Hotel, or the Mountain View Hotel. The hotel opened just a few months after the railroad was completed through the Cook Springs area. This was a part of the Georgia Pacific Railway linkage (later Southern Railway) from Atlanta, Georgia, to Birmingham, Alabama, and on to points west.

No doubt another inspiration for building the hotel was the availability of naturally occurring mineral springs in the area. Vacationers came to partake of the water for its alleged health benefits.

LaFayette Cooke, founder of Mineral-Springs Hotel Resort in Cook Springs.

The concept of building hotel resorts was a popular one in that day and age. Some of these hotels were built near mineral springs, which became quite an attraction. Some other hotels were not near mineral springs, but they were near railroad stops. Other vacation hotels flourished around the nation with neither mineral springs nor train-stop convenience as a feature. In the case of LaFayette Cooke's Mountain View Hotel venture, he had all three things going in his favor — a hotel that was (1) a luxury facility, (2) located at a train stop, and (3) featuring mineral springs.

Patsy and the Hotel in Cook Springs

Patsy Carter recalled a Cook Springs hotel resort that still had some of the same amenities and challenges in the 1920s as it had when it opened in the 1880s. She recalled that it took a lot of work to keep it going, and Patsy was called on to handle some of the chores.

Some of her vivid hotel memories came from the time she was 11, 12 and 13 years of age. She had chores she didn't mind so much, and she had others she could have done without.

The Good Chore

One chore that wasn't bad at all for young Patsy was bringing springs-water to the guests.

"It was my job to get the water and place it in all the hotel rooms for the guests during the summer," she said. "I would get pitchers and fill them with water and take those pitchers of water back to the guests' rooms in the hotel. We had three kinds of water. There was the 'black sulphur water' and the 'white sulphur water' and then the 'freestone water.'"

She said both kinds of sulphur water looked alike, both clear, and both had a strong odor and a pungent taste — the black sulphur stronger than the white sulphur.

"Now, the freestone water was what everybody liked the best," she said. "But if I took the water into the rooms and let it stand awhile before the guests used it, enough evaporation took place that the sulphur water didn't seem to taste quite as bad."

The Bad Chore

As glamorous as the hotel was, there were some unglamorous sides. Typical of 1920s conditions in much of rural America (and in many urban areas as well), there was no running water at the hotel. This meant using rather primitive toilet facilities.

Among Patsy's chores was the cleaning of the hotel's two bathrooms. "The hotel had bathroom facilities built way down in the dirt," she said. "They kept some boxes of lye that people dropped down in there. But still it would get to smelling. And when it did, Daddy would have me go down and kind of tend to it. That was a chore I had that I hated. I really hated that!"

Getting to Know the People in the Area

In addition to operating the hotel and cottages, Patsy Carter's father also ran a grocery store/general store near the hotel, adjacent to the pavilion. "Also in Daddy's grocery store was the mail drop-off," she said. "There was a lady there who tended to the mail."

Mrs. Carter said it was in her father's grocery store where she got exposed to people living in and around Cook Springs who came to shop for groceries and other supplies.

"There would be people who lived in the Cook Springs area and other areas nearby — like up on a nearby mountain — who would come to Daddy's store maybe twice a year to stock up on groceries," she said. "I remember some of these local people walking through the downstairs area in the pavilion building, where the pumps were, to get to the grocery store. Some of those families had lots of kids. There was this one family I remember in particular that had so many kids; I just can't tell you how many kids they had! And I remember this mother who would come into Daddy's store and buy a whole bolt of material, of fabric, and the next time you saw the family all the girls in that family would have identical dresses made from that bolt of material."

Preston H. Lewis, 1920s hotel manager and founder of Chula Vista community.

Preston Lewis in Cook Springs and Chula Vista

When Patsy Carter's father decided to lease the hotel resort complex from LaFayette Cooke in the 1920s, that move was consistent with her dad's tendency to undertake diverse business ventures.

Patsy Carter's father was Preston H. Lewis, known to many as P.H. Lewis. He was a flamboyant, risk-taking, natural-born salesman and entrepreneur who became a well-known figure in the history of the Cook Springs-Chula Vista area of St. Clair County, Alabama.

Although he grew up in Alabama, Lewis in young adulthood became a vagabond and made his temporary home in states including Kentucky, West Virginia, Ohio, Texas, and New Mexico, before he returned home to Alabama. Through the decades, he was a commercial photographer, a rancher, a hotel proprietor, and the developer of a small community in St. Clair County (Chula Vista). He married three times. His second wife was Patsy Carter's mother, Ida.

"Daddy was a take-charge type of person," said Mrs. Carter. "For example, in his family he was always taking care of his older brothers. And, when it came to business, Daddy could always make something out of a business venture."

In St. Clair County, Lewis was known as an entrepreneur. After a few years of operating LaFayette Cooke's mineral-springs hotel resort in Cook Springs, Lewis ventured a few miles away to undertake the early development of a neighboring community he named Chula Vista.

"Daddy owned some property in the area that came to be called Chula Vista,' said Mrs. Carter. "Daddy just went up there on the mountain in the woods in Chula Vista and just started developing things. He named it Chula Vista because the name meant 'beautiful view.' When he first started building out in those woods, he built a grocery store. Well, everybody thought he had lost his mind building a grocery store way out in the woods like that.

And then the state people came through and put a road right in front of Daddy's grocery store. I always figured Daddy must have known someone in Montgomery who told him that road was coming."

The grocery was not the only business her dad built in Chula Vista. "Daddy also built this dance hall in Chula Vista," said Mrs. Carter. (Later, in the mid-1930s, the dance hall burned, and there also was much talk in the area about an unsolved murder of a man who apparently had rented the dance hall building for a time.)

"Now, I don't know anything about any murder. But I do know that this dance hall building Daddy had built caught on fire and burned up," said Mrs. Carter. "And I know from the start that some of the people around that area didn't like the idea of that dance hall being there because they didn't think people ought to be dancing. I've wondered if maybe it was some of them who disapproved who set the dance hall on fire. You see, Daddy already had been holding dances on Saturday nights at the pavilion next to the hotel at Cook Springs, and people in the community seemed all right with having those dances at the pavilion. But that dancing at the pavilion

Early 1930s view of country store in Chula Vista, founded by Preston H. Lewis.

had been going on a long time, back to when Mr. LaFayette Cooke ran the hotel, long before Daddy was involved. And people had gotten accustomed to dancing at the pavilion. Now, when Daddy opened that dance hall up in Chula Vista, having a real dance hall in the community was new to everybody. What he had up in Chula Vista was an actual dance hall, not just a pavilion next to a hotel. And I think some people felt like that kind of thing should not be part of their lives.

"In addition to the dance hall and the grocery, there was also this house on some property up there in Chula Vista that Daddy had bought. As I understand it, Daddy would invite some men over to play cards and gamble on the weekend. Daddy called that his 'clubhouse.'"

As time went by, Preston Lewis used his country store in Chula Vista as a centerpiece for a little community trading post that also included an "eating place," filling station, and soft-drink stand. He became proud that the area was beautified with flower beds and that it had a lovely windmill that also had a practical use of pumping water to houses in the area. Lewis sold off some of his property to attract other residents into the area. Preston Lewis became known to many as the "Father of Chula Vista."

Mrs. Carter said her father was proud of the Chula Vista community and very much believed in giving back to the community. "Even though Daddy didn't go to church himself, I know he donated some property to be used as a church-building site."

Leaving Cook Springs and Returning

Back in the mid-1920s, when Patsy Carter left Cook Springs the first time, she was around age 14. It was not her idea that she leave. It was her father's.

Her leaving Cook Springs was a sad memory — another memory in the life of a young girl who had known a lot of change.

Patsy and her younger brother, Forrest, lived at the Cook Springs hotel resort in a blended family situation. After Patsy and Forrest's parents had divorced, their mother began operating a boarding house in Birmingham. This was during the same period that their dad and his third wife, Alice, were operating the hotel complex in Cook Springs. For several years, Patsy and Forrest visited back and forth with their mother in Birmingham but spent most of their time in Cook Springs with their dad and Alice. The Lewis family in Cook Springs expanded when Alice gave birth to Patsy and Forrest's half-sister, Mary.

Very attached to Cook Springs — to the hotel life, to the community, and to teenage friends she had made there — young Patsy had no desire to leave. However, as she gained solid footing with her teenage years, her dad felt he could not deal with a strong-willed teenage daughter. The final straw came one day when Patsy sobbed uncontrollably after her dad told her she could not go to a school dance with a teenage boy who was a classmate. Although she would continue to feel a close bond with her father down through the years, she felt heartbroken when he sent her away from Cook Springs to boarding school (in a Catholic convent).

When she returned decades later to again reside in Cook Springs — as a resident in the Springs Manor assisted-living section of the Village at Cook Springs senior-living community — Mrs. Carter vowed she had returned to the beautiful area to stay. She loved the Village. She participated in many activities there. She baked muffins for newcomers at the Village, for the new residents moving in. In 2002, she won a top honor there, being named Ms. Springs Manor. She became friends not only with fellow residents but also with members of the staff. "They are so durned good to all of us here that I don't plan to go anywhere else, ever!" she said. "I'm back at Cook Springs for good. You see the sign on my door, don't you?"

The sign on the door of her apartment had been posted by Patsy Carter herself, by the grown-up version of the young girl who 80 years previously had frolicked and handled chores at a resort hotel in Cook Springs. The wording on her sign was "Carter's Last Stand."

3

LaFayette Cooke and His Mineral-Springs Resort in Cook Springs

"Looking back, I still am impressed at what good condition that wooden hotel structure remained in for decades after Grandpa built it."
—Herbert Cooke, grandson of LaFayette Cooke

Herbert Cooke said his first memory of the imposing Cook's Springs Hotel dated back to the mid-1920s, when Patsy Carter's father, Preston Lewis, was leasing and operating the hotel.

Around 10 years old at the time, young Herbert was fascinated to see this hotel that had been built in the 1880s by his well-known grandfather, LaFayette Cooke.

Before and after that period, Herbert heard his granddad talk about the days of building and operating the hotel.

"Grandpa was pleased that he built the hotel with lumber that had been cut in his own saw-milling operation located up there in those hills close to Cook Springs. Grandpa had a pretty big saw-milling operation during those days," he said in a 2005 interview. "Also, Grandpa was very proud that he was able to complete construction on the hotel so quickly. He would say, 'I built that hotel in about a year's time!'"

Although Herbert Cooke was just a boy when he made this visit during the 1920s, his impressions of the hotel remained vivid and were enhanced as the years went by. Reared in Mississippi, he moved to Alabama to live in the Cook Springs area for a time during the 1930s, before moving to Louisiana to launch a long career working for oil refineries. At the time of his 2005 interview, Herbert Cooke was living in Sulphur, Louisiana, and was approaching his 90th birthday.

For a short period during the mid-1930s, Herbert lived with two of his brothers in one of the vacation cottages his grandfather had built near the

Unidentified woman in front of Cook's Springs Hotel, between rocks painted with hotel name. Note whitewashed tree trunks, a practice sometimes employed for appearance and sometimes in an effort to ward off insects and tree diseases.

hotel. "Looking back, I still am impressed at what good condition that wooden hotel structure remained in for decades after Grandpa built it," said Cooke.

LaFayette, the Driven Businessman

LaFayette Cooke was focused on developing businesses.

He started his career in the Cook Springs area where he had been reared, deep in the heart of St. Clair County, Alabama. In the 1870s, he became a farmer and saw-miller in Cook Springs. In the 1880s, he built the Cook's Springs Hotel mineral-springs resort. After operating the hotel resort for two and a half decades, he left his hotel enterprise in the hands of others who leased and/or managed it. He moved on in the early 1900s to the nearby town of Pell City, which became one of two county seats in St. Clair County. It was in Pell City where he owned a telephone company and where he became founder and president of a bank, the Pell City Bank and Trust Company. He also invested in a bank in the St. Clair County town of Odenville. Then, in the 1920s, he moved to Florida, where he lived the rest of his life. Based in the Miami area, LaFayette Cooke had a real-estate development business well under way before the Great Depression hit. Some of his real-estate holdings were used to develop Boca Raton, Florida.

"One of the business stories Grandpa told us over the years was about the suit he never bought to wear the day he married Grandma Cooke," said Herbert Cooke. "He said he had enough money saved to buy himself a new suit when he got married. But instead of buying a wedding suit, he invested that money in his business projects at the time. Back then, a man with a keen business sense could make a few dollars go a long way. Grandpa said he made sure his business projects got the most out of every dollar that he would have spent on that wedding suit."

The Highs and Lows of LaFayette's Business Ventures

As is the case with many businessmen who attempt a range of projects, LaFayette Cooke had a range of success with his businesses. Most of his ventures were profitable experiences.

Irene Carreker (of well-known Cook Springs family) pulls children in wagon near Pavilion at the Mineral-Springs Hotel Resort in Cook Springs.

Apparently no period in his life produced a bigger financial payoff than his real-estate investment period during the latter years of his life in Florida, when he was president of the South East Coast Land Company that he founded. His Florida years also brought a high measure of pride in the accomplishments of some of his relatives. For example, his youngest child, daughter Floy, joined with her husband, Joe Mitchell, in using her dad's land holdings for some of the early development in Boca Raton, and Joe served as Boca Raton mayor for 12 years.

There were business disappointments along the way for LaFayette Cooke. At one point, he had a short-lived unsuccessful venture in buying Texas cattle. And no doubt one of the biggest disappointments came when the Pell City bank he had founded in 1914 was among many banks ultimately falling victim to the Great Depression that ravaged the United States beginning in the late 1920s.

In terms of LaFayette Cooke business ventures that attracted the public's support and lasting media attention, there could be none with more grandeur or more romantic than his 1880s building of the Cook's Springs Hotel in Cook Springs, Alabama.

A Focal Point of Books

The Cook's Springs Hotel venture that LaFayette Cooke undertook in the 1880s has been spotlighted in several books. These are some examples:

LaFayette Cooke received attention in a genealogical book that traced Cook Springs pioneer Franklin Marion Polk, Sr. — father of LaFayette

Cooke's wife, Elizabeth, known as "Eliza." This 2004 book, *Franklin Marion Polk: Farmer, Soldier and Pioneer,* was written by John Russell Carreker. A grandson of Franklin Marion Polk, Sr., author John Russell Carreker was a member of both the Carreker and Polk families who were among the early families settling in Cook Springs in the 1800s.

In the mid-1990s, three St. Clair County historians joined forces to research and write a book that related the story of the Cook's Springs Hotel resort project and also some of the historical background of families and surroundings in the Cook Springs community. Published in 1996 by the St. Clair Historical Society, the book was named *Sparkling Waters* (for the mineral-springs waters). Its subtitle was *A History of Cook Springs in St. Clair County, Alabama.* The three authors were Daniel Stewart, director of the Pell City Library; Rubye Sisson, retired teacher in the St. Clair town of Ragland and the author of a Ragland history and other historical materials; and Joseph Whitten, a retired teacher in the St. Clair town of Odenville and the author of an Odenville history and other historical materials.

And dating back to 1960, LaFayette Cooke's mineral-springs hotel venture was one of 56 Alabama vacation havens that author James F. Sulzby, Jr., featured in his book, published by the University of Alabama Press and entitled *Historic Alabama Hotels and Resorts.*

The Popular Concept of Mineral-Springs Resorts

The concept of building hotel resorts that were located near soothing, healing mineral springs became a popular business model in various parts of the United States beginning in the late 1700s and gaining in popularity in the early 1800s. In various parts of the nation, one mineral-springs resort after another went into operation.

A combination of health retreats and entertainment centers, these resorts often tended to cater to upper-middle-class and wealthy patrons. Offerings at the resorts generally fell into two categories: Number one, guests could enjoy a range of recreational activities. And, number two, guests could gain alleged health benefits by drinking from and/or bathing in the mineral-rich waters.

Proprietors of the resorts touted the healing values of mineral springs as having long ago been discovered and validated. They noted that mineral-springs patrons included Europeans who indulged in soothing Roman baths and frequented fancy European spas. They also pointed out that American Indians used the mineral springs and valued their healing powers.

As additional mineral-springs resorts began opening in the United States, early popular sites included the area of the Eastern United States stretching from New England to Virginia.

In times to come, history would record the lure of many high-profile retreats in the United States that were associated with healing waters. Often visitors to these mineral waters chose neither to bathe in the waters nor to drink the waters; instead, these particular visitors seemed content to enjoy vacationing in the beautiful settings where the mineral springs tended to be located.

Several very high-profile springs resorts were developed in the South. Among them was the famous thermal-springs retreat at Hot Springs, Arkansas. There would be none more famous down South than Warm Springs, Georgia. The value of water therapy at Warm Springs would be associated with rehabilitation exercises for polio victim Franklin D. Roosevelt, the 32nd president of the United States. There was the big tourist draw of water meccas such as Silver Springs, Florida. And majestic hotel structures were built as centerpieces for a number of Southern springs resorts, such as the celebrated Ocean Springs Hotel in Ocean Springs, Mississippi.

When the mineral-springs business model began moving into the South, Alabama was ripe for this type of development. A key reason was that this Southern territory that would become the state of Alabama was an area dotted with mineral springs — many of them located in surroundings naturally adorned with the beauty of woods, lakes, and/or mountains. As an increasing number of white settlers began moving into various parts of Alabama in the early to mid-1800s, a number of entrepreneurs latched on to the mineral-springs resort idea that already had caught on in some other parts of the nation and was moving into the Southeast.

In the James F. Sulzby, Jr., book, *Historic Alabama Hotels and Resorts,* almost half of the 56 vacation havens that are featured are mineral-springs resorts. These mineral-springs resorts were located from one end of the state to the other, and most were developed between the mid-1800s and the first decade of the 1900s. Some were very modest, consisting of just a few rustic cabins and little or no entertainment, while others were elaborate and luxurious and offered several entertainment features. LaFayette Cooke's mineral-springs hotel development in Cook Springs, Alabama, featured one of the more beautiful hotels and was complemented by a network of nearby cottages and a wide range of entertainment features.

A major factor driving the success or failure of many of these mineral-springs resorts was transportation. In short, people had to have a way to get to these resorts. A transportation phenomenon that gave the resorts a big boost was the continued expansion of the railroads across America. In case after case, the locations of railroad stops gave birth to the locations of mineral-springs resorts.

Railroad tracks and old train locomotive paved way for mineral-springs resorts such as the one at Cook Springs.

An Idea from LaFayette's Father

LaFayette Cooke was not the first Cooke family member to create a mineral-springs resort in Cook Springs, Alabama. The first was LaFayette's father, William Praytor Cooke, Sr.

William Praytor Cooke, Sr., moved in the late 1840s into what would become the Cook Springs area of St. Clair County. He came there after having lived for several years in neighboring Jefferson County (Birmingham) and then in another part of St. Clair County.

Somewhat of an entrepreneur himself, William Praytor Cooke, Sr., had owned a store and rental houses in the Birmingham area. After he settled in the community that later would be named Cook Springs, he continued his quest for business ventures. Realizing that the property he had acquired there was rich in mineral springs, he decided to follow the example of a number of other businessmen around the state who were creating lodging facilities for guests who could come to relax and enjoy the springs.

While continuing to earn his living in Cook Springs mainly by farming and operating a grist mill, William Praytor Cooke, Sr., constructed a few rustic cottages that comprised the first mineral-springs resort on Cooke property. As the War Between the States was being fought during the early 1860s, this small resort enterprise became virtually inactive for a time. After the war ended, William Praytor Cooke, Sr., rejuvenated his small resort and continued to operate it on a low-key scale.

Teenage Boy Grows Up Quickly

When William Praytor Cooke, Sr., died in 1872, his youngest son, La-Fayette, was 18 years old. The eighth-born of nine children in the family, LaFayette had already known the grief of losing a parent. His mother had died when he was 7 years old.

LaFayette wasted no time in making the most of the modest inheritance he got from his hard-working father. At the time of his death, his dad owned somewhere between 200 to 300 acres in the Cook Springs area, which he divided equally among his nine children. LaFayette used his land to start a farm and a small saw-milling operation that grew into a rather big operation. As LaFayette Cooke's work began paying off, he saved his money to buy all the property he could.

As he moved on into his 20s, LaFayette joined business forces with two of his older brothers — John, the eldest in the family and 17 years older than LaFayette, and Osburn Byers, or "Obb," who was 13 years older than LaFayette. Together, the three brothers formed the Cooke Brothers Company and later the Cooke Brothers Mercantile Company.

One of the big objectives of the three Cooke brothers' enterprises was to acquire property. By some point during the 1880s, the amount of property the brothers' company owned in and around Cook Springs had grown to around 1,700 acres.

When the Cook's Springs Hotel project was undertaken in the 1880s, LaFayette was the brother who took the lead in the project — the one who actually built the hotel. However, the hotel was still listed in legal documents and in newspaper articles as a project of the Cooke Brothers Mercantile Company.

Within a few years after the hotel opened, LaFayette had bought out his brothers. That meant that LaFayette Cooke owned all 1,700 acres of Cooke-owned property in and around Cook Springs, including the hotel and any related facilities. From that point on, the hotel as well as certain other LaFayette Cooke businesses were operated by L. Cooke & Co.

Herbert Cooke said he questioned how much his grandfather's two older brothers ever were actually involved in hands-on operation of Cooke Brothers Mercantile Company in Cook Springs. "I always heard that those two older brothers moved out of the Cook Springs area quite early," he said. "I think Grandpa did a lot of things himself, from scratch — including the hotel."

A Girl Named Eliza Polk

The young woman with whom LaFayette Cooke fell in love was one of his neighbors in the Cook Springs community. Her name was Elizabeth Polk, known in her family as "Eliza." She was the oldest among 11 children who had been born to Franklin Marion Polk, Sr., and his wife, Mary Elizabeth.

The Cookes and the Polks had something in common in that both families were among early settlers in Cook Springs. It was just after the War Between the States, likely around 1867, when the Polks traveled from Georgia to settle in what would become known as Cook Springs. When the Polks arrived, it was almost 20 years after LaFayette Cooke's father came to the area. However, the Polks arrived at a time that was still very early in the history of the community. The Polks were very much considered community pioneers and quickly became community leaders. In fact, Franklin Marion Polk, Sr., served as the first postmaster in the community for a short time in 1882 and 1883, and for a few months before the community was named Cook Springs it was called Polk.

The Resilient Franklin Marion Polk, Sr.

Cook Springs pioneer Franklin Marion Polk, Sr., survived enough hardships for his life to have the makings of a dramatic movie.

Polk's difficult times came while he was serving in the Confederate Army during the War Between the States. Those hardships were detailed in a 2004 genealogical book written by Polk's grandson, John Russell Carreker, entitled *Franklin Marion Polk: Farmer, Soldier and Pioneer.*

Carreker detailed how his granddad battled the Union in hard-fought skirmishes during the early days of the war. He also detailed how Polk was captured by Union forces, who confined him to a tough Illinois prison for Confederate prisoners of war. In that prison, Polk was exposed to such cold temperatures that one of his eyes became paralyzed and he developed severe pneumonia.

After being returned to the Confederates in a prisoner exchange, Polk recovered somewhat in two Confederate hospitals in Virginia. Still in a weakened condition at war's end, Polk was discharged to make his way back hundreds of miles to his Georgia home — in a trek that required much walking.

Author John Russell Carreker described how Polk finally arrived at his home in such an exhausted state that he didn't have enough energy left even to give an enthusiastic greeting to his wife, Mary Elizabeth, who affectionately called him "Mr. Polk."

This is Carreker's description in his book concerning that post-war reunion between Polk and his wife: "One day his wife spotted him approaching their home on foot and went running down the road waving her arms, shouting and crying, 'Oh, Mr. Polk! Oh, Mr. Polk!' He embraced her and quietly said, 'Calm yourself, Elizabeth, now calm yourself. I'm too tired to celebrate.'"

Opposing a Courtship

It was said by many that Franklin Marion Polk, Sr., was a very strict, no-nonsense man. For whatever reason, when LaFayette Cooke came courting Polk's eldest child, daughter Eliza, Franklin Marion Polk was not a strong supporter. He did not approve of the idea of his daughter marrying LaFayette Cooke.

But LaFayette Cooke persisted. Just as young LaFayette already was recognizing what he wanted and going after it in business dealings, the same thing apparently was true in his personal life. Typical of LaFayette's tendency to pursue his goals even when facing obstacles, LaFayette's solution was to elope with 19-year-old Eliza behind her father's back. LaFayette Cooke later would tell his children and grandchildren that he saved the money he would have spent on a wedding suit. What LaFayette sometimes did not add was that it wasn't real noticeable that he wasn't wearing a proper wedding suit, because he eloped instead of having a formal wedding.

LaFayette and Eliza picked the evening of May 19, 1875, to take things into their own hands. The way events unfolded is described in the following excerpt from the Stewart/Sisson/Whitten *Sparkling Waters* book: "Shortly after LaFayette turned twenty-one, he saddled two horses and rode north four miles to meet Elizabeth Polk. They went to the home of a minister where they were married."

Franklin Marion Polk's reasons were unknown for resisting the marriage of daughter Eliza to LaFayette Cooke. However, Polk's reaction to the elopement was quite well known in family circles. The John Russell Carreker book indicated that Franklin Marion Polk was not forgiving about the elopement: "Mr. Polk never developed a rapport with (LaFayette) Cooke because he felt his son-in-law should have been man enough to come to him and ask for his daughter's hand instead of stealing her away in the night."

The feelings of Polk did not deter LaFayette and Eliza from having a long, full life together. The two would be very bonded, would rear six children, and have a marriage that lasted until death parted them some six decades later.

A Family Watches the Building of a Hotel

LaFayette and Eliza Cooke had been married only seven years when La-Fayette began making plans to build his big mineral-springs resort hotel in Cook Springs. LaFayette was 28 years old the year he got the project under construction, in 1882.

To make sure he could be nearby and be hands-on during the construction, LaFayette built a small house by the construction site and moved himself, his wife, and their children away from their Cook Springs farm to live in that house.

At the time, LaFayette and Eliza already had four children — a 6-year-old daughter, Jessie Mae; a 4 ½-year-old son, William Praytor, Jr.; a 2-year-old daughter, Henrietta, and a new baby boy just a few months old, John Franklin. The fifth child, daughter Pearl Christine, came in 1884, shortly after the hotel construction was completed. Pearl later would laugh and tell people that the locomotive brought her. (The hotel would be in operation several years before the 1889 arrival of LaFayette and Eliza's sixth and last child, baby girl Floy.)

When the idea starting churning in LaFayette's mind in the early 1880s that he wanted to build the hotel, he was motivated by learning that a railroad was coming to Cook Springs for the first time. The coming of the railroad was magical. LaFayette knew the time was right to construct a big-time mineral-springs resort — a mineral-springs resort that would be mammoth compared to the small one his dad had first started a quarter of a century earlier. His dad's project to build a few cottages indeed had been a small-scale concept. At the very most, his dad could only expect a trickle of guests. In his dad's day, there had been no major transportation to bring guests to Cook Springs. The coming of the Georgia Pacific Railway line to Cook Springs was about to change that.

From the start, LaFayette Cooke knew where he would build his hotel. It would be right at the railroad stop in Cook Springs. When guests arrived, they would be within a short walking distance of the entrance to the hotel. In other parts of Alabama where rail lines already were in place, some owners of other mineral-springs resort hotels had experienced a booming business when they built their hotels next to railroad stops.

So, as Georgia Pacific was putting the final touches on laying tracks for its railroad line through the Cook Springs area, LaFayette Cooke was putting the final touches on his hotel. The core construction of the hotel actually was completed in late 1883, about the time the rail line was completed.

This notice appeared in Pell City's *Southern Aegis* newspaper on July 16, 1884: "Messrs. Cooke Brothers have completed a large and well-furnished hotel at this place. They are prepared to accommodate quite a number. Why cannot Cook Springs be made one of the best summer resorts in the South as the climate is mild and the water of various kinds first class."

A Hotel Showplace

When LaFayette Cooke's dream hotel opened for business, there could be no doubt that it was among the upper-end of mineral-springs resorts of the day.

The exquisite hotel was a real match for the fine clothes that guests wore as they disembarked from the passenger-train cars connected to the huffing-and-puffing, steam-engine-driven locomotives. The men sported their best suits and hats, and women wore long fashionable dresses accented by matching hats and gloves. Filled with anticipation about the upscale vacation that awaited them, they walked a short distance from the railroad-stop platform across a bridge that LaFayette Cooke's construction crew had erected to lead them straight to the hotel. (Although this bridge became an added attraction, it had been a necessity to provide a walkway that crossed a deep ravine in front of the hotel.) To top off the aura of excitement that greeted arriving guests, Cooke often would have a band on the platform playing hit tunes of the day as guests made their way from the train to the hotel.

The spectacular two-story wooden hotel that greeted the guests was set off with 1,000 feet of veranda. It had 60 guest rooms, plus a spacious lobby area and dining-room accommodations big enough to seat 200 people for a meal. Situated high on a steep hillside in the wooded, mountainous terrain of Cook Springs, the hotel afforded its guests a breathtaking view that kept many guests returning time after time. One of Cooke's early mottos for his hotel resort was "Here we rest."

An effective "partner" to the mountainous Cook Springs view was the weather. The weather tended to be cooler and brisker in this mountain setting than in many Alabama locales during the hot summer months, which made up the busiest season for the resort each year. Also, guests liked the fact that pesky insects such as mosquitoes did not seem to thrive well in those mountains.

As was true of many of its competitors, the Cook's Springs Hotel (or Mountain View Hotel, as it was called for a time) was much more than a hotel. The resort boasted other components as well. Some of those components were for lodging. Other components were for entertainment.

In the category of lodging, LaFayette Cooke followed a popular mineral-springs resort model of the day by also building a group of new cottages near the hotel. In this sense, he was following in the footsteps of his father, who had started the resort decades before with a group of cottages.

In the category of entertainment, one of the big attractions of the Cook's Springs Hotel Resort was the nearby pavilion used for dances, roller-skating, and other social activities. The pavilion was situated above the "springs house" where the pumps were located that accessed the mineral-springs water.

And then there were the extras. Some of these didn't come right away. They were added as the years went by. There was a swimming pool, a bowling alley, and an early version of tennis courts on the hotel lawn.

So, for typical guests, the options for enjoyment soon became quite extensive. Guests could sit around the hotel, chat with friends, enjoy board games, and partake of great food in the dining room (food that included fresh vegetables from Cooke's garden). Then the guests could go for a swim, find a good spot at a nearby stream and do a little fishing, take a hike in the woods or do some mountain-climbing, enjoy a game of bowling, play a little tennis or croquet on the lawn, go skating, and dance the evening hours away at the pavilion while talented string-band musicians played their favorite tunes. In quest of a wide range of health benefits, hotel guests could drink the "magical" mineral-springs waters and also enjoy hot sulphur baths.

In 1908, this hotel resort being operated by L. Cooke & Co. was being billed as the Mountain View Hotel. In an advertising campaign directed toward the public and used in newspaper ads, the proprietor listed what were called the "Five Important If's" as reasons for someone to visit the mineral-springs resort in Cook Springs, Alabama:

"If it's health

"If it's pleasure

"If it's a delightful climate

"If it's to avoid mosquitoes

"If it's to get away from work and worry and take a real vacation, recuperate, build up your system and be assured of perfect health during the winter,

"Then come to Cooks Springs and get all these at a nominal cost."

A look back at this overall mineral-springs resort concept was offered by LaFayette Cooke's great-grandson, Raymond Cooke (son of Herbert Cooke's deceased twin brother, Hubert). At the time he was interviewed in 2005, Raymond Cooke lived only a short distance from where his ancestor LaFayette Cooke had operated the resort. He was the only descendant of LaFayette and Eliza Cooke who still lived near the Cook Springs area.

"If you think about what my great-grandfather's Cook's Springs Hotel resort was all about, it was really a vacation resort with lodging that offered guests some of the same activities that the country clubs of later years would offer. And my great-grandfather's resort started operating in a time before the country clubs were well-developed," said Raymond Cooke. "My great-grandfather was just one of these entrepreneurs who had access to mineral springs and who saw value in this concept — particularly once the railroad came and there was a way to transport the guests to these resorts."

Pavilion located near Cook's Springs Hotel, used as community meeting place and for dances and other special events. Pumps for three kinds of mineral water were located on the bottom level of the Pavilion.

The Making of Lasting Memories

The Cook's Springs Hotel was not open for long before it was creating lifelong memories for many of its guests. One of those guests was a little girl named Delia Truss. Delia lived with her parents and her younger sister in the community of Riverside. By later standards, Riverside would not be considered very far from Cook Springs. However, when Delia and her family were journeying to the Cook's Springs Hotel for summer vacations beginning in the late 1890s, it was quite a trek.

Delia Truss (a relative of the founders of Trussville) grew up to marry John Robert, and they both became close friends of the parents of Arlene Henley. When Delia Truss Robert was in her elder years, Birmingham resident Mrs. Henley helped care for her. "She would share memories of her childhood. And among them were such fond memories of the time she and her family spent vacationing in Cook Springs," said Mrs. Henley. "She would talk about how nice it was at the hotel and how it was so great to go there. Going on vacation to Cook Springs was such a big event in her life."

The Drawing Power of Mineral-Springs Waters

Health benefits of the mineral-springs water were always at the center of what drew many guests to the Cook's Springs Hotel and other similar mineral-springs resorts.

Similar to some other business-minded proprietors of mineral-springs hotels, LaFayette Cooke marketed the mineral-rich water in more ways than one. He made the mineral water available to his hotel guests. Also, he sold the mineral water around the nation — bottling and shipping it in large quantities. Thus, if a hotel guest was sad about going home and leaving the mineral water behind, he could purchase some mineral water to take home with him or order it by mail.

Different mineral-springs resorts boasted different types of mineral-springs waters. There were waters reputed to be rich in sulphur or iron. Others were advertised for their content of magnesia, lime, carbonic gas, or lithium salts. Some waters were said to contain health-promoting combinations of several of these minerals.

During various times in the history of the Cook's Springs Hotel, this resort's mineral-rich water was divided into first one set of categories and then another.

Sometimes the Cook's Springs Hotel operators divided the water into three categories. That was how Patsy Lewis Carter recalled the water classifications during the 1920s, when her dad was leasing and operating the hotel. Then the hotel had "black sulphur water" and "white sulphur water" and "freestone water."

At other times, the mineral water available in Cook Springs was divided into four main categories — sulphur magnesia water, chalybeate (containing iron salts), alkaline healing water, and Blue Ridge lithia water (water containing lithium salts, also known as "freestone water"). Those were the four categories described by author James F. Sulzby, Jr., in *Historic Alabama Hotels and Resorts*. Below is Sulzby's description of those four water categories and the human-body ailments and needs toward which they were directed. In parenthesis are some clarifications added by this author (Anita Smith):

"The best-known water at Cook's Springs was the sulphur magnesia, which was highly recommended for indigestion, stomach troubles and insomnia of the worst form.

"The chalybeate water was recommended for chronic intestinal catarrh (inflammation), lung and kidney troubles, eczema, nervous disorders of all types, seminal weakness (diminished sexual performance; impotence), and in any case of convalescence when a tonic was required.

"The alkaline healing water was used for the cure of constipation, liver, kidney and bladder trouble, and was unsurpassed for dyspepsia (indigestion), nervous disorders and rheumatism. This water was also recommended to build up the system, give strength and vigor to the entire body, clear the complexion, and set the organs right.

"The Blue Ridge lithia water, which came direct from under one of the spurs of the Blue Ridge, was recommended as a fine agent in the treatment of dropsy (swelling; fluid buildup in the body), gastritis, diabetes, and Bright's disease (at that time, a catchall term referring to various kidney diseases). It was supposed to quiet the nerves and act as a fine restringent (control agent) in cases of chronic diarrhea."

The following excerpt shows how the values of the Cook Springs mineral-springs waters were described in a 1908 advertisement brochure produced by L. Cooke & Co.:

"The beauty of the waters at Cook's Springs is that one does not have to drink them the entire season before they find out whether they are going to be benefited. Twenty-four hours is usually long enough to tell, as ninety per cent of the people who come here for health and recreation improve from the day they arrive, without any loss of time. Life is too short to lose much time, and especially while regaining one's health away from home at the Springs. And again, the medicinal properties of these waters are so accurately compounded by nature, till they are very palatable, the most delicate stomach has no difficulty in taking them, and the very superior virtues of these waters are vouched for by the thousands of people who have tried them during the past eighty years, and found them to contain exactly the right proportion of each ingredient to be easy to take and give forth the most benefit to the user. A trial will convince anyone that the virtues of the waters at Cook's

Springs are second to none. No malaria can exist here."

Mineral-Springs Resorts Thriving in Alabama

When LaFayette Cooke's father built the few simple cottages in the 1850s that started the Cooke family in the mineral-springs resort business, he got in on a business that was already well-grounded in the state. Several other mineral-springs resorts had started up in Alabama dating back as early as the 1820s and 1830s.

After the War Between the States ended, the mineral-springs resort business would grow much faster than before the war. No one single factor fueled that business more than did the coming of the railroads. Prior to the railroads, resorts had to depend heavily on people being delivered by stagecoach or horseback, or sometimes coming a short distance by horse-drawn buggy or wagon. Steamboat travel helped deliver guests to a couple of resorts in South Alabama located near the Tombigbee River.

One only has to read through the 1960 book by James F. Sulzby, Jr., to get a picture of the widespread prevalence of mineral-springs resorts in Alabama during the 1800s and early 1900s.

Some resorts, such as the one in Cook Springs, were very elaborate and featured beautiful hotel structures and a network of cottages and quite often a pavilion and other amenities. (One Alabama resort even had an amphitheatre.) Other resorts were quite modest, consisting of very plain cottages and simple-life opportunities for guests to drink and bathe in the mineral-rich waters, eat good food, breathe fresh air, and enjoy peaceful surroundings.

In addition to Cook's Springs, 24 other mineral-springs resorts were listed by author Sulzby in *Historic Alabama Hotels and Resorts*. These resorts were located from one end of Alabama to another. Several were in coun-ties adjacent to or near Cook Springs in St. Clair County. Resorts in this Alabama network of mineral-springs retreats included:

• Alabama White Sulphur Springs, first known as Hanna Springs, was located in DeKalb County, a couple of counties to the northeast of

St. Clair County. It was built in 1871.

• Aus-Kel Springs Hotel in Geneva County, in southeastern Alabama, was built in 1908.

• Bailey Springs was in Lauderdale County, in the northwestern corner of the state. It was one of the early developments, starting in the 1840s.

• Bellevue Hotel, which opened in 1889, was reorganized in 1910 as the Mineral Springs Hotel Company. It was located near Gadsden in Etowah County, bordering on the northeast of St. Clair County.

• Bladon Springs, which opened in 1846 in Choctaw County in south-western Alabama, was located in a valley near the Tombigbee River.

• Blount Springs was located in Blount County, a county in north central Alabama bordering on St. Clair. This was one of Alabama's earliest mineral-springs resort developments, starting around 1825.

• Blue Springs, opening in 1890, was near Clio in Barbour County in southeastern Alabama.

• Bluff Park Hotel was located in the Birmingham area, in Jefferson County that bordered on St. Clair. The hotel opened in 1907 to succeed a smaller resort on the same property that had been known as Spencer Springs.

• Borden-Wheeler Springs was a resort that opened around 1900 in Cleburne County, near the Georgia-Alabama line — a couple of counties to the east of Cook Springs.

• Butler Springs, located in Butler County in south central Alabama, was said to have its roots in springs believed to have been discovered by hunters around 1830.

• Chandler Springs, with beginnings dating back to the mid-1800s, was in Talladega County, a county bordering on St. Clair.

• Clairmont Springs was located in Clay County, 18 miles from Talladega, between Talladega and Ashland. First known as Jenkins Springs, this was among the later developments to get on board. The hotel opened in 1909.

• Cullom Springs was located about one mile from Bladon Springs, also in Choctaw County. Development there began in the 1850s.

• Healing Springs, which began in the 1870s, was located in Washington County in southwestern Alabama.

• Ingram Wells was located in Calhoun County, which bordered on St. Clair to the east. This resort had its beginnings in 1897 as a business to ship lithia water and then was expanded eight years later with the building of a hotel and cottages.

• Mentone Springs Hotel, later known as the Loring Springs Hotel, was located atop Lookout Mountain near the towns of Mentone and Valley Head in DeKalb County — a couple of counties to the north of St. Clair, in the northeastern edge of the state. This resort had its beginnings in the 1880s.

• Piedmont Springs resort was constructed in the late 1880s on a mountain site in Calhoun County, bordering on an eastern edge of St. Clair County. This resort was just a few miles from Borden-Wheeler resort in Cleburne County.

• Shelby Springs was in Shelby County, bordering to the southwest of St. Clair. This resort was located between the Shelby towns of Calera and Columbiana. It started with cabins as early as the 1830s and then expanded with a hotel and new cottages in 1855.

• St. Clair Springs resort was located in St. Clair County, the same county where Cook's Springs Hotel was located. With a history dating back to this site being called Sulphur Springs, the location was drawing guests who vacationed in tents back in the 1830s before a hotel was ever built. One hotel, the St. Clair Springs Hotel, came to St. Clair Springs in 1875. Then a second hotel, the St. Clair Inn, came to St. Clair Springs in 1902.

• St. James Hotel was located in Selma in Dallas County, in west central Alabama. Opened in 1837, the hotel was known for its large mineral wells in the hotel courtyard — mineral water that also was the source of drinking water for hotel guests. Proprietors said the water brought beauty to the fountain in the courtyard and good health effects to hotel guests.

• Talladega Springs was located in Talladega County and was the earliest of at least three springs resorts in and around the town of Talladega.

This resort was known by names of Talladega White Sulphur Springs and later as Sulphur Springs or Franklin and finally as Talladega Springs. This, too, was one of the early mineral-springs resort developments, dating back perhaps as far as 1839. Legend had it that the springs in this area were discovered by one of the soldiers in Andrew Jackson's Tennessee troops during the Creek Indian War.

• Valhermoso Springs, beginning in 1823 and featuring the Cedar Hotel, was located in Morgan County, three counties to the northwest of St. Clair.

• Wilcox Mineral Springs was located in Wilcox County, in the south central part of the state. This resort opened in 1902 and had two hotel buildings.

• Windham Springs was located about 25 miles north of the city of Tuscaloosa, in Tuscaloosa County. The resort started around 1850 in this west central Alabama county — a couple of counties to the southwest of St. Clair.

The James Sulzby book also gave insight into events that marked some of the mineral-springs resorts with extra touches of individuality.

Some of these earlier mineral-springs resorts in the state had a history that in some ways became intertwined with the War Between the States. One was Windham Springs in Tuscaloosa County, which was stormed during the war by Union soldiers, who inflicted extensive damage on the hotel. Another Alabama war-linked mineral-springs resort was Shelby Springs in Shelby County. During the War Between the States, the Shelby Springs resort was converted first into a Confederate recruiting center and training site for cadets and then was used as a Confederate hospital.

Some resorts were the scenes of never-forgotten events. Such was the case at the plush Bladon Springs resort in Choctaw County, about 85 miles north of Mobile. On a night in 1891, gunfire erupted to awaken the hotel guests and signal the beginning of a series of events that would come to be known as the "Sims tragedy." This is what unfolded: Among the guests staying overnight that particular evening at Bladon Springs were a marshal and a prisoner he was escorting, a man by the name of Bob Sims. Shielded by the darkness, some of Sims' relatives arrived to set him free. In the fighting that ensued, a guard and the prisoner's son were killed at the hotel that night. The next day, the prisoner's brother was hanged. As for the prisoner himself, he had managed to escape. He joined with some cohorts and, according to the legend, went on to kill several members of a family he said had reported him to the law. Ultimately Sims and five of his male relatives who allegedly were assisting him were captured and, as the story goes, all six were hanged from the same tree.

There were several trends and changes that tended to follow these mineral-springs hotels — trends and changes that author Sulzby detailed in his book. LaFayette Cooke's hotel resort in Cook Springs would become a part of some but not all of these trends. These are examples:

A dismal trend — one that never affected LaFayette Cooke's development — was that many of these wooden hotels ultimately fell victim to fires. For some hotels, the fires came after they had operated only a few years and

Sofa from old Cook's Springs Hotel is in the historical collection housed in Ashville Museum & Archives. (Sofa donated by Bill and Judy Castleberry. Grandparents of Bill Castleberry managed the Cook's Springs Hotel during its latter days.)

were still in their prime. For others, the fires came after the hotels had operated for decades or had ceased to operate as resorts. Among Alabama mineral-springs resort hotels in which part or all the facilities ultimately burned were Bladon Springs, Borden-Wheeler Springs, Butler Springs, Chandler Springs, Cullom Springs, Shelby Springs, St. Clair Springs, and Wilcox Mineral Springs.

Another trend was that, as time went by and these resorts became less profitable, there was a tendency for the owners either to sell the resorts to someone else or to turn the resorts over to others to lease and/or manage. Although LaFayette Cooke did not sell his resort, he did begin making arrangements for others to manage and/or lease it, beginning in the first decade of the 20th century. Among the managers for a time were his eldest daughter, Jessie, and her husband, Henry Riggan.

Religious involvement related to some of the mineral-springs resorts also was a trend of sorts. Although not a prevalent trend, it was one that would touch LaFayette Cooke and his mineral-springs resort in Cook Springs. After the Great Depression of the 1930s wrote the last big chapter in the heyday operations of the mineral-springs hotels, devoutly Baptist LaFayette Cooke would donate his hotel resort, complete with its various facilities and all the property, to an evangelical group — to be used for religious training. Prior to his making this decision, there already had been at least two religion-linked precedents involving other Alabama mineral-springs hotels. At the South Alabama mineral-springs resort of Healing Springs in Washington County, a Baptist minister had built a church-linked school. And in North Alabama, a group of Baptist leaders had acquired some of the Mentone Springs development to use for faith-based assemblies, including for the youth. One could only speculate that those developments might have helped give LaFayette Cooke some ideas concerning the destiny of his hotel resort in Cook Springs.

4

Two Cooke Sons

"One of my early memories as a little boy was that when it came time for Daddy's trial, they loaded up all of us kids and hauled us up to Ashville to the St. Clair County Courthouse."—Herbert Cooke, grandson of LaFayette Cooke

The Cooke family became the highest-profile family in Cook Springs. Many who lived in the area naturally assumed that the two sons of LaFayette Cooke would carry on some of their father's business ventures and then pass them on to future generations.

It was not to be.

There would be sparks of business ability among the four daughters, most notably with the youngest Cooke daughter, Floy. But the business ventures of the two Cooke sons would be short-lived.

The only two sons born to LaFayette and Eliza Cooke indeed did go to work in prominent positions in businesses founded and funded by their father. However, both Cooke sons soon became central figures in tragic stories.

The Younger Son

In the first decade of the 20th century, the younger Cooke son — John Franklin Cooke — became general manager of the telephone company his father bought in Pell City. John Franklin's wife, Jessie, became the first

Twin grandsons of LaFayette Cooke as children, and then as adults, Herbert and Hubert Cooke. (Herbert is on the left in both photos.)

telephone operator John Franklin hired at this company.

Then, in 1910, John Franklin died of typhoid fever. He was 28 years old. He and Jessie had been married two and a half years.

John Franklin Cooke left behind not only his young widow, Jessie, but also their baby daughter, Julia, who was born the same year her father died.

The Elder Son

The only other son of LaFayette and Eliza Cooke was William Praytor Cooke, Jr., who became a physician. William Praytor was the second-born Cooke child and the elder son. Named for his paternal grandfather, he would become involved in his father's business enterprises in a number of ways.

A graduate of the Tennessee medical school operated at the time by The

University of the South at Sewanee, he was a physician in his dad's Cook's Springs Hotel for a short time after his medical school graduation in 1901. One of his physician roles at the hotel was to advise guests on the kinds of mineral water to drink for various ailments. (Having a hotel physician on hand to advise the guests and treat their ailments was one of the services offered by many top-echelon mineral-springs resorts such as the one at Cook Springs.) In addition to his short stint as a hotel physician, young Dr. Cooke rode on horseback to make house calls on patients in a more conventional medical practice.

However, true to the business roots of his father and grandfather, William Praytor Cooke, Jr., was more interested in business ventures than in practicing medicine. For a time he helped operate the bank in which his dad had invested in the St. Clair County town of Odenville, a few miles from Cook Springs. William Praytor Cooke, Jr., was industrious. During World War I, he also helped run a small business related to making barrels. During that time, there was a big demand for wooden barrels, to use as containers for everything from gunpowder to farm supplies and food products.

Then, soon after World War I ended, William Praytor Cooke, Jr., found himself at the center of one tragic event after another.

The Sadness of Dr. William Praytor Cooke, Jr.

The first tragedy to hit Dr. William Praytor Cooke, Jr., came in January 1919. Mable Cooke, his wife of 15 years, died of a combination of childbirth complications and influenza. She was among victims of the massive influenza epidemic that had begun sweeping the nation the year before. Severely weakened by the flu, Mable gave birth with much difficulty on January 7, 1919, to a baby girl who was named for her. Mable died the same day her baby was born. The baby died the following day.

Mable Cooke's death at the hands of influenza and childbirth came when she was 36 years of age. When she and William Praytor had met and fallen in love, she had been only 21 and was just starting a school-teaching career in her home state of Mississippi. As was true of many couples in that day and age, they had a large family. The baby daughter who died the day after her was their ninth child. In the wake of Mable's death, her 41-year-old widowed husband, Dr. William Praytor Cooke, Jr., was left with three motherless daughters and five motherless sons — a daughter not quite 14, daughters ages 12 and 10, sons ages 9, 7 and almost 5, and twin sons who had just turned 3.

Their son, Herbert, (one of the twin boys), believed the death of his mother and newborn baby sister so devastated his father that it helped set his dad on the downhill spiral that followed. He said that spiral was fueled by his dad's drinking to excess after his wife died. In the early 1920s, his dad re-married, to a woman considerably younger than he — a young woman named Liza Jane. Soon thereafter, in an incident apparently related to Liza Jane, Dr. William Praytor Cooke, Jr., shot a man — a fellow physician.

Herbert Cooke shared his own collection of information about what transpired: "From what I've been told, the commotion was stirred up because this physician there in St. Clair County allegedly made some remark about Daddy's new wife, Liza Jane — a remark that Daddy didn't like a little bit. Well, Daddy got his gun and went out looking for the doctor and proceeded to shoot him. He didn't kill him, but he wounded him. Now, given what I've heard about Daddy's drinking along about then, I wouldn't be surprised but that Daddy's drinking could have figured into the shooting.

Historic St. Clair County Courthouse in Ashville, which is still in use. Courthouse building has a history dating to 1844, and Ashville became a county seat in 1822. (Since 1902, St. Clair County has had two county seats – Ashville and Pell City.)

"At any rate, later on Daddy went on trial for this shooting up at the courthouse in Ashville, the county seat of St. Clair County. One of my early memories as a little boy was that when it came time for Daddy's trial, they loaded up all of us kids and hauled us up to Ashville to the St. Clair County Courthouse. Now remember, there were eight of us kids. I think that was to get sympathy with the jury."

All in all, Herbert Cooke said his dad got off lightly in some ways. He remembered that the aftermath involved some suspended sentence for William Praytor, and then, later on, a short confinement in an Alabama penitentiary. However, he said his dad also paid dearly in terms of his business reputation in the community. "That shooting and the trial kind of wound up my dad's career in businesses in St. Clair County," he said.

During the years that followed the shooting, his dad spent some time outside the United States — including a couple of stints as a ship physician on cruises near South America, plus a period actually living in South America trying to make a go of a mahogany business. "Grandpa Cooke sent some money down there to Daddy for that mahogany venture, but it didn't go well," said Herbert Cooke.

In the 1930s, William Praytor Cooke, Jr., returned to his St. Clair County birthplace. In his 50s at the time, William Praytor tried his hand at being a farm foreman on property located not far from the hotel his dad had built in Cook Springs and near the Odenville community where he had once lived. During this time after his dad's return, Herbert Cooke was in his late teens and was living in St. Clair County. Herbert worked some with his dad on the farm, and he remembered how much he admired his father's work during that period. "Daddy was good at being a foreman. Those days, Daddy was getting up before 5 a.m. every day and was out there on the farmland supervising some sharecroppers. Daddy knew how to supervise, and he also knew how to do things himself. Although I was young, farming was something I had done a lot of. Still, Daddy could show me things. You see, after Mother died and things went the way they did with Daddy, my brothers and sisters and I had been reared in Mississippi on Mother's parents' farm. So I had been working on a farm doing one thing or another since I was 8 years old. And I thought I knew just how to do things on a farm. But during that time in the 1930s when I was working some with Daddy on that farm in St. Clair County, I saw that even though he was in his 50s there were times when Daddy physically could outdo me. I particularly recall one day I was out there with a hoe thinning out the corn. Daddy came over to me and said, 'Give me that hoe!' Why, Daddy went to work with that hoe in a way that made me look like a little boy with his first-grade reader!"

Tragically, the return stay of William Praytor Cooke, Jr., in St. Clair County and his venture in farming lasted less than two years. One night in the late spring of 1934, Cooke and a man who was his longtime friend were returning home from a trip to Birmingham. In the post-midnight darkness, at around 1 a.m., Cooke's roadster collided with a pickup truck. The accident occurred on a curvy, treacherous stretch of the two-lane Bankhead Highway (Highway 78) near the community of Prescott. Cooke's friend was killed. A few weeks later, William Praytor Cooke, Jr., died of critical injuries he had sustained in that accident. An article about this tragic incident appeared in *The Birmingham News* later the same day of the accident — on Saturday, May 5, 1934. The article described both victims — Cooke and his friend — as being "widely known in this section of the state." Cooke's friend was well-known Preston H. Lewis, the same man who had leased and operated the Cook's Springs Hotel in the 1920s and who went on to establish the St. Clair County community of Chula Vista. Preston Lewis was the father of a vivacious daughter named Patsy who had worked and frolicked at the Cook's Springs Hotel during the 1920s and whose memories are featured in Chapters 1 and 2 of this book. Preston Lewis died a few weeks shy of his 65th birthday. William Praytor Cooke, Jr., died at age 56.

5

An Attraction for Nearby Neighbors

"There were people in Leeds who would go to Cook Springs just for a one-day outing, either taking along a picnic lunch or eating in the dining room of the Cook's Springs Hotel."–Marie West Cromer, former president of the Leeds Historical Society and the St. Clair Historical Society

In the "glory days" of the Cook's Springs Hotel, there were hotel guests who traveled quite a distance by train to enjoy fun times at the hotel and its pavilion. There also were guests who traveled just a few miles from neighboring communities to enjoy outings there.

Among those neighboring residents who made their short pilgrimages to LaFayette Cooke's showplace hotel were citizens of Leeds — a town with the distinction of being located in parts of three counties (St. Clair, Jefferson, and Shelby).

In her years of research about Leeds and surrounding areas, historian Marie West Cromer discovered a number of interesting facts about the lure that the Cook's Springs Hotel had for the people of Leeds. Mrs. Cromer said it saddened her somewhat that the hotel stopped functioning as a resort spot before she was born. However, she was able to live vicariously through what she uncovered in the stories that people recalled and in newspaper articles that were passed down through generations in her native Leeds.

"When the Cook's Springs Hotel was in operation, it was not uncommon in Leeds to see a group of residents gathered at the Southern Railroad

Depot buying tickets to leave Leeds for a weekend in 'the country' in Cook Springs," said Mrs. Cromer. "Now, although Leeds residents were traveling only a short distance on the train to reach Cook Springs, to the people of Leeds it seemed that Cook Springs was way out in the country. It was quite an adventure for them to board that train in Leeds and go out to the resort in Cook Springs. And how far were they riding on that train to get there? About 8 to 10 miles."

Mrs. Cromer ran across many details about the Cook's Springs Hotel during years she served two terms as president of the St. Clair Historical Society and the Leeds Historical Society, having been the organizer of the latter group in 1998. She also uncovered details during her decades of working on newspaper staffs.

The Cook's Springs Hotel in fact was a source of interest and pride for many people throughout St. Clair County, and the hotel attracted visitors from various parts of the county, said Mrs. Cromer. She said people in the county were proud of the grand hotel there. They also were proud of the prevalence of mineral-springs in the county as a whole — springs located in such areas as Cook Springs, Springville, and St. Clair Springs.

"There were people in Leeds who would go to Cook Springs just for a one-day outing, either taking along a picnic lunch or eating in the dining room of the Cook's Springs Hotel," she said. "And the hotel was a popular place for special gatherings, for special occasions."

She gave an example that was recorded in an entry in the 1924 yearbook of Leeds High School. "The Senior Class picnic was held in Cook Springs. The class left Leeds by train at 6:30 a.m. and returned at 9 p.m. The outing was educational as well as enjoyable. The mineral water was examined at one of the springs. Dinner was served at the hotel at 7 p.m."

After growing up in Leeds and attending college at what then was Jacksonville State Teachers College (later Jacksonville State University), Marie West Cromer lived in other parts of the nation after she married her educator husband. When the Cromers returned to Alabama in 1969, they settled not far from where Mrs. Cromer had grown up in Leeds. In 2005, she was living in the St. Clair County community of Moody. And she still was as fascinated with the history of the old Cook's Springs Hotel as she had been when she first heard about it during her growing-up years in Leeds.

"Oh, I wish that resort hotel in Cook Springs was open and ready to receive guests still today," she said. "I know I would love to go board a train and ride it 8 to 10 miles and spend the day at that beautiful hotel resort. I would really enjoy having the resort's band playing there on the platform when I stepped off the train at the hotel, and then visiting the different mineral springs, and eating in the dining room of the hotel. Wouldn't that be neat? Those days of the Cook's Springs Hotel were grand, grand days that brought such good times for so many people."

Section Two

~

*Early Years of a County
and a Community*

6

The Rich Historical Legacy
of St. Clair County, Alabama

"St. Clair County has had a very rich history. There is a tremendous interest among many people in St. Clair County in researching and preserving the county's history. In several areas of the county you will actually find someone who specializes in the history of that particular area."–Joseph Whitten, Odenville, Alabama, a St. Clair County historian

A small fire was ablaze in the historical county-seat town of Ashville. The fire had been set on purpose. People were on hand to watch it and control it, to make sure it burned only what was intended to be burned. The fire was part of a housecleaning process to rid the basement in the historical Courthouse building of some old papers that had been declared no longer of use.

Suddenly two women ran out of the stately white Courthouse structure located on what was called "the square" in Ashville. The women waved their arms, called out in protest, and headed straight for the fire. The women were longtime St. Clair historian Mattie Lou Teague Crow and county archivist Elizabeth Lonnergan.

"According to this story that has been passed down, Mrs. Crow and Miss Lonnergan ran right up to that fire and, unmindful of any burns they might suffer as a result, they reached into the fire and started pulling out papers and records they felt were important for the county to save," said Charlene

Simpson, archivist at the Ashville Museum & Archives, which became based in the Ashville Courthouse. "As I understood it from hearing this story, Mrs. Crow did suffer a few burns as a result of this incident, although nothing serious. I also was told that she and Miss Lonnergan were successful in retrieving from the fire most of the items they were trying to save."

For years after that incident, both Mrs. Crow and Miss Lonnergan continued their diligent work to preserve St. Clair history. At the time Mrs. Simpson recalled this story in 2005, it had been several years since the deaths of Mrs. Crow and Miss Lonnergan. However, their reputations and their love for St. Clair history continued to outlive them — including this story that long had been passed around among historians' groups in St. Clair.

For Mattie Lou Teague Crow and Elizabeth Lonnergan, the history of St. Clair County not only was something they were trying to preserve. It was something they and their families actually had lived.

Mrs. Crow's father had been a pioneer leader in education in St. Clair County, dating back to the 1800s. She married a man who became a St. Clair County sheriff. A schoolteacher and librarian, Mrs. Crow became a researcher and writer of St. Clair history, including *The History of St. Clair County, Alabama*, published in 1973.

Miss Lonnergan was a descendant in a family that for many years owned one of the oldest historical homes in the county, the Looney House, that later was turned into a museum. An employee in the Ashville Courthouse, Miss Lonnergan became the first to be employed in the county's archives there. She lived out her later years in the historically rich St. Clair community of Cook Springs, at the Village at Cook Springs retirement center.

The passion that Mattie Lou Teague Crow and Elizabeth Lonnergan felt and showed for St. Clair history was not unique in that county. In fact, it was typical of a history-driven fervor for research and preservation that prevailed from one end of St. Clair County to the other.

"St. Clair County has had a very rich history. There is a tremendous interest among many people in St. Clair County in researching and preserving the county's history. In several areas of the county you will actually find someone who specializes in the history of that particular area," said

Joseph Whitten, a retired high-school English teacher who taught in the St. Clair town of Odenville and who still lived in Odenville at the time of this interview. Whitten had showcased St. Clair history in several books he had written or co-written and on a website he maintained. He also volunteered his help at the Ashville Museum & Archives and was a devoted member of the very active St. Clair Historical Society.

The History They Preserved

In preserving the history of St. Clair County, historians were treating with tender loving care the artifacts, records, and research data of a county known for its valuable natural resources, for the glorious natural beauty of its sites, for the pivotal events that had taken place on these sites, and, in some cases, for the structures that still remained as reminders.

It was a county respected in part simply because it was one of the state's older counties. It was a county whose own history would forever be tied to the Creek Indian War and the War of 1812 and to names such as Andrew Jackson and Fort Strother. It was a Southern county that wore the name of a Northern statesman, a county that ironically would generate a mixture of Southern and Northern views during the War Between the States, also known as the Civil War. And St. Clair County was, perhaps above all, a county of independence, individualism, and diversity whose citizens came together for common causes.

The Birth of St. Clair County

As was true with much of Alabama's development, the way was paved for the creation of St. Clair County when lands formerly occupied by the Creek Indians were opened up for white settlers. The total of these former-Creek lands that created much of Alabama and Georgia amounted to 23 million acres. The lands were relinquished by the Creek on August 9, 1814, through the Treaty of Fort Jackson — a treaty in which Andrew Jackson led the negotiations.

This treaty was negotiated after the end of the War of 1812, at a time when the Creek found themselves with virtually no negotiating power. The reason was that the Creek had made two fatal mistakes in response to the encroachment of the white man on their territory. Number one, a faction of the Creek had gone on the warpath and attacked white settlers, including the infamous 1813 Massacre at Fort Mims, located in Baldwin County, Alabama. Number two, these attacks by the Creek were part of moves made by a warring Creek faction to take sides with the British against the colonial soldiers during the War of 1812, and the British would lose the war. Luring the Indians into this alliance was a promise from the British to protect the claims of the Indians to their lands — a promise that would be kept on the condition that the Indians would help the British defeat the colonial soldiers in battle and thus help the British to win back the colonies. And, since the colonies defeated the British in war, that promise to the Indians was not kept.

The actual birthdate of St. Clair County on former Creek-occupied lands in north central Alabama was listed as November 20, 1818. This made St. Clair no doubt one of the older pioneer counties in the state even though it was born 18 years behind Alabama's firstborn county, Washington. Officially older than the state of Alabama, St. Clair became a county more than a year before Alabama became the 22nd state to enter the Union, on December 14, 1819.

The creation of St. Clair County occurred amidst a backdrop of a drawing and re-drawing of land boundaries in the years immediately following the signing of the Treaty of Fort Jackson. Actually, it was a Congress-authorized re-drawing of land boundaries in 1817 that divided the Mississippi Territory, resulting in the creation of the Alabama Territory and paving the way for the creation of the state of Alabama.

St. Clair County itself was carved out of a division of Shelby County, after a small number of counties became divided into a bigger number of counties in what was then the Alabama Territory. There would be considerable changing of county lines as things settled down with the distribution and re-distribution of the millions of acres of Creek land.

As the boundaries gradually took shape for what ultimately would be 67 counties in the state, an elite group of counties emerged to be representative of Alabama's earliest county-molding pioneers. In singling out those early counties that were "the pioneers," some pointed particularly to the counties that were officially established in times preceding Alabama's own official statehood. There were 29 of these counties, including St. Clair. Among other Alabama counties sharing that distinction of being established prior to the state of Alabama were St. Clair's nearby neighbors of Shelby, Blount, and Tuscaloosa Counties, all three of which were established during the same February month more than nine months prior to St. Clair. As for Jefferson County, St. Clair's next-door neighbor to the south and the county that would become Alabama's most populous, that county's birthdate would be listed as December 13, 1819, more than a year after St. Clair was born and one day prior to Alabama's entering the Union.

Wearing the Name of a Northern Statesman

During the rapid development of the South in the 1800s, it was not uncommon for a Southern geographical area to look northward in choosing its name. After all, there were sections of the North that were decades ahead of the South in development. There were areas of the North that in the 1700s had produced military heroes and statesmen during the emerging nation's bid for independence during the Revolutionary War and then during the initial structuring of the federal government in the years that followed.

St. Clair County, Alabama, was among those Southern areas that picked the name of a leader in a Northern part of the nation. The leader was General Arthur St. Clair.

Having come to the emerging United States from Scotland, Arthur St. Clair had settled in what became Pennsylvania. During the Revolutionary War, St. Clair served as an officer under George Washington's command and rose to the rank of major general. After that war, St. Clair represented Pennsylvania in the Congress of the Confederation. In 1787, Arthur St. Clair's star continued to rise rapidly. Early in that year he served as president of the Congress of the Confederation. Later that year, he became governor of the Northwest Territory.

General Arthur St. Clair was among those who had come to the "new country" from Great Britain early enough in his life to have the experience of fighting first on the side of the British and later against the British. Several years before fighting against the British in the Revolutionary War, St. Clair served as a British Army officer during the French and Indian War.

In a 2005 interview, St. Clair County Commission Chairman Stanley Batemon made some clarifying statements about the name of St. Clair County. "In naming our county for Arthur St. Clair, early settlers here named it for a man who spelled the first part of his last name as 'St.' and not 'Saint,'" said Batemon. "Some people are not aware of that. There are some who incorrectly believe that officially this county should be spelled out as 'Saint Clair County.' In fact, I've heard some people say that they feel that the listing of Alabama tag numbers for Shelby and St. Clair counties should be reversed to put St. Clair in front of Shelby, to reflect the spelling of our county as 'Saint Clair.' The Alabama tag-number order is correct as it stands — with Shelby as Number 58 and St. Clair as Number 59. That order correctly reflects that our county was named for General Arthur St. Clair."

General Arthur St. Clair died in December 1818 at age 82. His death came the month after St. Clair County was established and named for him.

Fort Strother and the Creek Indian War

If one were conducting a survey among St. Clair County historians about key places and events that shaped the county's history, virtually all would mention a place called Fort Strother.

Located at the extreme western edge of St. Clair County, Fort Strother became one of the most meaningful sites related to the Creek Indian War (often called the Creek Campaign), which in turn was closely related to the War of 1812.

If one were looking for the Fort Strother site, he or she would travel to a wooded place not far from the St. Clair town of Ragland, to an area along the Coosa River near the Neely Henry Dam and just across the river from neighboring Calhoun County.

"But, once someone gets to that place, there is very little to see," said

St. Clair County Commission Chairman Stanley Batemon. "Except for a marker that stands there to commemorate the spot, one would have a hard time finding this site without having had archeological experience."

Standing on this site during the Creek Indian War were buildings that made up a stockade known as Fort Strother.

The stockade was built in late 1813 by General Andrew Jackson and the men under his command. Jackson and his men used Fort Strother as a garrison to store their guns, ammunition, and other supplies as they prepared to fight the Creek Indians in the pivotal Battle of Horseshoe Bend on March 27, 1814 — the deciding battle that defeated the Creek during the Creek Indian War. The battle was fought near what became the towns of Dadeville and Alexander City in Tallapoosa County, Alabama — an area that would be charted by boundary lines as being located three counties to the southeast of St. Clair.

Fort Strother in St. Clair County, Alabama, was described by the Tennessee State Library and Archives as "the main rendezvous point for the American armies during the Creek War." It was a place where anywhere from hundreds to thousands of soldiers gathered at various times between the building of the fort in November 1813 and the Horseshoe Bend battle four months later. Gathering with Jackson's men from time to time was a group of Indians who fought alongside Jackson against the warring Creek Red Sticks. There likely were around 2,500 men total in Jackson's forces when they gathered in full force, plus a couple of hundred Creek and Cherokee Indians who were their allies.

It was a powerful fact of geography that no doubt led to the building of Fort Strother on that particular site — the fact that the site was located on the Coosa River. By operating out of Fort Strother, Jackson and his men could move supplies down to Horseshoe Bend via the river system, from the Coosa River on into the Tallapoosa River that accessed Horseshoe Bend. During the months Jackson operated out of Fort Strother, there was a gathering at Horseshoe Bend of around 1,000 Creeks from the Red Sticks who had been on the warpath against white settlers.

In naming Fort Strother, Jackson chose to honor one of his officers whose all-important work played a vital role in the selection of the fort's location. This officer also played a key role in charting Jackson's march from Tennessee that led him in the fall of 1813 from Fayetteville, Tennessee, down through Alabama's sites of Huntsville and Fort Deposit on to the site where Fort Strother would be built. The treasured skills for which this officer was so valued didn't have to do with his strategic ability to plan a battle or his bravery on the battlefield through expert marksmanship or hand-to-hand combat. This officer instead was an indispensable topographer — a skilled specialist in creating the maps and charts of the unfamiliar wilderness that surrounded the men who fought under Jackson's command. Fort Strother was named for Captain John Strother (later promoted to major), who was the chief topographer for Andrew Jackson from September 26, 1813, until February 26, 1814.

Long after Jackson's men waged successful war against the Creek and years after the buildings of the Fort Strother stockade no longer were standing, a chapter of the Daughters of the American Revolution (DAR) in Anniston, Alabama (Calhoun County) took steps to erect a marker to commemorate Fort Strother's site. The timing for putting the marker in place was in November 1913 — one century to the very month after Jackson's men had arrived at the Fort Strother site on November 3, 1813. The marker was erected by what was known to some as the Frederick William Gray DAR Chapter and to others simply as the Fort Strother DAR Chapter. The marker reads: "Here stood Fort Strother, a defense against the Indians, built by General Andrew Jackson and occupied by him and his Brave Men during the Creek Campaign, November 3, 1813. Erected by the Frederick Wm. Gray Chapter DAR of Anniston, Alabama, to preserve the memorial of Faithful Service, November 13, 1913."

St. Clair Commission Chairman Batemon noted that in more recent years other steps had been taken to research and preserve the history of Fort Strother. "There has been a University of Alabama archeological team out there at the Fort Strother site, working at what we know to be a cemetery that became a burial ground for some of Jackson's soldiers and some of the Indians who were helping them."

There were historians in St. Clair County who would like to see more done to commemorate Fort Strother, much more.

"Fort Strother is so significant in the history of our county and our nation that efforts have been made to get a national park made out of it," said Rubye Sisson, retired schoolteacher and active St. Clair Historical Society member who had written a history of the town of Ragland, located near Fort Strother. Mrs. Sisson's late husband, Harold Sisson, developed an interest in Fort Strother and conducted research to locate the cemetery there.

Batemon said that efforts to obtain government funds for restoration and commemoration at Fort Strother had not been successful. "There are just so many historical sites in this nation," he said. "The reality of it is that the money usually goes to sites that are more identifiable."

St. Clair County Commissioner James S. "Jimmy" Roberts got the "history bug" about Fort Strother when he was a Pell City High School ninth grader writing a report on the fort. "That fort has stuck in my mind ever since," said Roberts, who became a leader on the political end in trying to get a major commemoration project accomplished at the Fort Strother site. "Back when I was a ninth grader, I had a hard time finding any information on the fort. I went to hunt information on the fort and had much difficulty. But in the years since, I've learned that there are a lot of people interested in that fort." When asked what kind of commemoration he would like to see at Fort Strother, Roberts was quick to respond. "That's easy," he said. "I'd like to see a reconstruction of the fort, one that would get as close as we could to duplicating the original site. And I'd like to see a campground built close to the fort site, so that visitors could come and see the fort site and spend a few days in St. Clair County." He praised two men who had done considerable research about the fort's history — Robert Perry and Charlie Brannon. "They've done the research. And I've been trying to keep something going about Fort Strother on the political end. Although we've run into roadblocks trying to get the commemoration that we want at the fort site, we certainly have not given up on it."

In the meantime, regardless of whether the Fort Strother site ever would become the object of a site reconstruction, or a national park, or a campground, the stories of the fort and its leader, Andrew Jackson, remained alive and flourishing in St. Clair County.

Some of the stories had to do with agonies sustained by both sides during the battles near the Fort Strother site — such as the Battle of Talladega, and the destruction of Indian villages in the area by Jackson's men. One of the villages that Jackson's forces destroyed a few days before they reached the Fort Strother site was Littafatchee, on Canoe Creek, not far from where Fort Strother soon would be built.

One of the more touching stories had to do with a little Creek boy that Jackson found and decided to adopt while he was in St. Clair County. The boy was named Lincoya. His mother had been killed. Jackson initially had the boy sent to a friend's house in Huntsville; later Jackson and his wife, Rachel, took the child into their own home to rear as their own. The adopting of a child in need was nothing new to Andrew and Rachel Jackson. Although they never had children of their own, the Jacksons adopted one of Mrs. Jackson's nephews soon after birth (Andrew Jackson, Jr.). They also helped rear two more of her nephews and a grandnephew as well.

No doubt some of the most colorful stories about Andrew Jackson while he was in St. Clair County revolved around his fiery personality. This was consistent with a strong historical spotlight on the no-nonsense toughness of this man called Andrew Jackson who in 1829 would become the seventh president of the United States. Among the more popular of these stories about his days in St. Clair County related to the interaction between Jackson and his men, who were called the Tennessee Militia or Tennessee Volunteers.

St. Clair County historian Joseph Whitten recalled a favorite tale about Jackson from during Jackson's days at Fort Strother. It was a tale that left no doubt as to why Jackson's men gave him the nickname of "Old Hickory" after observing that he was as tough as hickory.

"One of the problems that Jackson's men faced while they were at Fort Strother was that they would run out of provisions," said Whitten." In addition, some of Jackson's men thought they already had fulfilled their time of service anyhow, and that since they were hungry the thing to do was to get away and search for food and try to go home. Well, the time came when some of the men decided to go ahead and rebel, to just leave. Jackson found out in advance about this planned rebellion from some of his other men who were loyal to him. Those loyal men told him the rebellion of the others would occur during that very night. So, Jackson got on his horse and, armed with his gun, positioned himself in the middle of the road out here in what is now our St. Clair County. This of course meant that in order for any of Jackson's rebellious men to leave by that road, they first would have to get past Jackson. Now, in a previous battle Jackson already had sustained an injury to his arm. Since his arm was sore, as he sat on his horse in the middle of that road he protected his sore arm by laying the barrel of his gun between the ears of his horse. I've always felt sorry for the poor horse if it had been necessary for Jackson to fire his gun. As it turned out, Jackson didn't have to fire. Just as he had been informed would happen, his men indeed did start leaving. As the men rounded the curve, there Jackson was to confront them. Jackson yelled out to them a commanding 'Halt!' The men halted. Jackson yelled out, 'About face!' The men about-faced. Then Jackson ordered them, 'Now forward march, every damned one of you!' And all the men marched back to camp at Fort Strother. In a day or two, provisions arrived and they had food to eat. That ended the rebellion."

A Divided St. Clair County During the Civil War

During the War Between the States, or Civil War, there were split feelings in St. Clair County about allegiance to the Confederate forces of the South and the Union forces of the North. There were holdouts — healthy St. Clair County men who would not support the Confederate cause and who stayed home during the war, sometimes posing as women working out in the fields. Gangs developed. There were deserters.

"With the divided feelings, there were numbers of cases in St. Clair County in which the divisions occurred within families — cases in which there was brother fighting against brother, one for the South and one for the North," said Ashville archivist Charlene Simpson.

In terms of war-time divisions spawning gangs, gunfire erupted in St. Clair County at the hands of a group known as the Springfield Gang. "This

Springfield Gang was a group of men who had deserted the Confederate Army and had become Northern sympathizers," said Mrs. Simpson. "At one point, there was a meeting being held in the Courthouse building here in Ashville, and members of the Springfield Gang hid under a house and shot a man who had come to town for this meeting. I mean, if you go back and read some Northern newspapers around that time, Ashville was described as a wicked place. Of course, the Southern account was quite different."

One much-talked-about chain of events in St. Clair County during the War Between the States involved desertion, a murder, and revenge. This saga was fueled by the murder of the Reverend Hezekiah Balch Moor, Jr., of the Moody-Leeds area and by the subsequent revenge waged by his young son. The story, as passed down through Moor family descendants, was reported in a 1998 book, *The Heritage of St. Clair County, Alabama* (by The St. Clair County Heritage Book Committee). As summarized in sections from this book compiled from Moor descendants' information, this is how the chain of events unfolded: Reverend Hezekiah Balch Moor, Jr., had pastored a Baptist church in St. Clair County prior to the outbreak of the War Between the States. Hezekiah was 40 years of age when he enlisted in the Confederate army. After serving two years, he came home on furlough because he had been quite ill. Soon after he returned home and got somewhat back on his feet health-wise, Hezekiah embarked on a mission that had to do with tracking down a Confederate deserter near where he lived. Hezekiah had been informed that a local boy there in St. Clair County had deserted a Confederate unit headed by Hezekiah's own brother. So Hezekiah set out to locate this deserter and return him to his brother's unit. However, instead of catching the deserter, Hezekiah was ambushed and killed by the 20-year-old deserter — on June 28, 1863. The deserter was hiding in a tree on Moor family property near Moody. When Hezekiah passed beneath the tree on horseback, the deserter shot Hezekiah dead in his saddle. When this tragedy occurred, Hezekiah and his wife had an 8-year-old son, Joe. This boy sank into such a state of despair following the murder of his father that soon his grief planted the seeds for a growing, burning desire for revenge. The fifth-born of the seven Moor children, Joe began planning how he could avenge his dad's killing as soon as he felt he was old enough. At age 14, feeling he had waited long enough, Joe set out looking for the man who had murdered his daddy. It didn't take Joe long to learn that the man he sought was in Texas working as a cowboy in cattle drives. So Joe went to Texas, got himself jobs working in cattle drives, and waited and watched as cowboys with various herds joined at night to camp together. It took Joe three years of looking to find his prey. Finally the night came when Joe spotted the man for whom he had searched so long. Although it had taken Joe three years to find the man, it didn't take him long to act on his finding. As paraphrased by historian Joseph Whitten, a member of the committee of historians who put together *The Heritage of St. Clair County, Alabama*, this is how the revenge played out: "That night, after the cowboys had rolled up in their blankets and gone to sleep at their overnight camping spot, Joe slipped out of his own bedroll, took out his knife, crept over to the bedroll of this man he had sought out, and proceeded to slash this man's throat. Joe killed the man instantly. It was said by a contributor to our St. Clair history book that Joe's action represented 'vengeance at last.' After slashing the man's throat, Joe saddled his horse that very night and headed back home to St. Clair County, Alabama." Joe Moor took up residence on familiar family soil in the St. Clair community of Moody — where he married, reared a large family, and lived to be 81 years of age.

A History Driven by Valuable Geography

Much of the history of St. Clair County would become embedded in the county's geography — in its terrain, its striking beauty, and its abundant natural resources.

Located at the foot of the Appalachian Mountain Range, and cradled to the east in the arms of the powerful Coosa River, St. Clair County possessed endless acres of rich soil, hundreds of thousands of acres of forestland, breathtakingly beautiful mountains, and rich minerals and metallic elements that peppered its water and infiltrated its soil.

In early-day St. Clair County, natural resources paved the way for many a citizen to make a living off the land and river — through farming, hunting, fishing, saw-milling, or working in the coal mines. The Coosa River was a county lifeline, providing a way to transport products to market and cutting a lifestyle path that made ferries, bridges, barges, and locks a familiar part of everyday life. As the decades passed, and with the coming of two interstates and two dams, St. Clair County's geography also would transform the county into a recreational paradise and a mecca for new industries.

The county's geography itself wielded considerable power in dictating much of the development of the county.

The Coosa River and how and where it flowed drove decisions. "In the very early days of this county, there were communities that developed in certain locations because it was such an issue to get from one side of the river to the other," said St. Clair County Commission Chairman Stanley Batemon. "Once a group of people got to one side of the river, they sort of tended to stay, to settle and make their homes there. It was too hard to get back across. So in some cases, a community developed in a particular spot for that reason."

The mountains also had their power. It was the challenge of traveling from one side of a mountain to the other side that gave birth to the unusual situation of having two county seats in St. Clair County. The original county seat was historic Ashville. A town with impressive historical buildings that resembled a postcard from the past, Ashville was incorporated as the county seat in 1822. The town was centered by a courthouse building dating to 1844 that represented one of the oldest courthouse structures in the state. However, in the early days of St. Clair, many citizens in the county experienced great difficulty traversing Backbone Mountain to reach Ashville to conduct their business at that courthouse. So, as a result of an election in the county in 1902, Pell City was authorized as a second county seat to be added to share county-seat responsibilities with Ashville. "What we have in St. Clair County is not one county seat and a branch. We actually have two county seats — one county seat in Ashville, and a second county seat in Pell City," said County Commission Chairman Batemon. "Setting up a branch of a county seat is not all that unusual. All that is necessary to create a branch of a county seat is for members of a county commission to vote among themselves. By contrast, the decision to have two county seats in St. Clair County came about through a constitutional amendment authorized by an election of the people. To reverse that and go back to having one county seat, we would have to have another constitutional amendment authorized by an election of the people. While our two-county-seat system is not unique, it is unusual."

Within this county of two county seats, there developed through the years a rivalry between the county's Northern Division (Ashville-based) and the county's Southern Division (Pell City-based). That rivalry was usually friendly, but not always friendly. Fueling the rivalry were the two distinctly different personalities of Ashville and Pell City — Ashville with its deep roots and sense of history, and Pell City as the more industrialized newer kid on the block. As time went on, the Northern Division and Southern Division increasingly tended to come together for various common causes, including economic development.

"St. Clair County is so, so rich in history. There are all kinds of historical threads in St. Clair County that are just fascinating!" said historian Marie West Cromer, who was an organizer and a president of the Leeds Historical Society and also served as president of the St. Clair Historical Society. She said contributors to that fascination included (1) the county's status as one of Alabama's older counties, (2) the fact St. Clair had started out as such a big county and then was sub-divided into several counties, and (3) the fact that its own history was so strongly linked with early Indian history in the area.

Communities Entrenched in Individuality

Although the towns and hamlets of St. Clair County came together to form one county, they were not the products of any form of homogeneous mix. As had been true from the time that St. Clair County began, each town or hamlet stood on its own in terms of personality. These community units were as their ancestors had been — products of individualism in their appearance, attitudes, lifestyles, and history.

While celebrating their common ties as a county, many in St. Clair found their closest identity within their own communities. People who grew up in these communities took pride in the history that had bred and fed them and their ancestors.

Those who grew up in towns such as Coal City and Ragland knew that the coal mines had given birth to their hometowns. In the case of Ragland, the townspeople knew their town was fed first by the mining of coal and later by the making of cement.

Even as the community of Riverside developed over the years into an area noted for recreation, those who had deep roots there knew that Riverside had an earlier entry into economic growth that was fueled by saw-milling and lumber. A key to the success of the saw-milling and lumber business there was Riverside's strategic location on the Coosa River, which was used for transporting the lumber products by water.

In the small community of Cook Springs, in several ways the natural resources were never something to be taken for granted. The local people made their living from the saw-milling in the hills and mountains. The town also became nationally famous because of the mineral springs that paved the way for the construction and success of the Cook's Springs Hotel. In addition, the town became the scene of some thriving little sand businesses, since the sand in the Cook Springs area had a consistency that was ideal for use in cast iron foundries.

For some towns, it was the determined spirit of the people that was celebrated. Such was the case with Pell City. Although Pell City would become the largest town in St. Clair County, the town had to have two births to stay alive. Pell City was established initially in the late 1880s. The town died as a result of an economic panic in the mid-1890s. Then, beginning in 1901 and 1902, the town was reborn with the help of its hero, Sumter Bogswell, and a cotton mill.

Making History REALLY Come to Life

The occasion was Pioneer Days, one of the historical celebrations in St. Clair County. It was hosted by the St. Clair Historical Society. The event was being held in the John Looney Pioneer Museum between Ashville and

Ragland, a historical home that also was referred to as "the Looney House," with a history dating back to the 1820s.

On this particular day, elementary school children from the county were touring the facility and listening to some teachings about the history of the Looney House and its occupants of long ago. One of those serving as a combination tour guide and teacher was Historical Society member and retired Ragland schoolteacher Rubye Sisson.

Dressed in the long-dress attire of a pioneer woman, Mrs. Sisson used her school-teaching and theatrical skills to present a program to the schoolchildren. As the children gathered around her, Mrs. Sisson took on the role of Mrs. Looney, who had moved into St. Clair County as an early settler so many years ago.

As she played out the part of Mrs. Looney as a stage actress would do, Mrs. Sisson began talking about "her" life — which was really the life of this Mrs. Looney, who had lived more than 180 years in the past. "When I moved down here to St. Clair County, Alabama, I didn't really want to come," Mrs. Sisson told the children. "I was afraid of the Indians. It was so cold in the winter. As you can see, we had to get all our heat from these two fireplaces. And in order to go to our bathroom, we had to go outside in the bitter cold." She continued, explaining in detail how difficult St. Clair pioneer life had been.

As it turned out, Mrs. Sisson apparently gave an award-winning acting performance. Her play-acting became so real to one young St. Clair elementary-school girl that the child forgot that Mrs. Sisson was just pretending to be Mrs. Looney.

As soon as Mrs. Sisson finished telling about Mrs. Looney and her hardships, this little girl walked over to Mrs. Sisson and tugged at her long dress. Showing great sympathy about the hardships Mrs. Sisson had described, the little girl looked up at Mrs. Sisson and whispered to her, "You know . . . . if you want to, you can just come and live with me and my family."

History's Strong Advocates in St. Clair

The story of Rubye Sisson and the little girl at Pioneer Days became one among many stories associated with St. Clair County residents who had a strong commitment to preserving history in St. Clair County.

That commitment was so strong that the commitment itself began to evolve as an important added chapter in the county's history.

Some of the leaders in this St. Clair historical-preservation movement noted that they were not just preserving the past for the sake of the past. They also were preserving the past as a roadmap to show how St. Clair had arrived at its present and how it could go forward with its future.

This commitment to historical preservation was seen in influential groups, organizations, and places in the county. It was seen in historical buildings that already had been preserved or were in the restoration process. It was seen in special history-marking events. It was seen in historical compilations and books put together in the county.

The two most powerful historical-linked groups in the county were the St. Clair Historic Development Commission and the St. Clair Historical Society. Two leading centers for the encouraging of historical preservation were the Ashville Museum & Archives in Ashville and the Pell City Library in Pell City.

The St. Clair Historic Development Commission was appointed by the St. Clair County Commission to receive and distribute funds to maintain the county's history, including historical buildings.

The St. Clair Historical Society had a history dating back to 1972. It was formed in response to a desire on the part of a husband and wife to donate some property they owned for historical purposes. That property was the Looney House. The husband and wife were Colonel Joseph Reuel Creitz and his wife, Polly. At the instigation of avid historian Mattie Lou Teague Crow, an organizational meeting was held on April 8, 1972, for citizens with an interest in banding together to preserve St. Clair history. As evidence of the widespread interest in history among St. Clair County residents, by August of that year the charter membership in the St. Clair Historical Society had reached 275 people.

Teaching the Children

One of the priorities of the St. Clair Historical Society was to involve St. Clair children in researching and writing about the county's rich history.

Fourth-grade students in St. Clair are among those who were touched by the St. Clair Historical Society. "Every year in February, the fourth-graders in St. Clair County are given the opportunity to participate in the Historical Society's project on St. Clair history," said archivist Charlene Simpson of the Ashville Museum & Archives. "Each participating child is asked to write a short article and create an exhibit relevant to some aspect of the county's history. Children have selected topics such as the county's historical Looney House, Andrew Jackson and the Creek Indian War, Fort Strother, Hog-Dressing Day, Logan Martin Dam, and genealogical projects relevant to the students' own families."

Winners of the contest were selected from the schools, and then an overall county winner was selected. Mrs. Simpson said this has been great for the children and also for their parents.

"Particularly with so many new people moving into St. Clair County in recent years, this project has given both children and adults a chance to learn information they didn't know about St. Clair history," said Mrs. Simpson. "Since the Ashville Museum & Archives works with these children in their research and exhibits for this project, I have the opportunity to interact with the children while they are learning about St. Clair County's history and doing their projects. It is a joy for me, an absolute joy!"

Ashville Museum & Archives

As Mrs. Simpson spoke in a 2005 interview, she sat in a section of the Ashville Courthouse that had become the historical haven known as the Ashville Museum & Archives. (In months following this interview, plans progressed to renovate the Courthouse. As a result, the Ashville Museum & Archives became slated to relocate in 2007 to a former bank building across the street from the Courthouse.)

A combined small museum and a storage place for precious records, the Ashville Museum & Archives stood in 2005 as a testimonial to the commitment that county officials felt for historical preservation. The large amount of use this facility attracted stood as a testimonial to the value placed on the combined museum and archives by its patrons. The Ashville Museum & Archives drew a steady stream of historians, families researching their genealogy, schoolchildren doing papers and exhibits, title researchers looking up mineral-rights deeds, and visitors with an assortment of other missions.

In the memorabilia room there were precious artifacts, including an old medical bag and medicine bottle, saddlebags, typewriter, a spinning wheel, and old books. There was a sofa from the Cook's Springs Hotel. There was a handmade wooden fiddle from a recently deceased St. Clair basket-weaver/storyteller/fiddler named Ernest Mostella.

In adjacent record rooms, preserved in climate-controlled conditions, were rows and rows of beautifully bound volumes, some dating back to the beginnings of St. Clair County in 1818 and 1819. There were estate records, county commission records, and records pertaining to births, deaths, marriages, divorces, property lines, deeds, probate minutes, condemnation proceedings — anything one would find in a probate office and more.

"When I look around the room that is our museum, it's more like a memories room to me," said Mrs. Simpson. "Then, when I go to the part that contains our archives, our records, I am just fascinated with some of the entries contained in these historical volumes."

She gave some examples:

"In one of our archives volumes, there is an account of the first divorce in St. Clair County. It was in 1819, and the divorce actually was granted by the Alabama Legislature.

"In regard to old wills in the county, we have archival information about a will written back in the 1800s that particularly caught my attention. In this will, a St. Clair County man had stipulated that after his death his widow could have continued use of the household's kitchen utensils and the bed in their house — that is, as long as she didn't remarry. And this man who had authored the will had named his next-door neighbor as guardian of his property and his wishes — to oversee his money, and to make sure his stipulations were carried out about the limits to the rights of the widow."

Filling in Gaps in History

Leading historians in St. Clair County did not limit their activities to preserving historical buildings and records that already existed. When they saw a need, they created new records.

Such was the case in 1996, when the St. Clair Historical Society published a book on the history of the Cook's Springs Hotel and its mineral-springs waters. The book also provided information about the history of the St. Clair community of Cook Springs, including genealogical information on some of the community's pioneer families. The title of the book was *Sparkling Waters.* The subtitle was *A History of Cook Springs in St. Clair County, Alabama.*

The Historical Society was motivated to sponsor the researching and writing of this book because its members felt there wasn't enough information available to the public about historical Cook Springs.

Book co-author Daniel Stewart saw the need for such a history from his view as director of the Pell City Library. As was the case with archivist Charlene Simpson at the Ashville Museum & Archives, Stewart and the staff he supervised at the Pell City Library helped schoolchildren who were researching information about St. Clair's history. He said assisting those children as they tried to gather facts about the county's history served to identify gaps in the county's historical information. "Since our St. Clair Historical Society was supporting these county history projects among fourth-grade children, we began to realize that there simply weren't enough books on the history of the county," said Stewart. "So we began talking about what we as a Society could do to fill in some gaps. The subject of Cook Springs' history came up. And we decided to do that book on Cook Springs."

The idea to name the book *Sparkling Waters* came from book co-author Rubye Sisson.

"I got the idea for our book's title from a brochure that was used a century ago to advertise the hotel and the mineral-springs waters in Cook Springs," said Mrs. Sisson. "In that brochure that was put together by the people running the hotel at the time, there was this material about how the waters from the springs could cure all these different ailments. In that brochure, they referred to the waters located near the hotel as 'sparkling waters.' When

I saw that description, I said, 'Hey, that's good. I like that. That will be a great name for this book we're writing on Cook Springs.'"

What Drove Them to Preserve the Past

A range of motivators drove avid historians to devote their time and talents to the preservation of St. Clair's history.

Some were motivated because they have lived in St. Clair County most or all their lives, had contributed to the county's development, and were proud of the history. There were some whose ancestors had lived in the county since St. Clair's early days and had helped plant pioneer seeds for the county's success.

On the other hand, there also were newcomers to the county who became enchanted with St. Clair's history and wanted to help preserve it.

Joseph Whitten was one of those who was not a lifelong resident of St. Clair County. In fact, he had been partly driven to preserve the county's history because he moved there as an outsider and was so well received. Whitten came to feel that he was adopted by the people of the St. Clair town of Odenville, where he took up residence and taught English in local schools, first in junior high and then in senior high. "The people accepted me. I was at home. I loved the people. And the place interested me." To Joseph Whitten the term "place" came to mean not only the town of Odenville but all of St. Clair County. "When you fall in love with a place, you want to help. For me, I wanted to help write down the history."

For some St. Clair historians, a deep love of history was within itself enough of a motivating force to enlist their support in preserving St. Clair's rich history. But, here again, St. Clair's historical groups had members with diverse track records as history lovers. Some of them had been turned on to history since childhood, while others had just caught the history bug in recent years.

Although Rubye Sisson was among the county's historians who had spent much of her life in St. Clair County, she was not among those who had had a lifelong fascination with history. "My favorite subject definitely had not been history," said the longtime teacher of math. It was through genealogy that Mrs. Sisson became a history buff. "Oh, I'll tell anyone that for me this interest I now have in history goes back to my getting involved in genealogy. You see, I became interested in finding out about my own family roots years ago around the time when there was an increased awareness about genealogy all over the nation. And from there, I became so, so interested in history." Mrs. Sisson began doing historical research and writing. She began spending hours meticulously and patiently searching for historical facts in libraries, archives, courthouses, and cemeteries. She not only researched and wrote a history of Ragland but also researched and wrote studies of early marriages and early landowners in St. Clair County. "I am convinced that genealogy can motivate many people to become more aware and more interested in history," she said. "When schoolteachers begin assigning students to do their family trees, the students find out who their ancestors are and from there many of them tend to become interested in other aspects of history."

Within Mrs. Sisson's own family, the recording of history found another advocate — Mrs. Sisson's daughter, travel writer Lynn Edge. A native of St. Clair County, Ms. Edge later moved to Birmingham, which she used as a home base for writing for a number of travel publications scattered over the United States. "As I write travel stories, there is no doubt that history plays a big part in many of these articles," said Ms. Edge. "It seems that when I go into some town or city to write about it as a travel site, history becomes an important part of the story — no matter where the town or city is located. People want to tell you the history of where they live. They want to tell you about the historical buildings in their town and about the accomplishments of local citizens in developing the town. Residents of a town are proud of their town's history."

Tom Waldrop was the 2005-06 president of the St. Clair Historical Society. He said he had had a longtime interest in history. A native of Jefferson County who had moved to St. Clair in 1989, he said he was especially captivated by St. Clair's history. Waldrop made his home near Ashville in Beaver Valley. Prior to moving to St. Clair, he had been in the restaurant equipment supply business. As a part of that business, he had done some restaurant-related construction. He had building in his blood; his granddad had been a builder. So, after moving to St. Clair he combined his interest in building and his love of history in projects he undertook to restore older buildings. He restored homes and other buildings in and around St. Clair areas where he lived. One of his restoration projects was the Masonic Lodge Building in Ashville. "It has been so interesting to me to see how and why the original settlers moved to St. Clair County, how the county progressed at different times in its history, how the economy has changed and continues to change here," said Waldrop. "I think it's important that we remember these original settlers, why they came here, and what they accomplished."

St. Clair County Commissioner James S. "Jimmy" Roberts agreed with Waldrop. A proponent of historical preservation, Roberts said, "I think it's important that we see how people lived in our county in the past and compare that with how we're living here today. We need to know about and understand the struggles and the heartaches and the progress of those who came before us."

Buildings That Had Survived

Glimpses into the rich history of St. Clair County could be seen in a number of historical buildings that had been preserved in the county.

Those buildings had weathered the test of time with the help of determined members of groups such as the St. Clair Historic Development Commission, the St. Clair Historical Society, and the Sons of Confederate Veterans.

The aura that surrounded the historical buildings was linked to the buildings' respective ages, to the purposes for which they were used, to the people who had inhabited them, and/or to the uniqueness of the structures themselves.

And, in some cases, the aura became even stronger when enhanced by the stories of the individuals and groups that fought so hard to preserve the historical structures.

Four examples of historical-building treasures in St. Clair County were the John W. Inzer Museum in Ashville, the John Looney Pioneer Museum between Ashville and Ragland, the Ash-Newton Cabin some four miles south of Ashville, and the old Masonic Lodge Building in Ashville:

• JOHN W. INZER MUSEUM IN ASHVILLE. Beginning in 1866, a dozen years after this house was built, the structure became the home of John Washington Inzer, one of the county's most illustrious citizens. (John Washington Inzer became an early probate judge in St. Clair County, represented St. Clair County in the secession convention in 1861, served as a Confederate officer, was captured and became a prisoner of war, and after the war served in the Alabama Senate.) After the Inzer home had been in the possession of Inzer's descendants for generations, the home came into the hands of the Sons of Confederate Veterans to use as a museum.

• THE JOHN LOONEY PIONEER MUSEUM. Often called "the Looney House," this early-day St. Clair residence became a preservation project of the St. Clair Historical Society. A home with a history dating back to the 1820s, this house was viewed as a real historical gem because it was one of the earliest houses in St. Clair, because its builders were linked to Andrew Jackson, and because the house had unusual architectural features. It was built by John Looney and his son, Henry, who were members of Andrew Jackson's Tennessee Militia fighting forces when they first came into St. Clair County. The Looneys loved the area so much they decided to move other family members there and to carve out new lives for themselves in this beautiful wilderness land. After picking the spot where they would settle, John and Henry Looney built a two-story log cabin that had a design that would be a real focal point more than a century and a half later when the St. Clair Historical Society began opening the cabin to the public. By the time tourists began visiting the structure, it would be one of the rare buildings left standing that had a "double dogtrot" — referring to the so-called "dogtrot" hallway going straight through the middle of a house. In the case of the Looney House, there was a dogtrot both on the downstairs level and the upstairs level.

• THE ASH-NEWTON CABIN. Believed to be the oldest house still standing in St. Clair County, this log cabin on Highway 411 outside of Ashville had a history dating to 1817–1818. As historians spoke of it in 2005, they talked of the need to push forward with further restoration of this small historic structure. This was a cabin that bore the names of John Ash (for whom Ashville was named) and Ash's father-in-law, Presbyterian minister Reverend Thomas Newton. Ash was a progressive man who became a St. Clair political leader, an early-day St. Clair representative in Alabama's Senate. As the legend had been passed down, it was a tragedy rather than a planned occurrence that caused the Ash and Newton families to locate in St. Clair County. The two families were just passing through the area on a wagon train headed west. However, when the wagon train reached what later became St. Clair County, a young girl in the Ash family, Betsy Ann, was thrown from a wagon and killed. The child's family could not bear the thought of leaving her grave. So they stayed there and settled.

• THE MASONIC LODGE BUILDING. This historical two-story frame building in Ashville formerly had been used as a combination Methodist Church and home of the Masons. With a history dating back to the mid-1800s, this building had been moved from its original location and then moved again to still another location. The building's main savior, the person who persuaded powers-that-be not to tear it down and who found people to raise money to move and restore it, was historian Mattie Lou Teague Crow.

Mattie Lou Teague Crow Strikes Again!

A legend was born out of the successful battle that Mattie Lou Teague Crow waged to save the Masonic Lodge Building in Ashville.

Mrs. Crow began to draw her battle lines when word got out that the lodge building was in jeopardy. The site where the building was located was needed for other purposes. Since the Masonic Lodge Building was so old, the decision was made to tear it down.

Archivist Charlene Simpson personally witnessed what unfolded. Mrs. Simpson recalled this account of how the determined spirit of history-heroine Mrs. Crow prevailed again:

"At the time all this took place, I was working in a small room in the library in Ashville, and the Masonic Lodge Building was located just across the street from the library. Well, one day Mrs. Crow walked in the door of my office and asked who was responsible for plans she had just heard about to tear down the Masonic Lodge Building. I told her I didn't know. She said she was going to City Hall to ask about it. She walked over to City Hall, and she talked to the mayor. He told her it wasn't him. So she came up to talk with the county commission chairman. He was not in his office. The ladies told her that they expected him in shortly. She said she was going across the street to the drugstore and that, when the commission chairman came in, to please ask the chairman to come over to the drugstore and meet her there.

"A while later the county commission chairman walked into the drugstore to join Mrs. Crow. The commission chairman and Mrs. Crow had their meeting there in the drugstore. As the meeting wore on, Mrs. Crow told the chairman the history of the Masonic Lodge Building and how important it was, what an asset it would be to the community, and how awful it was that they were destroying it.

"Before the chairman left the drugstore, he promised to give Mrs. Crow the lodge building — that is, if she could raise the money to have it moved.

"The next week, Mrs. Crow called me and asked me go across the street and measure the lodge building, for me to also look and see what kind of foundation the building had, and to call her back. I told Mrs. Crow it was raining. She told me I wouldn't melt.

"So, I looked across the street and began thinking about how I would measure the building. I called my husband and his partner — my husband being a timber buyer and his partner being in real estate. They came down and looked the lodge building over. They sort of gave an estimate as to how tall the building was and looked under it to see what kind of foundation it had. I called Mrs. Crow back and gave her the information. Based on what I told her, she said she knew she could have it moved successfully.

"Then Mrs. Crow started looking around for help. She went to the Historical Society. But they disagreed with her. They told her the lodge building was too far gone, that it could not be restored. Then she went to the American Legion. They told her they thought that building would just not move at all, that it would probably fall apart going down the street and that also they didn't have the funding to help her.

"A real-respected lady in Ashville happened to walk into my office at the library one day soon afterward, and we were talking about Mrs. Crow's efforts with the lodge building. The lady told me, 'Well, I'm afraid Mrs. Crow has lost this one. I don't think she's going to be able to save that Masonic Lodge Building and get it moved.'

"Why, it had not been more than two hours after that lady told me that when I looked out across the street, and there was my husband up in a window in that Masonic Lodge Building doing some measuring. Then I saw that there were a couple of other men out there measuring that building, too. So I walked across to see what they were doing. They told me not to bother them, that they were working for Mattie Lou Crow. It seems that Mrs. Crow had decided that if she couldn't move the building all in one piece she would have it torn down and then put back together on a smaller scale. So they were measuring to see about that.

"As it turned out, Mrs. Crow didn't have to do it that way after all. She found a group of ladies who decided they could raise the funds to try to move the whole building. They did that; they raised the money. Mrs. Crow knew who to pick to raise money, and those ladies she picked could raise money! Now, the next thing that Mrs. Crow had to do was to get the building moved without it breaking apart.

"Needless to say, many people around Ashville kept saying the building would fall apart when they started to move it. There were people in all these little coffee groups that met over at the drugstore here in Ashville who were talking about that building, about how what Mrs. Crow was trying to do would never work, that she couldn't save that old building.

"So the day came when the building was being moved. Why, that building just went down the street perfect! It didn't even shake as it was being moved. And Mrs. Crow had even managed to get a nearby lot donated that she could have the building moved to. Just as Mrs. Crow had intended, the building was moved, the building was restored, and the building is still here today."

7

The Close-knit Community
of Cook Springs

"There is just something that is ongoing about the Cook Springs community."
—Faye Howard, longtime resident, Cook Springs area

A mule-drawn wagon made its way down a bumpy wide path called Ferguson Road in the community of Cook Springs. Along the way, the driver pulled the wagon to a stop to allow grateful passengers to climb aboard. The driver was Frank Polk. At his side was his wife, Maude. They were on a regular "run" to pick up friends, neighbors, and family members — to take them to church services at Cook Springs Baptist Church.

This was a flash from yesteryear out of the memories of this couple's granddaughter, Shirley Polk Estes. "My grandparents would take their wagon a couple of miles down Ferguson Road to pick up both children and adults in the community, to take them to church for services on Sunday and then for prayer meeting on Wednesday night," said Mrs. Estes.

Mrs. Estes' recollections came from the late 1930s and 1940s, when she was growing up in Cook Springs. "Sometimes I would be on that wagon with my grandparents and others who got aboard. I even remember the names of the mules pulling the wagon — Kate and Mary."

She noted that similar occurrences had been taking place in Cook Springs long before she was born. "Back before my grandparents were picking up people in the wagon and taking them to church at Cook Springs Baptist, my great-grandparents were doing the same."

What Mrs. Estes described were typical scenes out of the history of the close-knit community of Cook Springs in St. Clair County, Alabama. It was the history of a community where generations of the same families made their homes, where people supported one another and the institutions around them — such as Cook Springs Baptist Church.

Mrs. Estes and her family were examples of those trends. Shirley Polk Estes was the great-granddaughter of early Cook Springs pioneer Franklin Marion Polk, Sr., the community's first postmaster. Shirley Estes' grandfather, Frank, had been the last of 11 children born over a period of 27 years to Franklin Marion Polk, Sr., and his wife, Mary Elizabeth. The firstborn of those 11 children (Shirley Polk Estes' great-aunt) was Eliza Polk, who in 1875 eloped to marry fellow Cook Springs resident LaFayette Cooke — founder of the widely known Cook's Springs Hotel.

Born and reared in Cook Springs, Shirley Polk Estes moved away from Cook Springs in her youth and decades later returned to make her home there. As she spoke in her 2005 interview, she lived, worked, and worshiped in Cook Springs. She was employed in the activities program of the Springs Manor assisted-living facility that was a component of the Village at Cook Springs senior-living campus. She also was the organist at Cook Springs Baptist Church. It was in this church's first home, a log cabin, where Mrs. Estes' great-grandparents began attending worship services not long after they arrived in Cook Springs in the mid-1800s.

Cook Springs Baptist had played an important part in the lives not only of Mrs. Estes' family but of many families in Cook Springs. Church members enjoyed one another and welcomed one another into their home-lives as well as into their church-lives. "I know there were many times over the years that my grandparents would take the church's minister and other church members back home with them to eat meals after church services," said Mrs. Estes. "My grandparents had this big long dining table that as I recall would seat at least eight people on the benches that ran along each side of the table. Why, those benches were so slick that you could reach

Churchgoers file into Vacation Bible School at Cook Springs Baptist Church, mid-1950s. (Note truck and cars of that era.)

your place at the table real quickly by just sliding right down a bench! At my grandparents' dining table in Cook Springs, there always seemed to be room for one or two more."

A Church at the Center of a Community

In 2005, the Cook Springs Baptist Church still stood within a stone's throw of where one of the church's earlier structures was built in the 1880s. The church, the pastor's home (parsonage) next door, and the cemetery located behind the two structures occupied property adjacent to where the old Cook's Springs Hotel once stood. The church and the parsonage faced a narrow street that still bore the name of hotel founder LaFayette Cooke, just across from the railroad tracks where the train once brought guests to the old hotel.

With an organizational history dating to 1858 and a first meeting place a few years later in a Cook Springs log cabin, Cook Springs Baptist Church had developed as the most durable anchor in Cook Springs. Beginning in the 1880s, the church's stability was helped along as a series of sturdier church structures succeeded the log cabin.

The 2005 layout for the Cook Springs Baptist sprawling piece of sanctuary-parsonage-cemetery property was slightly changed from past decades. For example, in early days the main church building had been located near the site where the parsonage was added in the late 1940s. Also, the 21st century church was a more modern version of the church's older buildings constructed on that same group of lots in the 1880s, 1930s, and 1960s. However, much remained the same on this site of a church that continued to serve as the only church in the community. Cook Springs Baptist still stood as an enduring place of worship, a church whose members gave insight into the spirit of a closely linked community.

In terms of the people of the church, deep historical threads still were much in evidence in the 21st century. Those historical threads were embedded into the family roots of some of those who filled the pews for services — church members whose families had lived in the Cook Springs area for generations. Those historical threads also were in evidence on the tombstones in the cemetery that adjoined the church — in many cases, tombstones of the ancestors of current church members.

The names on those grave markers served as an inventory of some of the early Cook Springs pioneering families, a number of whom had roots in the community dating back into the 1800s. There were graves for families whose names were household words among longtime Cook Springs residents. Examples included Cooke, Polk, Carreker, Beavers, Shurbet, Davis, Ferguson, Reeves, Stevens, Goodwin, Fincher, Brock, Isbell, Cline, Brown, and Williams.

"There is just something that is ongoing about the Cook Springs community," said Faye Howard, who made her home on Cook Springs Mountain and had deep Cook Springs family roots. Her mother was a Fincher, a descendant of members of the Fincher family who first came to Cook Springs in the 1800s. "When I attend services at Cook Springs Baptist, I'm very aware that I'm a member of a church where my relatives have worshiped for years and years," said Mrs. Howard. "There are people in our church, including my sister and myself, who can look out at that cemetery and see the graves of their relatives from long ago who have passed on. Some can look out and see the graves not just of their parents but also their grandparents and even their great-grandparents before them. There's something comforting about that — something that is, like I said, ongoing."

A number of the families in Cook Springs had become linked through the decades not only by friendship but also family ties, said Mrs. Howard. "I've heard our pastor at Cook Springs Baptist say on a number of occasions, 'Now if you're in Cook Springs, don't go saying anything bad about somebody. Because the chances are you easily could be talking to one of that person's relatives!' "

Bonds of Familiarity

For many longtime Cook Springs residents in the early 21st century, there was something comforting about being able to walk on ground where their ancestors had walked, about being able to visit with neighbors who were descendants of their ancestors' neighbors. Even in a few cases where old, historic buildings no longer existed (such as the hotel and the old com-

Crowd gathers at Cook Springs Baptist Church for the wedding of Sara Polk and Alvin Livingston, 1956. (Note guest at left arriving by bicycle.)

munity school), the sites where the buildings had once stood still looked a lot like they had in the old days.

Esta and Ed McLaughlin had that feeling of familiarity everywhere they turned in Cook Springs. They didn't have to drive far from their Cook Springs home on U.S. Highway 78 (Bankhead Highway) to see places they held dear.

Among the senior members of Cook Springs Baptist Church, the McLaughlins could reflect on how the church's appearance had changed. "I helped cut timber to use in constructing a new Cook Springs Baptist building back in the 1930s," said Ed McLaughlin.

If the McLaughlins departed the church and turned left down toward Cook Springs Road, or old Ferguson Road, Ed had reason to appreciate how much better the road was nowadays than in decades past. "Why, I can remember when this was just a dirt road, a mud-hole you might say. I used to travel this road in a mule and a wagon. That was the only thing that could get over it in the wintertime!"

If the McLaughlins drove out of the Cook Springs Baptist parking lot and turned right, they drove by the site where Esta Goodwin McLaughlin had attended a two-room school that since had been torn down.

If they drove a very short distance further, they passed the site where Esta's grandmother once had been postmistress at an early-day version of the Cook Springs Post Office. Esta was a member of a family that included 1800s pioneers in Cook Springs. Her postmistress grandmother had married a Shurbet, the grandmother's father had been a Carreker, and the grandmother's mother had been a Reeves — all much-respected pioneer names in Cook Springs.

At age 78, Esta McLaughlin in 2005 was clear as to why she felt happily grounded in Cook Springs. "My whole family has been here in Cook Springs. My parents and my grandparents before them, and on back before, were members of the church that my husband and I still attend, a church I've attended all my life and where I became a member when I was nine years old. We've raised our children in Cook Springs. We just never have found any place we liked any better than Cook Springs."

Age Not an Issue

Common bonds that held many people together in Cook Springs were a potent blend of family ties, long friendships, and community spirit and pride. Cementing these bonds was a history of local people coming together to share the good times and the bad, and to reach out to help and support one another. The results were resilient people connections, the kind of connections that tended to cut through boundaries of age and generation gaps.

"Age means nothing around here in Cook Springs," said Faye Howard. "You can talk with someone who is 25 years older or younger than you and feel as though you're talking to someone your own age. For me, Cook Springs is a place where I can go to church, go to the Fire Hall or some event in the community, and see people I've known forever. These are people with whom you can sit around and talk and socialize. I just feel a special connection. How old they are doesn't matter."

In 2005, one example of shared experiences between Cook Springs generations came in the connection between 61-year-old Shirley Wallace and 93-year-old Myrtis Ferguson. The two women shared several things in common. They were neighbors, living a short distance from one another on the same road in Cook Springs. They were relatives, Mrs. Wallace being a daughter of a sister of Mrs. Ferguson's husband, Vernon. But the forever-binding connection between these two women occurred the day that Shirley was born. "I brought Shirley into this world!" Mrs. Ferguson said proudly. For a number of years in days gone by, Myrtis Ferguson was an old-time nurse-midwife. She was a woman who became expert at helping doctors deliver babies, and in delivering them herself if the doctor didn't get there in time. With no formal training except what was given to her by family doctors and another Cook Springs nurse-midwife (Shirley Estes' grandmother, Maude Polk), Myrtis Ferguson helped deliver quite a number of babies in and around Cook Springs. "I couldn't tell you how many babies I helped deliver if my life depended on it. But it was plenty," said Mrs. Ferguson. In 1944, when she helped deliver Shirley Moss Wallace as the seventh and last baby born into the Moss household, she delivered baby Shirley into a home on what first was called Ferguson Road and later Cook Springs Road. Mrs. Wallace laughed in a 2005 interview and said she had not moved far from where Mrs. Ferguson delivered her. "I was born on what now is called Cook Springs Road, and I still live right here on Cook Springs Road."

Still a Tiny Spot on the Map

Although longtime Cook Springs residents marveled in 2005 about how much the area had grown up and developed in recent decades, the community still by all measurements was a little hamlet. There was no city hall, no mayor or city council, no local schools, no hospital, no shopping center. The fire department was a volunteer one. The biggest local employer was a senior-living community, the Village at Cook Springs, a much larger version of a small nursing home that had been founded more than a half century ago.

In its earlier years, Cook Springs consisted at the most of a few hundred people, even if one included some of the families who lived in the most remote nooks and crannies up in the mountains in the area. Over the years, as transportation had improved, Cook Springs had more and more become a "bedroom community." As motor vehicles and roadways had improved (including the coming of an interstate), there were increasing numbers of people who made their homes in Cook Springs but commuted to work in Birmingham, Lincoln, Pell City, or other surrounding locales. This had not meant that Cook Springs had experienced a big population boom, but it had meant that the community had its share of new residents and recently constructed homes. Still, the new homes that had been built in the area blended in appearance with those that had been there for decades. In 2005, Cook Springs still retained its wooded terrain, its country-setting atmosphere, and its imposing signature mountains, Bald Rock Mountain and Cook Springs Mountain.

Cook Springs resident Gale Bunt, sister of Faye Howard, described modern-day Cook Springs: "Today when we speak of 'downtown Cook Springs' we're still not talking about anything very big. We're talking about the Cook Springs Baptist Church and the parsonage, the office for the water authority (located on the site once occupied by the Cook's Springs Hotel), the Post Office, the tunnel (a one-lane tunnel, a real community attraction), and one store." The one store, an old-fashioned country general store selling everything from soft drinks to a few groceries to hardware items and gifts and collectibles, was J's Retail — owned by Gale Bunt's husband, Jeter Bunt.

A Two-Way Impact

With such a small number of institutions and residents in Cook Springs, a clear-cut pattern of mutual influences began emerging as far back as the community's 1800s beginnings.

On the one hand, the institutions in Cook Springs greatly impacted the lives of the residents of Cook Springs. These institutions near residents' remotely located rural homes became the places of worship, learning, caring, work, and fun that helped to mold their very lives.

And, on the other hand, the residents of Cook Springs greatly impacted the institutions that developed there. Simply put, the residents helped make the institutions what they became — by becoming the local institutions' members, students, employees, and clients.

It was a two-way street of mutual impact.

Cook Springs was a compact community. Many of its residents, particularly early-day residents, put the most trust and value in what happened close to their homes. Contributing to that feeling in early-day Cook Springs was the fact that travel was so limited back then and much of life for the residents took place close to home.

Life-molding community impact was seen particularly with two institutions in the community — the Cook Springs Baptist Church, and a small school that operated in the community for decades (Cook Springs School).

Far-reaching influences on the community's exposure, lifestyle, and image were seen with the high-profile Cook's Springs Hotel, hotel founder LaFayette Cooke, and other members of the Cooke family. The community was proud of the mineral springs and of the mineral-springs resort that LaFayette Cooke founded. The springs and Cooke's resort in fact brought the community its greatest identity in the eyes of the outside world. It was a very positive identity of a beautiful, quaint garden spot where people could get away from their stresses.

Deep influences on Cook Springs also were seen with members of other pioneering families in addition to the Cookes. Cook Springs in fact was comprised of families who cared about their community and contributed to it.

Life in Cook Springs in many ways was a charmed life. Even back in times of widespread economic hardships, dusty roads, and dawn-to-dusk hard work, Cook Springs was a place surrounded by natural beauty and alive with interesting goings-on — a place where unforgettable, colorful memories were born and nurtured.

A Cook Springs Resident Remembers

It was in late 1923 when Myrtis Ferguson first became a resident of Cook Springs. At the time, she was Myrtis Davis, and she was going on 12 years old. When she moved to Cook Springs, Myrtis initially spent some time living in the home of her grandparents, saw-mill owner A.B. Davis and his wife, Sarah.

It was from her vantage point in her grandparents' home that young Myrtis had a front-row seat to the excitement surrounding the Cook's Springs Hotel when it still was in its heyday. The reason she gained such insight was that during the time she was living with her Davis grandparents in the 1920s, the Davises were making their home in one of the Cook's Springs Hotel cottages, located a short distance from the hotel. Myrtis thus lived in a cottage that was part of the network of vacation cottages that LaFayette Cooke had constructed to supplement his hotel in providing lodging for the guests who came to his resort.

"By the time I came to Cook Springs, they weren't using all these cottages for guests. They were renting out some of them for Cook Springs residents to live in," said Mrs. Ferguson in a 2005 interview. "The cottages were furnished with furniture, and you had to supply your own towels and sheets and things like that. There was a number of those cottages up and down the road, sometimes situated near one another kind of two-deep. In

Above, the landmark one-lane tunnel in Cook Springs. Below, the landmark railroad tunnel in nearby Chula Vista.

some places it seemed that wherever there was a spare spot of ground, there was a little cottage."

As a resident living in one of the resort cottages so near the hotel, young Myrtis Davis had a bird's-eye view of the operation of the Cook's Springs Hotel, at the time being managed by Preston H. Lewis.

"When I came here in the 1920s, that hotel was going full-blast in the summertime," said Mrs. Ferguson. "When those people got off the trains there at the hotel, they were all dressed up — the women with hats and gloves and everything!"

As young Myrtis moved through her teenage years, the hotel-and-cottages resort continued to make vivid impressions on her. She was touched by the mineral water, the good food at the hotel, and perhaps most of all, by the pavilion that was the hotel's main recreation facility.

"The water was pumped out of the ground up there out of the pumps at what we called the Springs House. Now, the water was different kinds. That freestone water was really good water. But I'll have to say that to me the sulphur water tasted like rotten eggs!"

Meals served in the large hotel dining room were nothing short of delicious, said Mrs. Ferguson. She came to know the cook at the hotel, a woman who lived there in the Cook Springs community. "At the time, that woman was cooking most all the meals they served in the hotel's big dining room, and I can tell you that she fixed some of the best meals you ever tasted in your life. And that woman worked! Also, she would walk to work at the hotel, quite a distance from where she lived way down the road here in Cook Springs. Now, I wondered why this woman's husband couldn't give her a ride to work. I mean, that man had a good team of mules and a wagon — that's how people around here traveled back then. But that poor woman would walk up to that hotel to cook those wonderful meals for all those people — lugging a 24-pound bag of flour and an eight-pound bucket of lard!"

The pavilion near the hotel created memories for Myrtis Davis Ferguson in many ways. The pavilion was a site for dances — something to entertain hotel guests, and also a pastime for some in the community.

The pavilion was a place for chit-chat — and not just for chatty females. "Down underneath this two-story pavilion was this open area where they had some chairs and benches. The thing I recall was that some of the men would gather down there and, as I say, would sit around and gossip," said Mrs. Ferguson. These were not just men who were guests of the hotel, but also men who lived in the Cook Springs community.

Too, she remembered the pavilion as the site for some memorable community events. "The very first bridal shower I ever saw — actually, the first bridal shower I ever heard of in this community — was given up there at the pavilion." That bridal shower was given for Lewis Polk and his bride, Verna. The young Polk couple later moved into a cottage that was part of the hotel resort. It was in this cottage, in 1935, where the couple's only child, a baby daughter, was born. This was a daughter named Shirley (Shirley Polk Estes).

When Myrtis Ferguson was interviewed for this book, she was living on a main road running through Cook Springs — a road now known as Cook Springs Road but for years before called Ferguson Road (for her husband's deeply rooted Cook Springs family). At age 15, three years after she had come to Cook Springs, Myrtis had married Vernon (J.V.) Ferguson, a young man who went to work for her grandfather in his saw-mill. Vernon and Myrtis had four children — thus continuing the tradition of producing more Fergusons to live in Cook Springs.

Relaxing on front porch of Cook Springs combination Post Office and General Store. From left, Postmistress Louise Glidewell, Frank Polk, and Polk's daughter, Sara Polk Livingston, 1950s.

As she shared her memories, Mrs. Ferguson gazed pensively out a window of her home, looking out at the woods and the chirping birds. Her face broke into a smile as she recalled her grandparents, her parents, her deceased husband, Vernon — all people with whom she had shared life in Cook Springs in times gone by. Her smile became even brighter when her telephone rang and she heard the voice of her youngest child, daughter Sammie Ferguson Wade, who lived a short distance down the road from her on Cook Springs Road. For Myrtis Ferguson, this was all welcome continuity in motion. Mrs. Ferguson noted that there still were generations of Fergusons living on this road that once bore the family's name. "Oh, I do love it here in Cook Springs," said Myrtis Ferguson. "You know, I've been here a long time."

Shortly after Myrtis Ferguson's interview in June 2005, she changed her place of residence. She moved into a senior-living community, the Village at Cook Springs. She still had the birds and the woods just outside her

A newer version of Cook Springs Post Office, built in late 1950s. (Note school bus making its stop.)

window. She was only a short distance from the home where she formerly resided. After all those decades, she was still living on Cook Springs Road. In 2006, Mrs. Ferguson was accorded a high honor, when she was crowned Ms. Village at Cook Springs during an annual pageant hosted by the Village's nursing home section. That honor came only two months prior to Myrtis Ferguson's death on June 28, 2006.

Cook Springs School

For more than 70 years, Cook Springs had its own school — a school that carved a permanent soft place into the hearts of those it touched.

Myrtis Davis Ferguson was a student there for a time in the 1920s. Esta Goodwin McLaughlin was a student there in the 1930s. And Shirley Moss Wallace and her sister, Sarah Moss Wells, were Cook Springs School students in the 1940s and early 1950s, respectively.

"I attended the first and second grade at Cook Springs School, during

Cook Springs School, smaller building at left, was located next door to Cook Springs Baptist Church. The school closed in the early 1950s, and the school building later was torn down. The church, with roots dating to 1858, has gone through several building programs and is still an active church.

the school's last days in the early 1950s," said Mrs. Wallace.

During that period, young Shirley saw the last days of both the Cook Springs School and the nearby Cook's Springs Hotel.

"The Cook Springs School was located close to the Cook's Springs Hotel, with just the Cook Springs Baptist Church property in between," she said. "By the time I was a student in the Cook Springs School in first and second grades, starting in September 1950, the Cook's Springs Hotel was so old and rundown that it was empty and was really starting to fall in. It would soon be torn down." At ages 6 and 7, young Shirley was among the school children fascinated with the hotel. "Sometimes in the afternoons I would stop to play in that old hotel when I was on my way walking home from Cook Springs School."

The reason the Cook Springs School closed its doors was that the school no longer had enough students to justify its existence. "By the time I went to school there, there just weren't enough kids in the community in the lower grades," said Shirley Wallace. From its beginnings, Cook Springs School served students only in lower grades. To attend junior high and high school, students went to other schools, mainly to Pell City. "After the Cook Springs

School closed, Cook Springs students in all the grades went off somewhere else to school, like to Pell City," said Mrs. Wallace.

The first version of a Cook Springs School dated back to sometime in the 1870s. Land for that school, next to Cook Springs Baptist Cemetery, was donated by Russell Alexander Carreker. That school functioned in the same building until some point around 1914. Then the first building was replaced by a bigger two-room school building, near the site of the first school, on property donated by LaFayette Cooke and his wife, Eliza. It was that school that remained in operation until the school closed in the early 1950s.

From all indications, the first school building was so primitive that it fell on decidedly hard times before a replacement school building was built. One early-1900s glimpse into hardships related to the first Cook Springs School structure was recorded in John Russell Carreker's book that chronicled the family history of the Polk and Carreker families — a book entitled *Franklin Marion Polk: Farmer, Soldier and Pioneer.* This book recalled the school's hardships through the memories of a Carreker relative, Lillie Alma Morton Batson, who taught in the original building used as the Cook Springs School. Mrs. Batson's memories came from a period in her late teens (likely

Cook Springs School. The school's first building opened in the 1870s and was replaced in the early 1900s by this building, which was demolished several years after the school closed.

around 1913). "I taught there (at Cook Springs School) for three months in a dilapidated one-room school building," Mrs. Batson recalled in her memoirs in the Carreker book. "There were two wood-burning heaters, one in each end of the room. The boys would take turns coming early to get the fires started, and the men in the community were supposed to make sure we always had a supply of firewood, but they didn't always do it." Mrs. Batson said the reason the first Cook Springs School building was closed soon thereafter (and replaced by a second structure) was "because it was so dilapidated."

When a replacement building was constructed for the Cook Springs School in the early 1900s, it was a sturdier, more spacious facility. The wooden two-room replacement structure had large windows, a foyer-like hallway in between, a big pot-bellied stove that provided better heating, and a bit of space set aside for a coat closet.

"When I went to school in that Cook Springs School building in the 1920s, children were coming from miles around to attend that school. They walked to school from all over the mountains," said Myrtis Davis Ferguson. "We had these two rooms in the school, and we were supposed to have two teachers — one for students in each room. But part of the time we only had one teacher, and when we only had one teacher we just used one room."

During the 1930s, Esta Goodwin McLaughlin studied hard and made straight A's during the time she went to the Cook Springs School in grades one through six.

"Both rooms of the school were in use when I went to Cook Springs School, and we had two teachers," said Mrs. McLaughlin. "We had first, second and third grades in what we called the Little Room, and fourth, fifth and sixth grades in the Big Room. When the teacher was teaching first, second and third grades in the Little Room, she would take a certain amount of time with the children in first grade, and then those in second grade, and then in third, and she'd start over again. I remember we had to buy our own books and furnish all of our school materials."

The 1930s brought in a large supply of students for the Cook Springs School, said Mrs. McLaughlin. "I imagine there were 100 or more students going to school there then — really a crowd of students. The bus brought some kids there from the nearby community of Brompton. Some children walked up Cook Springs Road, three miles or so, from back on the mountain."

When Sarah Moss Wells attended grades one through six at the school in the 1940s, the teaching arrangement was much like it had been in the 1930s. "A teacher would teach one grade a little while and then teach another, like an hour or two at a time with each," she said. Mrs. Wells said she really did not want to leave that school behind and go to Pell City after she finished sixth grade at Cook Springs, the last grade taught there. "The idea of going to that bigger school at Pell City was scary," she said.

Even by the time the Cook Springs School reached its final days in the 1950s, it still in many ways was the same rustic school that had opened years before. Students such as Shirley Moss Wallace loved their school. "For our water, we still had hand pumps outside. And we still had some of that old mineral water that tasted funny," said Mrs. Wallace. "We had no indoor bathrooms; we still had the outhouses." And, for enjoyment during play period outside, there was a simple swing set.

For years after the Cook Springs School closed, the small wooden school building was used as an activities building for the Cook Springs Baptist Church. Then the school building was demolished.

"During the time Cook Springs Baptist used it as an activities building, the building was used for things such as ping-pong games and for church socials," said Cook Springs Baptist member Gale Bunt.

Mrs. Bunt said she thought about the school building and the old Cook's Springs Hotel both in the same vein, in that she hated to see them torn down. In the case of the school building, Mrs. Bunt and her sister, Faye Howard, had special personal ties. "Our mother, Grace Fincher George, started going to the Cook Springs School around 1918," said Mrs. Bunt. "That school building would have made a wonderful historical building in the community. But by the time it was torn down, the school building was really old. After the church took over the school building, there was the issue of the church having to keep paying insurance on that old building." Some remnants of the old Cook Springs School building still existed in the community in 2005. In her home in Cook Springs, Shirley Polk Estes had a treasured piece of furniture, a hutch, that had been made out of some of the timber from the Cook Springs School.

Cooke Family Imprints

The Cooke family had tremendous influence on Cook Springs in at least three ways:

• The naming of the community for the Cooke family.

• Lifestyle exposure in the community, mainly through what the Cook's Springs Hotel and its network of cottages brought in terms of entertainment, culture, reputation, pride, and new experiences.

• Members of the Cooke family who personally touched others and/or influenced community lifestyles. It was said, for example, that LaFayette Cooke owned the first car in Cook Springs and one of the first cars anywhere in St. Clair County.

The Saga of a Community's Name

Beginning in the 1850s, when the Cooke family was becoming entrenched in the Cook Springs area, that area informally was referred to by many as Cooke Springs. (*Note:* Cooke, with an "e.")

The tendency to call the area "Cooke Springs" was intensified when William Praytor Cooke, Sr., (LaFayette Cooke's father) began developing his small mineral-springs resort that was based on "the springs" in the area.

However, it was not until late 1883 that the community was officially given the name of Cook Springs. (*Note:* Cook, without an "e.")

The timing of this late-1883 official naming of Cook Springs came in conjunction with two developments.

The first development had to do with when the first post office actually was established in Cook Springs. Although families gradually had been moving into the community since the early 1800s, it wasn't until 1882 that Cook Springs got its own post office. Prior to that time, the community's mail had been handled by the post office in a neighboring community. For a few months after Cook Springs got its own post office, the post office was called Polk Post Office. This was in honor of the community's first postmaster, Franklin Marion Polk, Sr., who also was LaFayette Cooke's father-in-law.

The second development having to do with officially naming the community and post office in honor of the Cooke family related to the timing of when LaFayette Cooke completed a second version of a mineral-springs resort in Cook Springs. This was a resort much more expansive and more spectacular than the original small, rustic one founded decades before by his father. The decision in late 1883 to name the post office and community for LaFayette Cooke coincided with the time when he completed construction on the hotel that was the centerpiece for this resort — and which put the community on the map. One could speculate that it would only seem practical that since LaFayette Cooke would be advertising his hotel far and wide that the name of the community should match the name of the hotel.

When the community officially was named for the Cooke family, there was a discrepancy in how the name was spelled. The spelling of the Cook Springs post office and community didn't exactly match the spelling of the family for whom it was named. The "e" on the end of the Cooke family name was omitted in the community and post office name. Down through the years, there would be some who would think that was a mistake, an oversight. Others would say it was done on purpose but they didn't know why.

Raymond Cooke, great-grandson of LaFayette Cooke and, in 2006, still a resident of the Cook Springs area, had this view: "I have heard it said, and I know it has been written, that this difference between the spelling of our Cooke family name and the spelling of the Cook Springs community's name was because my great-grandfather decided to change his name and take the 'e' off of it. That never happened. The spelling of our family name was never changed. The real story is this: They had to leave the 'e' off our family-name spelling when they named Cook Springs because the entire family name wouldn't fit on the postal cancellation stamp at the Cook Springs Post Office."

The version that Raymond Cooke gave was the same as that given in the 1996 history of Cook Springs entitled *Sparkling Waters*, published by the St. Clair Historical Society and written by Daniel Stewart, Rubye Sisson, and

Joseph Whitten. According to these authors, a brief unsuccessful attempt was made to match the community post office name with the Cooke family name. This is the report from that book: "The post office was established as Cooke Springs but had to be changed because it was one letter too long for the postal cancellation stamp, so it became Cook Springs."

Even after the post office settled on Cook Springs as the name for the community, there were various slight differences in how the community name was spelled when referring to LaFayette Cooke's hotel. The hotel was alternately marketed as Cook's Springs Hotel (the more popular listing) and, occasionally, without the apostrophe, as Cooks Springs Hotel.

However, as time went on, the version of Cook Springs for the name of the Cook Springs community finally would stick.

LaFayette's Survey

From all accounts, if LaFayette Cooke had not become distracted by other business interests in the early 20th century, he might well have launched developments in Cook Springs that could have resulted in even more far-reaching changes in the community.

As the owner of some 1,700 acres in the Cook Springs area, and with the buying power to purchase even more property, LaFayette was in a position to influence land-use in the area. In 1911, he had a large area in Cook Springs surveyed. Conducted by Wheelock Engineering Co. in Birmingham and signed by surveyor Charles Wheelock, this survey produced a map complete with designated lots and streets in Cook Springs. On the survey, the streets were called by such names as Chestnut, Pine, and Cherry.

One could only speculate that the Cook Springs development LaFayette Cooke had on his mind at the time did not materialize, partly because his business and personal life moved on to other locales. Beginning around the time he had the survey completed in Cook Springs, LaFayette Cooke was already becoming more and more involved in business ventures in nearby Pell City — business ventures including his owning of a telephone company and a bank.

A decade later, when he was in his late 60s, LaFayette Cooke would be moving to Florida, to spread his wings in the real-estate business and to make his home in Miami.

Generations of Cookes and Cook Springs

There could be no doubt that mineral-springs resort magnate and successful businessman LaFayette Cooke was the most high-profile member of the Cooke Family. However, the community of Cook Springs felt the presence of other Cookes — in generations before, during, and after LaFayette's time.

Family members who made particularly strong marks in the community included LaFayette's father, one of his sisters, one of his daughters, one of his nephews, and one of his grandsons.

A Cooke Father, a Cooke Sister, and a Cooke Daughter

LaFayette Cooke's father, William Praytor Cooke, Sr., would forever be known as one of the early Cook Springs pioneers, dating back to the 1840s. He also would be known as the founder of the original small version of a mineral-springs vacation spot in Cook Springs, in the 1850s.

LaFayette Cooke's older sister, Jane, became a much-loved resident of Cook Springs. Known to many of her family members and friends as "Aunt Jane," she was nine years older than LaFayette. When she was 16, a major life-molding event occurred in Jane's life when her mother died. While her four older brothers helped their father carry on, Jane, as the oldest girl, took on a motherly role with her three younger sisters and her younger brother, LaFayette. Although Jane would never marry and never have children of her own, in a sense she became everyone's mother. She became deeply tied to Cook Springs life and to the people in the community. For a time she served as the postmistress at the Cook Springs Post Office. A dedicated member of the Cook Springs Baptist Church, she was the church's organist and started the church's Sunday School and served as its superintendent and as a teacher. LaFayette Cooke's grandson, Herbert Cooke, remembered well how much his Great Aunt Jane loved Cook Springs: "After Grandpa and Grandma Cooke moved down to Miami, Florida, Aunt Jane went down there and spent some time living in Miami. But then I recall that

Black & White Gardens restaurant was founded during Depression era by Jack Cline, LaFayette Cooke's nephew. The restaurant gained national attention during the 1940s and early 1950s. The restaurant and a motel that was added were converted to St. Clair Nursing Home.

during the mid-1930s, during a time when I was living in Cook Springs, Grandpa and Grandma Cooke came up from Florida to Cook Springs to bring Aunt Jane back there to live. Aunt Jane wanted to live out her senior years there in Cook Springs." Jane Cooke still was living in Cook Springs when she died in 1940, at the age of 94. She was buried in Cook Springs Baptist Cemetery.

Among LaFayette and Eliza Cooke's six children, the one who became most visible to Cook Springs residents was their firstborn, daughter Jessie Mae. As was true of her Aunt Jane, Jessie served for a time as Cook Springs' postmistress. Too, during early years of the 20th century, when her father began concentrating more on his developing business interests in Pell City, Jessie and her husband, Henry Riggan, for a time managed the Cook's Springs Hotel.

A Cooke Nephew

Jack Cline, a colorful entrepreneur nephew of LaFayette Cooke, became the proprietor of one of the best-known roadside restaurants in the United States. The eating establishment was known as the Black & White Restau-

BREAKFAST

SERVED FROM 7:00 A.M. TO 11:00 A.M.

JUICES

Fresh Orange Juice	15c	Grapefruit	10c
Tomato	10c	Prune	10c
Milk	15c	Chocolate	10c

Coffee — 10c

CEREALS

ALL CEREALS, SERVED WITH MILK 25c

Rice Krispies   Pep   Corn Flakes
40% Bran Flakes   Oatmeal

SMOKED HAM (2) EGGS 75c
SMOKED HAM (1) EGG 65c

PAN SAUSAGE (2) EGGS 75c
PAN SAUSAGE (1) EGG 65c

Served with Grits, Buttered Toast, Jelly and Coffee

BACON (2) EGGS, Hominy Grits, Buttered Toast,
Jelly, and Coffee 65c
BACON (1) EGG 55c

TWO EGGS, Grits, Toast, Jelly, Coffee 40c
ONE EGG, Grits, Toast, Jelly, Coffee 35c
BUTTERED TOAST, Jelly, Coffee 25c
ORDER OF BACON, HAM or SAUSAGE with Toast,
Jelly, and Coffee 50c
PANCAKES, SAUSAGE, SMOKED HAM or BACON, with
Maple Syrup, Butter, Coffee 75c
PANCAKES, TWO EGGS, Coffee 75c
PANCAKES, Coffee 40c

MILK AND CHOCOLATE EXTRA ON ALL ORDERS

★ ★ ★

PLEASE PAY WAITRESS
Waitress cannot change an Order after given to kitchen

PLANKED T-BONE STEAK

Service For One—$3.25   For Two—$6.00
A Delicious Western Steak Seared On Both Sides
Then Broiled Slowly Until Done

WITH THIS WE SERVE

Potatoes   Celery Hearts   Salad   Sliced Tomatoes
Coffee — Tea

Time: 45 Minutes

LUNCHEON SUGGESTIONS

CUBED STEAK $1.00
HAMBURGER STEAK, 1 Vegetable 1.00
VEAL CUTLETS with Cream Sauce .... .90
CHICKEN PLATE, 1 Vegetable
2 Pieces Chicken (no choice) .... .90
ONE PORK CHOP — ONE EGG, 1 Vegetable .... .90
CHICKEN LIVERS, 1 Vegetable 1.25
CHICKEN GIZZARDS, 1 Vegetable 1.00
CALF LIVER AND ONIONS 1.00
LAMB CHOPS 1.00
BLACK AND WHITE FAMOUS CHICKEN DINNER
One-Half Milk-Fed Fryer 1.25
FRESH LEAN PORK CHOPS 1.00
FRESH PORK HAM STEAK 1.25
HAM DINNER, Smoked Ham 1.00

ALL ABOVE ORDERS SERVED WITH FRENCH-FRIED POTATOES,
SALAD, COFFEE OR TEA

rant, or, more often, as the Black & White Gardens. It became popular with travelers from far and wide and was praised by nationally known guidebook author Duncan Hines.

The restaurant was located in the community where Cline had been born — Cook Springs, Alabama.

A man who marched to his own drummer, Cline went west to be a cowboy in his early-adult years, and then he lived a decade in Canada. Later he returned to his native St. Clair County soil. Beginning during the Great Depression of the 1930s, Cline tried to eek out a living in the Cook Springs community by setting up a restaurant on U.S. Highway 78, also known as the Bankhead Highway.

In being called the Black & White Gardens, the eating establishment was an obvious match for its name — because part of the restaurant was painted white and part of it was painted black. As the story went, the unusual paint job came about when Jack Cline was short on cash during the Depression.

Menu from Black & White Gardens restaurant, late 1940s or early 1950s. Hamburger steak with one vegetable, French-fries, a salad, and coffee or tea was $1.00. For 65 cents, a patron could purchase two eggs with bacon, grits, toast, jelly, and coffee.

Restauranteur Jack Cline.

He didn't have the money to buy enough white paint to paint his restaurant white or to buy enough black paint to paint it black. So he used the limited black paint and white paint he had on hand and alternated the two in painting the boards of the restaurant building.

A source of pride throughout St. Clair County, Cline's restaurant was the subject of considerable media coverage. A typical example was in an article in the *Pell City News* on October 23, 1947. The newspaper writer was describing how Duncan Hines had just listed the Black & White Gardens in his widely read book, *Adventures in Good Eating*. The article explained: "The significance and importance of this is attested to by the fact that only 14 restaurants and cafes in Alabama are listed in Mr. Hines' book."

The community of Cook Springs took special pride in Jack Cline's accomplishments for more than one reason. In addition to being known for his business success, Cline also was the product of a union between two pioneering families in the area — the Clines and the Cookes. Jack's parents were George Cline and LaFayette Cooke's sister, Mary Drusilla "Mollie" Cooke, the youngest of LaFayette Cooke's eight siblings. (The Clines and the Cookes were double-connected, because a brother of George Cline married another Cooke sister.)

After the Black & White Gardens became very successful, Jack Cline and his wife, Pauline, added a motel next to the restaurant. For years, they thrived. Then a business disaster struck — in the form of a new stretch of four-lane highway that was constructed through the Cook Springs area during the mid-1950s. That highway stretch was often referred to as part of the Birmingham–Pell City Highway; it later was converted to interstate standards to become a part of Interstate 20. This new four-lane highway section drew large amounts of traffic off of the old two-lane U.S. Highway 78 that ran in front of the Black & White Gardens. "It was like turning a water faucet off," Jack Cline would later tell the *St. Clair News-Aegis* for an article published September 28, 1961. "Traffic in front of our place had been 1,500 to 2,000 cars a day. When the new road was cut in, we did well to have two dozen cars pass a day."

Ever the problem-solver, Cline converted his motel-restaurant into a small nursing home after the new roadway bypassed and devastated what had been a thriving business. The nursing home that Cline established initially was called the Jack Cline Nursing Home; it later became the St. Clair Nursing Home. Cline sold the facility in the mid-1960s.

When Cline announced his plans in the 1950s to go into the nursing home business, it was at a time when there was much talk about the need for facilities to serve an aging population. His announcement came just a few years after another nursing home facility had taken root a short distance away in Cook Springs — a facility that would undergo several changes before it ultimately became a sprawling senior-living community called the Village at Cook Springs.

A Cooke Grandson Named Hubert

Among LaFayette Cooke's grandchildren, the member of the Cooke family in that generation who was most associated with Cook Springs was Hubert Cooke.

"Hubert was my twin brother," said Herbert Cooke. "For a short time in the 1930s, Hubert and I were in Cook Springs together. I left Cook Springs to go out to Louisiana to live, while Hubert remained in Alabama — spending a number of years in Birmingham but still staying real close with those people in Cook Springs."

For a time in his younger years, Hubert Cooke was involved in the family sand-hauling business in Cook Springs. (The sand in the Cook Springs area was marketable for use in various processes used by foundries.) Also, Hubert managed a large farm in the Cook Springs area belonging to several members of the Cooke family. In addition, he purchased another smaller tract of property there. Early in his young adult life, Hubert Cooke became active in the Cook Springs Baptist Church. On April 10, 1937, when he was 21 years old, Hubert Cooke was ordained as a deacon in that church.

Raymond Cooke, son of Hubert and his wife, Lucille, said that his father visited Cook Springs often even after moving his residence to Birmingham. "When my sister and I were growing up in Birmingham, most every Saturday my father would drive us out to the Cooke Family farm in Cook Springs and spend the whole day out there. My father really maintained relationships with the people in Cook Springs."

Among two of Hubert Cooke's closest friends in Cook Springs were Vernon Ferguson and his son-in-law, Knox Wade, husband of Vernon and Myrtis Ferguson's daughter, Sammie.

"It was kind of something that was carried forward in our family — Sammie's daddy and then me becoming such good friends with Hubert Cooke," said Knox Wade. "Before and after Sammie's father died, I spent hours and hours with Mr. Hubert. He and I loved bird-hunting. Both of us also enjoyed the horses we rode when we went bird-hunting."

Wade recalled Hubert Cooke as a kind, gentle man "who was proud of everything at Cook Springs." Although Knox Wade was almost a full generation younger than Hubert Cooke, Wade could appreciate much of the Cooke family history in Cook Springs. Wade had grown up in nearby Chula Vista and had been exposed to the history since he was a boy. He became intrigued with stories about the early years of the Cook's Springs Hotel, the mineral springs, and the pavilion. Wade was fascinated to hear stories of how the trains had brought guests to the hotel and how the hotel had been such a popular destination. When time came for the Cook's Springs Hotel to be torn down, Wade was a young adult busy at work in the Cook Springs and Chula Vista communities. It was Wade who hauled away some lumber from the hotel when the hotel was torn down — lumber that was used in building some homes in St. Clair County. Knox Wade said there could be no doubt that the Cooke Family and the Cook's Springs Hotel brought experiences and exposures to the lives of local people that otherwise would not have existed. "I'll give one example of that from my view," he said. "As a kid growing up in Chula Vista, I well remember when I first heard they had been playing tennis at that hotel. Before then, I didn't even know that the game of tennis existed!"

In 2006, Knox and Sammie Wade lived on Cook Springs Road, not far from the site where the Cook's Springs Hotel once stood as a central part of the Cooke family legacy. In the backyard of the Wade home was a proudly displayed sign. It was the sign saying "Cook Springs" — the same sign that for years was at the railroad stop at the Cook's Springs Hotel. The historical sign had been a gift from Hubert Cooke to Knox Wade.

The first fire truck used by Cook Springs Volunteer Fire Department was loaned by City of Birmingham.

Hubert and Lucille Cooke, who died in 2002 and 2005 respectively, were buried in Cook Springs Baptist Cemetery.

Still a Cooke Presence in Cook Springs

In 2005, there was one member of the Cooke family living in the Cook Springs area — Hubert and Lucille's son, Raymond.

"For years there were no Cookes at all living in the Cook Springs area," said Raymond Cooke. "Today my sister, Linda Cooke Harrison, and I actually are the only members of the Cooke family left who live anywhere in Alabama. Linda lives in Hartselle, Alabama, and I live here in the Cook Springs area."

Section Three

~

*American School
of Evangelism*

8

Cook Springs Resort Property
Converted to Evangelistic Use

"No professor or teacher or lecturer is ever allowed to teach in said school the so-called modernistic, heresy, anti-Christ, or evolution doctrine."
–LaFayette Cooke, in a 1930 agreement he wrote and signed conveying his Cook Springs property to the American School of Evangelism

On November 23, 1929, LaFayette Cooke composed a letter to an evangelist who was a leader in a Mississippi-based organization called the American School of Evangelism. Cooke was confirming his decision to donate to this religious organization almost 1,600 acres of land in Cook Springs — the site of his once-grand mineral-springs resort anchored by the Cook's Springs Hotel.

The United States had fallen on hard economic times. Cooke composed his letter less than a month after the infamous "Black Tuesday" — October 29, 1929 — the day of a devastating stock market plunge that history later would define as signaling the official start of the Great Depression. On the whole, Cooke himself would continue to fare well financially in the Depression years. In 1929, 75-year-old LaFayette Cooke already was well-entrenched in a land-development and real-estate business based in Miami, Florida, where he and his wife, Eliza, had made their home for several years. The letter that Cooke wrote on that November day was hand-written on the stationery of

122

his South East Coast Land Company in Miami.

By the time the Depression arrived, the once-flourishing mineral-springs resort that Cooke had established in Cook Springs, Alabama, had begun to struggle. In fact, the glitter had worn off many of the once-popular mineral-springs hotels that, like Cooke's, had sprung up in the late 1800s and early 1900s around the initial building of the railroads. It had been years since Cooke personally had managed operations of his Cook's Springs Hotel resort that he strategically had located at a railroad stop on a line of the Georgia Pacific Railway (later Southern Railway). Cooke's tenure in presiding over the luxury hotel, beginning in late 1883, had been a grand time. It was a period when well-dressed guests arrived on the train and ate delicious meals in the elegant dining room, danced the night away at Cooke's nearby pavilion, and enjoyed daytime hikes in the tree-laden mountains. For a time after Cooke moved on to other business interests in nearby Pell City, Alabama, in the early 1900s, and then on to Florida, his family members had operated the hotel. Then Cooke had leased out the hotel to various operators. Now, with the arrival of the hard economic times of a nationwide Depression, it was apparent that the frills of resort vacations would not be a priority with Americans — at least not in the foreseeable future.

The Cookes' Religious Commitment

In decades to come, there would be those who would speculate as to how LaFayette and Eliza Cooke arrived at the decision to give this large tract of Cook Springs property to the American School of Evangelism for religious use.

Their grandson, Herbert Cooke, said he wasn't familiar with the specifics of their decision to donate their property to the American School of Evangelism. However, he said it came as no surprise to him that his grandparents chose to use the property to promote a religious cause. "When I was growing up, I knew Grandpa and Grandma Cooke to be very devout Baptists," said Herbert Cooke of Sulphur, Louisiana. "Actually, as religious as my grandparents were, what did come as a surprise to me — considering Grandpa and Grandma's strong Baptist beliefs — was that they had ever allowed all that dancing at the pavilion they erected at the Cook's Springs Hotel." But, after all, a "dance pavilion" was a prevalent component in the business model of many of the upscale mineral-springs resorts such as Cooke's.

Alabama "Springs-Linked" Evangelistic Precedents

By the time LaFayette Cooke decided to give his property for evangelical purposes, some strong precedents had been set for establishing religion-linked operations on or near mineral-springs properties. This included some Alabama precedents.

Notable examples in Alabama included a religion-linked school established near a mineral-springs resort in Washington County (in the lower southwestern corner of Alabama) and a Baptist summer-meeting gathering place established in what had been a mineral-springs hotel in DeKalb County (in the upper northeastern corner of Alabama).

The faith-based school in Washington County was established by a Mobile minister after he had a good experience as a guest at Healing Springs, a mineral-springs resort in that county. This minister had been suffering from an inflamed-eye condition, and he felt that the Healing Springs mineral water helped his condition. He decided that this type of healthy, beautiful environment would be a great place to build a school and educate young people. So he resigned his church pastorate and, with the help of a Baptist group, established the Healing Springs Industrial Academy for high-school-age students next door to the springs property. Although the school closed in 1914 due to financial struggles, it drew high praise for its educational standards during the time it operated.

The religion-linked development in the quaint north Alabama town of Mentone in DeKalb County involved the conversion of the old Mentone Hotel mineral-springs resort and its 200 acres into a site for meetings under the auspices of the Alabama Baptist State Convention. This faith-based development took root in 1920. To pave the way for the development, eight Baptist leaders formed a private corporation (the Mentone Springs Company) that bought the hotel and then leased facilities to the Baptists and other groups. Dormitory and classroom space were added to supplement the hotel facilities. In terms of the type of operation, this Mentone development would have some similar characteristics to the faith-based enterprise that eventually would result in Cook Springs after LaFayette Cooke donated his property. However, in terms of survival, the Mentone operation would have a much shorter life span than would the one at Cook Springs. While the Cook Springs operation would take root very slowly and struggle through the Depression years of the 1930s, it would emerge in the 1940s as a more thriving force. However, the economic pressures of the Depression would end the Mentone facility's life as a Baptist-linked operation in 1932.

A Link to Fighting Evolution

The organization to which LaFayette Cooke gave his Cook Springs property, the American School of Evangelism, was an evangelistic group based in Blue Mountain, Mississippi. A key leader in this group, the leader to whom LaFayette Cooke wrote his November 1929 letter stating his intentions to donate his Cook Springs property, was evangelist T.T. Martin.

Evangelist T.T. Martin and businessman LaFayette Cooke shared the same thread of strong opinions opposing the theory of evolution. As LaFayette Cooke followed up his 1929 letter with a 1930 formal agreement to donate his Cook Springs property for religious use, Cooke would make it clear he didn't want anyone teaching evolution on the land he was donating.

In T.T. Martin, LaFayette Cooke had found someone who not only espoused strong anti-evolution beliefs but who also had attracted national attention for waging an anti-evolution crusade. During the 1920s, Mississippi-born pastor and revivalist Martin had attracted considerable notoriety after he wrote a widely circulated book entitled *Hell and the High Schools*. In that book, Martin vehemently denounced any teaching of evolutionary thought, particularly in the nation's high schools.

Also referred to as "Darwin's Theory," the theory of evolution that both Cooke and Martin opposed was a theory about the natural evolvement of man that dated back to the 1800s writings of British naturalist Charles Darwin. The theory of evolution ran counter to the religious convictions of many. In fact, opponents of that theory often referred to evolution as

Darwin's "monkey theory," a reference to the concept of man being descended from monkeys.

At the time that LaFayette Cooke decided to give his property to the American School of Evangelism for use in religious teachings, there was renewed interest among many religious leaders and groups in waging a war against the theory of evolution. This stepped-up interest had been triggered by a much-publicized 1925 trial in the small town of Dayton, Tennessee. That trial often would be referred to by journalists and historians as the "John Scopes Monkey Trial." It involved a criminal case against Dayton schoolteacher John Scopes, who had been charged with teaching the evolution-based theory to Dayton high school students. This was a trial that pitted famed defense attorney Clarence Darrow against high-profile politician/newspaper executive/journalist William Jennings Bryan, who appeared at the trial on behalf of the prosecution. Scopes was convicted, but his conviction was overturned on a technicality.

As the Scopes trial unfolded during the hot summer days of July 1925, evangelist T.T. Martin joined the throngs of people who gathered in Dayton, Tennessee, to witness this controversial spectacle. Martin himself emerged as an object of considerable media and public attention during the days of the trial, as he lectured against evolution on Dayton street corners and sold and autographed copies of his *Hell and the High Schools* book.

The Agreement

Four and a half months after LaFayette Cooke sent his letter of intent to evangelist T.T. Martin, Cooke drafted and signed a formal agreement outlining his land-and-buildings gift to the American School of Evangelism. The handwritten agreement donating the Cook Springs resort property, complete with the hotel and outbuildings, was signed by both LaFayette Cooke and his wife, Eliza, on April 8, 1930. One of the witnesses was their eldest child, daughter Jessie Cooke Riggan.

In this agreement, LaFayette Cooke spelled out the specifications and conditions of his gift. He outlined the generous boundaries of the almost 1,600 acres. He outlined specifications about the land's resources — about

the handling of mineral rights, the cutting of timber. In the case of the Cook's Springs Hotel, the key building on the property, he noted that "the hotel shall always be kept insured against fire." (There had been a long-standing concern about protecting the wooden hotel building from fire. A number of similar wooden recreational structures around the nation, including several hotels located on remote forest-laden sites, had met their ends through fires.)

In regard to the mention of evolution in the agreement that LaFayette Cooke drafted and signed, Cooke was clear in his feelings. He referred to the teaching of evolution as a "forbidden doctrine." He specified that the property he was donating should never be used as a site for teaching this doctrine: "No professor or teacher or lecturer is ever allowed to teach in said school the so-called modernistic, heresy, anti-Christ, or evolution doctrine."

A Faith-Based Mission Taking Root in Cook Springs

After LaFayette Cooke donated the hotel and the property in Cook Springs, the mission that took hold there in the 1930s and 1940s had two components. The site provided faith-based camps for both youth groups and adult groups — the camps mostly being held in the summertime. Also, the site provided a place where religion-linked organizations could hold their meetings. At the beginning, Baptist organizations were the main ones to use the facility. As time went by, Methodists also became heavy users. Some other church denominations also participated.

A couple of decades after LaFayette Cooke donated the property, a third component would be added to the Cook Springs site. This third component, founded as a nursing home for retired ministers and missionaries, would evolve into a general nursing home and later would expand into a campus of several types of facilities for senior-adult living.

Immediately after LaFayette and Eliza Cooke signed over the property in 1930, the job of managing the property, and any operations conducted on the property, was assigned to a group of trustees who functioned as representatives of the American School of Evangelism. All the trustees lived

Campers file into Assembly Hall at early-day Cook Springs Campground, 1942.

near Cook Springs, mostly in St. Clair County. In the initial period after the trustees took over, they explored the possibility of establishing a junior college on the Cook Springs property, to use in educating ministers, missionaries, and other mission-associated representatives. However, this idea did not pan out. The trustees instead turned their focus to using the site for faith-based camps and religious meetings.

As the Great Depression tightened its vicious economic-turmoil grip on the United States, the trustees did very little with the Cook Springs site in the early 1930s. They proceeded very gradually. As the nation began to creep forward in the post-Depression years, the trustees began with modest religion-linked summer camps in the mid-1930s — using the hotel for lodging. When they started, they did so on an economic shoestring. For economic support, they had to depend heavily on churches and other Christian organizations that sent their members there. The churches and other organizations also had suffered financially during the Depression. So, to make the camps work, everyone who participated had to pitch in to help out with food and supplies — including the individual campers and their families.

Cook Springs Campers in the 1930s

Among the many who had religion-linked camping experiences at the American School of Evangelism's Cook Springs site in the 1930s were Elouise Wilkins Williams and Maizie White Bradford. At that time, both Mrs. Williams and Mrs. Bradford already had strong Baptist backgrounds. Both would go on to be leaders in various Baptist endeavors. In the mid-to-late 1930s, they came to Cook Springs with two different Baptist groups — elementary-age schoolgirl Elouise with the GAs (Girls Auxiliary), and young wife-and-mother Maizie Bradford with the BYPU (Baptist Young People's Union).

Maizie Bradford was in her 20s when she and her sister went to Cook Springs in the mid-1930s for a week-long faith-based camping retreat. These two young women had responsibilities as young wives and mothers, so they needed the help of their own mother to go away for a week. "Our mother babysat with my son and my sister's two sons so we could go to Cook Springs for that camping retreat. We really wanted to go," said Mrs. Bradford. Since their dad was a Baptist minister who had been a leader in churches in Jefferson and St. Clair Counties, the sisters had long been exposed to inspirational Christian programs and were looking forward to more in Cook Springs. They were not disappointed. Mrs. Bradford said some of the classes at the Cook Springs retreat were taught outdoors, in the beautiful mountains. "The first thing we did every morning was to have sunrise service. They had benches out there on the side of the hill, and we sat on those benches for our devotional every morning." As the day wore on, programs included a mixture of faith-based classes and songs. "All the programs we had there were religious in nature. Everything about the programs was Christ-centered," said Mrs. Bradford. She said in the afternoon there was free time, and for some campers that included hiking. "In the afternoon, we could walk up Bald Rock Mountain. Some did that, and others didn't. I was one of those who walked up that mountain. There was a trail that already was made for us. By the time I got to the top, I was really ready to sit down!" She said the view was so spectacular it was hard to believe. "You could see everywhere!"

Mrs. Bradford also recalled how campers had to pitch in to make the economics of the retreat work: "All of us who attended the retreat had to bring our own linens — our blankets, sheets, pillowcases, even our pillows. Also, we had to bring our own food. We had a list of the food we had to bring. This included bringing a pound of bacon, a pound of ham, a dozen eggs, some fresh vegetables and some canned vegetables, a jar of jelly or preserves, and a pound of meal and a pound of flour. They used that flour we brought to make us fresh biscuits every morning. And the workers there were all volunteers — the cooks, everybody. We had to go through a line and get our dishes washed — our plate, glass or cup, whatever. We carried our own plate to and from meals."

As Mrs. Bradford recalled the Cook Springs retreat in a 2005 interview, she was making her home in the same area where she had enjoyed that camping experience 70 years previously. She was a resident of an assisted-living facility (Springs Manor) that was part of the retirement community known as the Village at Cook Springs. At the Village, Mrs. Bradford had helped develop a chapter of the WMU (Woman's Missionary Union). Mrs. Bradford also had another tie to the history of the Village at Cook Springs. Her mother had a brother by the name of Mack Roper. As a trustee with the American School of Evangelism, Roper in the late 1940s led the effort to start a Cook Springs-based nursing home for retired ministers and missionaries. This was an endeavor that planted the seeds for what ultimately grew into the senior-citizens' retirement community called the Village at Cook Springs.

When Elouise Wilkins (later Elouise Wilkins Williams) came to Cook Springs for a Baptist GA camp in 1938, she was 10 years old. The camp was conducted under the auspices of the St. Clair County Baptist Association. Young Elouise lived in nearby Pell City, where her family was very active in the First Baptist Church. A little girlfriend of hers, a fellow GA member, was her roommate at the old Cook's Springs Hotel during the camp at Cook Springs.

"I just found everything so impressive, so different, when I attended the camp in Cook Springs that summer. And, since I was only 10 years old, I

was seeing it all through the eyes of a child," said Mrs. Williams. "I vividly remember the hotel as being this huge wooden structure. And that summer when we came, the hotel was almost vacant as far as being furnished. There was so little furniture in that hotel! My roommate and I were given a room with a bed and I think maybe also a chair. My little friend and I also had brought along a few other things from home that we placed in the room, and that made the near-vacant room look a little better while we were there. And we had brought our own linens as we had been instructed to do."

Mrs. Williams said there was little help in the kitchen that served the campers. So the campers had to help with chores. "When our meals were served, they had big pans of water, and each one of us would go through and wash his or her own plate." It was not the food she would remember from the meals; it was the water. "That sulphur water tasted like bad eggs!" she said with a laugh.

In terms of staying at the hotel, the main thing that would stick out in the mind of Elouise Wilkins would not be anything inside the big hotel structure. Instead, the big impression was made by what was outside the hotel — what periodically passed by outside, just a few feet from the front entrance to the hotel. It was the train. As a little girl not accustomed to that loud, shrill train sound, she found it exciting but a bit eerie. "Why, that hotel was so close to the railroad that during the night I sometimes felt sure that train was coming right through the hotel!" she said.

Young Elouise enjoyed the social activities at the camp. She also enjoyed the religion-linked teachings. "We had church at the camp. We had Bible study and religious discussions, just like you would have at any religious retreat. And these programs were led by people we already knew who were officers or other leaders of the St. Clair County Baptist Association."

At the time Mrs. Williams was interviewed in 2005, it had been decades since she and her attorney husband, Harold, had moved from their St. Clair County roots to make their home in Birmingham. Mrs. Williams had become a leader in a number of Birmingham civic and church endeavors, including the Samford Auxiliary that supported Baptist-linked Samford University.

The Two Hands-On Trustees

Although there were several trustees associated with the faith-linked operation in Cook Springs, there were two who were the most hands-on in day-to-day operations. One was Dempsey H. Moody, known to some as D.H. Moody. The other was Mack F. Roper.

Dempsey Moody in many ways became the caretaker of the old, and Mack Roper became the builder of the new. The names of Moody and Roper became so associated with the operation that some residents of the community referred to the faith-based development at Cook Springs as "what Mr. Moody and Mr. Roper have going on at Cook Springs."

Several years older than Roper, Moody was a resident of Cook Springs long before Roper lived there. During the 1930s period after the American School of Evangelism took over the Cook Springs property that had been donated by LaFayette Cooke, it was Dempsey Moody who served as the lead caretaker of the property (including the hotel). Meanwhile, during those Depression years and on into the 1940s, Mack Roper still resided in Trussville — where he ran first a large dairy-farm operation and later a hardware-appliance store. During the 1940s, Roper began coming to Cook Springs more and more to direct construction projects to build new buildings for the campground. During that decade, Roper closed first his dairy and then his hardware-appliance store. He then moved to Cook Springs. After he and his family took up residence in Cook Springs, Roper began directing the building of a nursing home for retired ministers and missionaries, which evolved into a nursing home for the general elderly population.

As Moody and Roper went

Dempsey H. Moody, longtime trustee of American School of Evangelism. Moody was a caretaker for Cook's Springs Hotel and worked with Mack Roper in operating Cook Springs Campground.

forward in this mission together, they became close friends and loyal working partners. The Cook Springs mission operation had its ups and downs financially — with some of the downtimes being real money crises. When those money crunches came, Moody and Roper took steps jointly to see to it that the Cook Springs mission survived.

Mack Roper's older daughter, Sarah Roper Smith, said she heard several stories about her father and Dempsey Moody struggling to make ends meet in Cook Springs.

"There was one time when Daddy and Mr. Moody were trying to get up some money for some pressing need regarding what they were doing at Cook Springs. So Mr. Moody took Daddy to the Moodys' home there in the Cook Springs community. Now, back then it was not uncommon for people to hide away stashes of cash in their homes — if they had stashes of cash, that is. Well, Daddy said when they got to Mr. Moody's house that Mr. Moody started pulling money out of all sorts of places! He was pulling money out of socks. He was pulling money out of pockets of old coats hanging in the closets."

Mrs. Smith also knew of a visit that her father and Dempsey Moody

made to a bank, to obtain a loan to help them through a difficult time with the Cook Springs mission. "They needed this money real badly to help out with a situation there in Cook Springs," said Mrs. Smith. "In order to get the loan, Daddy and Mr. Moody were going to have to stand good for the loan personally. Well, the bank took Daddy's signature, but they wouldn't take Mr. Moody's. The reason for that was so funny. And my mother really thought it was funny. You see, in the Moody family it was Mrs. Moody and not Mr. Moody who handled all the business for the Moodys. That guy at the bank told Mr. Moody, 'Now, your wife is the one I know!' So they had to send for Mrs. Moody. And Mrs. Moody had to come up to that bank to sign on the loan with Daddy, to get the money that Daddy and Mr. Moody needed to address whatever kind of pressing need they had in Cook Springs at the time."

The Ever-Active Dempsey Moody

Dempsey Moody was a small man who could rig up "fixes" for things. He was hardworking, a risk-taker, a man who marched to his own drummer. Even when he got himself into jams — which he often did — he maintained his cool and remained calm even if others around him fretted. He was carefree, funny, and the subject of many tales in the Cook Springs community.

When Moody took on the job as the trustee-caretaker at the American School of Evangelism's Cook Springs operation, he was just adding on one more role to his already varied work life. Some of that work was on his own. Some of his work was working side-by-side with his wife, Lizzie, who was the Cook Springs postmistress. On his own, he at times drove a truck for St. Clair County, hauling lime and fertilizer. He also handled truck-hauling of other items. He did some saw-milling. With wife Lizzie, he worked some in the small building in the center of Cook Springs that doubled as the community's post office and as a general-store type grocery that the Moodys operated.

A newspaper feature that focused on memories of Cook Springs appeared in the *St. Clair News-Aegis* on February 29, 1996 and recalled: "During the 1930s, Cook Springs residents frequented Dempsey and Lizzie Moody's general store, which also served as a post office. The Moodys were not averse to the barter system and would swap the community children's fresh farm eggs for all-day suckers."

That combination post office-general store was the source of fond memories for many. Shirley Polk Estes would later recall the store as a place that had a big stove in the back. "That's where we would go to keep warm while we waited for the school bus," she said.

In the rural Cook Springs community, the Moodys' general store was a place for one-stop shopping. Ed and Esta McLaughlin remembered the Moodys' store as a place where local folks purchased not only groceries and various household items but also gasoline for their automobiles.

"They would pump that gas by hand," said Esta McLaughlin. "And the gas would go up in a glass-looking thing, and it would measure the gallons. As Mrs. Moody put the hose into your vehicle, she could tell how many gallons she had."

Ed McLaughlin added with a laugh, "That thing would hold five gallons if you pumped it full!"

Some townspeople would describe the relationship between Lizzie and Dempsey Moody like something that later could have been the makings of a good television situation comedy/romance. In physical appearance, Dempsey and Lizzie were a real study in contrasts, he being quite small and she being a large, robust woman. They could bicker with one another. Yet they were very close, bound together by having shared times both good and bad.

As a daughter of trustee Mack Roper, Sarah Roper Smith came to know the Moodys well. She learned about their lives. One touching saga that she heard about had unfolded when Lizzie and Dempsey Moody were quite young — likely not long after they married and probably before the birth of their only child, a son.

"The story had to do with Mrs. Moody having tuberculosis," said Mrs. Smith. "You know, tuberculosis was quite a serious problem back then, and there was very little treatment being used other than rest and fresh air. It also was very contagious, and TB patients were supposed to be quarantined from other people. Well, for whatever reason — maybe money issues, maybe lack of access to any kind of treatment or convalescent or TB sanatorium facility — Mr. and Mrs. Moody just decided they would handle Mrs. Moody's tuberculosis care on their own. So they just left their home and moved up to an isolated spot on Bald Rock Mountain there in Cook Springs. They stayed there on the mountain for months. I don't know if they lived in a tent or a cabin or what. But Mr. Moody took care of Mrs. Moody. She rested. She got fresh air up on that mountain. And miraculously, she recovered. I've always thought that was the sweetest story."

Back in his youth, Ed McLaughlin worked some with Dempsey Moody when Moody was hauling various items in a truck. McLaughlin's brother, Fred, also worked some with Moody. McLaughlin said that Mrs. Moody worried about her husband being out so late at night in the truck. Mrs. Moody would fuss and fume. Her husband would remain calm, sometimes respond with some quiet wisecrack, and keep on doing whatever he was doing.

"I particularly remember one night when Mr. Moody and I had been out hauling something in this truck, and we were late coming in," said Ed McLaughlin. "Mrs. Moody was down at the post office when we got in. Mrs. Moody didn't want Mr. Moody fooling around with that old truck anyhow. She thought it was dangerous, him being out on the road, and she was afraid

Cook Springs Campground buildings, located in a picturesque setting. Note the steeple in right of photo. (Photo courtesy of Special Collections of Samford University.)

he'd get hurt. Well, that particular night when we were late she had been so worried about him that when we got in boy was she mad! She told Mr. Moody, 'You don't make the salt to go on your bread!' What she was telling him was that he was out there doing risky things and not making enough money to warrant it. He was just real calm, like always. He told her, 'Well, you get the bread, and I'll get the salt!' "

No one could question that Mrs. Moody had reason to worry about her husband. There was no telling what he would do, what kind of risk he would take, or what kind of a jam he'd get into.

Ed McLaughlin recalled one day when Dempsey Moody and his truck ended up in the Coosa River — with Ed's brother, Fred, as a passenger.

"This was a time when Mr. Moody and my brother were hauling bricks. It happened up at this ferry up near Coal City (in St. Clair County). Well, when you would drive off that ferry, there was a steep hill that you had to go up. And that old truck of Mr. Moody's got about halfway up that hill and choked down and ran back onto the end of the ferry. When it did, the ferry sank down. So Mr. Moody's truck was sitting out there in the Coosa River, with him and my brother in it. And the truck was really heavy, 'cause it was loaded down with all those bricks. Now, you know, that's real dangerous!

Mr. Moody and Fred had to crawl out on the hood of the truck that was still sticking out of the water. And they had to get a wrecker to come and drag the truck out of the water and up the hill. But you know, Mr. Moody just kept right on going. Mr. Moody didn't get excited over anything, and for that matter didn't seem scared of anything."

Dempsey Moody's finagling and patching way of doing things came in handy as the aging Cook's Springs Hotel required more and more upkeep. Dempsey Moody busied himself with repairs. He did most of the work himself, including repairing the roof. Since he was small, thin, and wiry, he scampered around the roof with ease. "Why, Mr. Moody was like a cat the way he climbed about!" said Ed McLaughlin's wife, Esta. It was quite a trick to reach the roof of the two-story structure, since the hotel's veranda-style porches and banisters protruded and got in the way. To reach the roof, Moody rigged up a ladder that leaned out away from the hotel structure — far enough out to clear those porches and banisters. Then he nailed in place some kind of make-do bridge-like fastener that linked the ladder to the hotel — hoping to make it strong enough to keep the ladder from falling backwards two stories down to the ground. Moody would climb that makeshift leaning ladder with a roll of roofing on his shoulder. He walked up and down the ladder with ease carrying tarpaper to patch holes. As far as anyone knew, he never fell, not once.

One day Ed McLaughlin got a big scare with that ladder Dempsey Moody had rigged up to reach the roof. "I was there at the hotel that day just meddling. I wasn't really doing anything. I just wanted to go up on the roof to see what Mr. Moody was doing," said McLaughlin. "To do that, I had to go up Mr. Moody's ladder. Now, all that Mr. Moody had holding this ladder in place were these two little old strips of something that he had nailed to the ladder and then nailed to a post on the porch of the hotel, with the ladder leaning back a ways from the building. Well, I somehow managed to climb that ladder to reach the roof. But after I got up there, I was scared to come back down that ladder — with that old ladder leaning back from the hotel building like that. I kept inching around on top of the roof, wondering how I would get down. Then I saw this tree. There was a great big old oak tree

Swimming pool at Cook Springs Campground. (Photo courtesy of Special Collections of Samford University.)

out there, and a limb of it ran out there over the hotel. I got out on that limb and came down that tree. I'll tell you that I didn't try to go up and down Mr. Moody's ladder again!"

Moody's ability to fiddle around helped fill a Cook Springs swimming pool with water for a while, said McLaughlin. He explained that Dempsey Moody built a wooden trough that ran from some of the freestone springs there in Cook Springs. He funneled the water from the springs down that makeshift trough about a quarter of a mile to the swimming pool. The trough was a big flat one, with a six-inch-wide bottom and two six-inch-wide sides. To support the trough, Moody built little posts to hold it up. "Now you talk about something that was hard to maintain!" said Ed McLaughlin. "In the summertime, it would get real hot and that lumber Mr. Moody had used to make that trough would dry out and shrink and crack, and all the water would start pouring out of those cracks. And Mr. Moody would have to shut up those cracks with rags and whatever. There he would be, chumping rags and everything up into those cracks."

Roper Leads Expansion

As the 1940s were ushered in, Mack Roper began driving from his Trussville home to Cook Springs on an increasing basis. He was directing some major expansions and improvements at the mission campground.

The campground was getting more use. More money was coming in. Despite the shoestring operation that trustees had been forced to run at the Cook Springs campground during the 1930s, the religious groups who came there were pleased with their experience with camping, retreats, and meetings. Religious groups now were willing to help the American School of Evangelism fund some expansion. It was time for new buildings — in fact, time to start building a whole new campground about a half mile from the old hotel.

"Beginning in the 1940s, the new buildings for the campground were constructed where the four-lane highway and then the interstate would be located a number of years later," said Sarah Roper Smith. "The camp buildings were rustic, unpainted — the kind you would expect at a rustic campground."

The first phase of construction, in 1941, consisted of a dining-hall structure and a building that had the dual purpose of being an assembly building and a classroom building. In a later phase, dormitories would be built — one for the boys and men and one for the girls and women. "And, out in the open space, there was this cross, with a trail leading out from the assembly hall to the cross," said Mrs. Smith. "Sometimes we would have our devotional services there by the cross."

As the first phase of construction got under way, there was much excitement in Cook Springs and surrounding communities. On May 8, 1941, the *Pell City News* carried a front-page article with the headline "Huge Church Convention Site Under Construction at Cook's Springs." Another headline read: "All denominations to hold summer meetings at former resort."

"M. F. Roper is in charge of a crew of men rushing some of the buildings to completion so that some of the state meetings expected to begin some time in June can be accommodated," the article noted. "The famed Cook's Springs water will be pumped to all buildings."

The article indicated who was sponsoring this expansion (including financial support). It specified the names of all trustees currently overseeing the operation, plans for use of the new buildings, and how the old Cook's Springs Hotel fit in with the new construction.

In terms of sponsorship: "The Baptists of Alabama in connection with other church associations are sponsoring the erection of a modern place where meetings, associations and religious and church conventions will be held during the summer months each year."

About the list of current local-based trustees for the American School of Evangelism who were involved with the Cook Springs operation: "Trustees of the estate are M. F. Roper, J. E. Griffin, W. I. Inzer, J. L. Mitchell, H. B. Woodward, D. W. Moody, and Judge H. L. Anderton, who also serves as attorney."

On plans for use of the new buildings: "When this long-range building program is completed, Methodists, Presbyterians, Episcopalians, and other denominations as well as Baptists who are sponsoring the plan, will use Cook's Springs as a place where summer meetings will be held."

About how the old Cook's Springs Hotel fit into the new construction: "The old Cook's Springs Hotel building has been remodeled and repainted and will be used for a girls dormitory. The hotel will accommodate approximately 300."

End of the Line for the Cook's Springs Hotel

The sounds of construction continued at the Cook Springs campground at various times during the 1940s. As the new buildings took shape, the old hotel was about to disappear. The stage was being set for the tearing down of the landmark hotel, then more than 60 years old. The hotel thus soon would travel the road of extinction that the mineral-springs resort's old pavilion building had traveled years previously.

For a time in the 1940s, the hotel continued to be used for campers in the summertime. But as new dormitories were built by Mack Roper's crew, that need disappeared.

Also for a time in the late 1940s, sections of the hotel were converted into an apartment building. Much like with the old cottages that remained as part of the mineral-springs resort, parts of the hotel were rented out to individuals who lived in the community. Several Cook Springs residents recalled family members living there in the late 1940s.

"My grandparents moved into that hotel after my grandfather had a heart attack," said Shirley Polk Estes. "The hotel had been made into an apartment building of sorts. As I recall, my grandparents had a bedroom, sitting room and a kitchen in their apartment at the hotel. My aunt also lived there at the hotel. Actually, I remember about four families living there at one time."

Sarah Moss Wells and Shirley Moss Wallace said their sister and her husband lived in an apartment in the Cook's Springs Hotel in the late 1940s. "They lived there right after they married," said Cook Springs resident Mrs. Wallace.

Toward the end of its existence, the hotel was no longer in use for anything. It was in disrepair and literally falling down in places.

"The hotel had been a beautiful building at one time. But it was time for it to be torn down. It had become a fire hazard," said Esta McLaughlin. "Mr. Moody had really worked to keep it up for years. But he was getting older and his health was failing, and it was really more than he could handle."

When the building was demolished, the American School of Evangelism sold the beautiful heart-pine lumber in the hotel to be used in constructing houses.

Several in the Cook Springs community put the time frame for the hotel's demolition in the early 1950s — likely around 1951 or 1952.

The hotel was still there but starting to fall down when Shirley Moss Wallace started to first grade at the nearby Cook Springs School in September 1950. She recalled playing in the hotel on her way home from school. She believed it was still there some in her second-grade year as well. But then it was gone.

Knox Wade believed the time frame for the hotel's demolition was likely in 1951 and no later than early 1952. "The reason I recall is that I hauled off some of that lumber from the hotel before I went into service (during the Korean Conflict)," he said. "Mr. Roper and Mr. Moody were the ones in charge of getting the hotel building torn down, and it was Mr. Moody who got some help for me to load up that hotel lumber so I could haul it off." Wade said the hotel lumber he hauled was used to build houses in Pell City.

One of those who bought some of the hotel lumber to build his own house in Cook Springs was longtime Cook Springs resident James Ritch. He built his house on old Highway 78, on a site a short distance from where the Cook's Springs Hotel had been located. As Ritch spoke in a 2005 interview, the house he had built from the hotel lumber still was standing, still was occupied, and was located next door to the house in which he currently resided. "I paid $500 to buy 14 rooms of pine lumber from that hotel — 7 rooms upstairs and 7 rooms downstairs," said Ritch. "I used that hotel lumber for most everything in my house except the rafters."

9

Building a Nursing Home
in Cook Springs

"Daddy awakened one morning and told Mother about a dream he had during that night. He told her this was the third time he had dreamed this same dream. It was a dream about building a nursing home in Cook Springs for retired ministers and missionaries."–Sarah Roper Smith, daughter of trustee Mack F. Roper of the American School of Evangelism

Mack Roper sat in his home in Trussville talking about a dream he had the night before. He was describing the dream to his wife, Grayce.

"Daddy awakened one morning and told Mother about a dream he had during that night. He told her this was the third time he had dreamed this same dream. It was a dream about building a nursing home in Cook Springs for retired ministers and missionaries," said Mack and Grayce Roper's older daughter, Sarah Roper Smith.

It was in the late 1940s when Roper shared this dream with his wife. By this time, Roper had served for years as a very hands-on trustee at the faith-based encampment and meeting ground in Cook Springs. In that trustee role, Roper had helped guide the operations at the campground in Cook Springs and had directed the construction of new buildings there. All the while, he and his family had continued to make their home in Trussville,

144

on the eastern edge of Jefferson County and just a few minutes' drive from Cook Springs. Roper devoted many hours to his trustee role in Cook Springs while at the same time managing his business interests in Trussville. For years he ran the large Roper Dairy Farm, and then he had a Trussville hardware and appliance store. When he was experiencing the dream of building a nursing home in Cook Springs, he already had stopped operating the dairy and was getting out of the hardware-appliance business.

As Grayce Stephens Roper sat and listened to her husband describe his dream, she felt his dream seemed more like a nightmare. She knew that her husband had his sights on an expansive new project that could be an all-consuming third career — building and operating a retirement home for ministers and missionaries. From several viewpoints, Grayce was not naïve about the implications.

"At first, Mother didn't like Daddy's idea," Sarah Roper Smith recalled with a smile. "Mother knew that if Daddy went forward with this plan, it was going to mean a lot of really hard work for both of them."

Grayce Roper was a smart, savvy, realistic woman who could envision in detail much of the planning, work, and hardships that would go along with her husband's dream. Her husband wasn't the only member of the family with a good business head on his shoulders. Grayce had a business track record as well.

Prior to marrying Mack Roper, Grayce held a very responsible job — particularly for a young woman in that day and age. She was head cashier of a large, upscale Birmingham department store. Having started out as a teenager working in this department store at the gift-wrapping counter, Grayce had worked her way up the ladder by her mid-20s to a job in which every single cashier in the large store reported to her. "Mother really had a good business mind and could have been good in any number of business fields," said daughter Sarah. "Years after she and Daddy married, Daddy's attorney would comment that he found it amazing how much Mother knew about law. That attorney said he felt that Mother would have made a good attorney."

When Grayce agreed to marry Mack, she was 27 years old and very secure

Cook Springs Nursing Home founders Mack and Grayce Roper, in the mid-1950s.

and happy in her career-life. "In fact, I heard Daddy say that he had been really afraid that Mother would back out of their wedding at the last minute," said Sarah.

But, despite her early aptitude for business and her quick success in a career, Grayce was in love with Mack Roper and did not delay or back out on their wedding in order to focus on a career. After she married Mack, she balanced her domestic tasks with assisting Mack in running the bookkeeping end of his businesses. Grayce became a dedicated wife and mother, an organized home manager, and such a superb cook that friends and relatives relished eating one of her meals. She was a deeply compassionate woman who reached out to help others, a woman who was deeply loved by those around her. In helping her husband keep track of business matters, Grayce continued also to be part-time businesswoman. Her efficiency was apparent in the precise manner she managed the books for Roper Dairy Farm, and then later managed the books for the hardware and appliance store her husband operated.

In the late 1940s, as Grayce listened to her husband talk about possibly starting a Cook Springs-based nursing home for retired ministers and missionaries, she had several specific concerns to ponder in addition to the workload itself. One consideration was age. Already deep into her 50s at the time and with her husband approaching 60, Grayce knew that just the physical stresses of establishing and operating a nursing home could prove to be especially demanding on a couple approaching their senior years. Another consideration was that if Mack went forward with this plan, Grayce likely would have to give up her home in Trussville and move to Cook Springs. She could see a lot of handwriting on the wall.

Mack and Grayce Roper's younger daughter, Martha Roper Saul, described the whole nursing home initiative as a major lifestyle change for her mother. "To support Daddy's dream of a nursing home, Mother would be giving up her own home, giving up everything," said Martha.

Grayce Roper was correct about how many events would play out. The next several years for her and her husband would be filled with hard work crammed into long days that often extended into the nights. However, what Grayce could not know in the late 1940s was that she would fall in love with the nursing home she would help her husband develop in Cook Springs, Alabama, and that she would fall in love with the patients and employees she met at that home.

The Energetic Mack Roper

Mack Roper was a sharp businessman and a hard worker, a man who seemed to have no bounds to his energy level. During the years he ran Roper Dairy Farm, he was awake by 4 o'clock in the morning and ready by 5 a.m. to supervise the milking of 110 cows. Then he oversaw other aspects of his dairy — a dairy that handled bottling of the milk and had delivery trucks to deliver the milk. At the end of the day, Mack Roper still seemed to have energy to spare.

"Daddy never seemed to just simply walk like other people did," said daughter Sarah. "He seemed to go in a half-run all the time, with those arms swinging at his side." She said her father loved to work. "Actually, the main reason Daddy decided to stop operating the dairy was not to retire from working. He stopped running the dairy because during World War II so many men were away in service that it was hard for him to find and keep help."

Mack Roper was a deeply religious man, very committed to his Baptist faith. He was a longtime member of Sulphur Springs Baptist Church, where generations of his family had attended. Although Mack's father had made his living as a farmer, he also had done some preaching. Mack Roper always seemed to have an eye toward helping others. As was the case with his wife, Mack Roper was loved by those around him.

In his role as a trustee of the American School of Evangelism faith-based operation in Cook Springs, Roper was in the same situation as his fellow trustees in that his religious faith drove him to serve.

Mack Roper Converting his Dream into Reality

Mack moved forward with his plan for a nursing home in Cook Springs for Baptist ministers and missionaries.

"There were just a few facilities of that type at the time. Daddy had heard of some, had visited some," said daughter Martha. "When Daddy talked to the other trustees with the Cook Springs operation about his idea, they approved it."

She noted that the trustees believed in Mack Roper. He had been a leader among the trustees, had served in a role Martha Roper Saul heard referred to as Head Trustee. "Daddy already had done a lot to enlarge the camp in Cook Springs and keep it going."

As the trustees began to develop plans to build the nursing home for retired ministers and missionaries, they took a fact-finding trip together to gain more information. "This still was such a new concept that Daddy was undertaking," said daughter Sarah. "I know that Daddy and some of the other trustees made a trip to visit an Alabama facility that was taking care of retired ministers. It seems like it was down below Montgomery."

The One Condition

Before the trustees gave Mack Roper the go-ahead to launch the nursing home project, they placed one condition on their final approval.

That condition was that Mack and Grayce Roper must move from Trussville to Cook Springs — to be on-site to oversee the building and operating of the nursing home facility.

Martha Roper Saul smiled as she recalled a message the trustees sent to her mother. "The trustees told Daddy they wanted to make sure that Mother wouldn't be stuck with doing all this work in running the nursing home. They told Daddy to be sure to tell her they didn't want her to be stuck with a lot of work. But handling a lot of work is exactly what Mother ended up doing."

When Mack and Grayce Roper moved to Cook Springs in the late 1940s to start the nursing home project, they were a true husband-and-wife management team. They would run the nursing home together. In so doing, they would set a precedent for husband-and-wife management of that nursing home that would last for decades.

Uprooting a Family

In moving their family from Trussville to Cook Springs to launch the nursing home project, Mack and Grayce Roper were uprooting their two daughters — 15-year-old Sarah and 12-year-old Martha. (The oldest of the Ropers' three children, son Murray, was already grown and married.)

Even though the move meant big changes for the two Roper daughters, the girls were moving to a place with which they already were familiar and which they already liked. Although Sarah and Martha Roper had spent years living in Trussville, they also had been exposed to Cook Springs quite a bit during the years their dad had been helping with the faith-based camp there. The Roper girls had grown up with Cook Springs being a warm, enjoyable part of their lives.

"Why, by the time we moved to Cook Springs, I had been going to summer camp there for years," said Sarah. "I think it was around 1943, when I was 8 years old, when Mother and Daddy first let me stay overnight with kids at the camp. During that camping experience, I stayed in the old Cook's Springs Hotel along with other campers. Of course, since Daddy was involved with the camp, he was there at Cook Springs while I was camping there."

In the late 1940s, Mack Roper was already busy with the camp in Cook Springs and then also was embarking on the nursing home construction project. During that period, the Roper family lived fulltime during a summer in one of the old Cook Springs cottages that had been built by LaFayette

Cooke as part of his resort back in the late 1800s.

"Daddy said he needed to be there in Cook Springs all the time around that period, instead of having to drive back and forth to and from Trussville," said Sarah. "The cottage where we lived in Cook Springs that summer was one of those cottages that had survived from those days way back when Mr. Cooke built that hotel. Now, when we lived in the cottage for that short summer period, I can remember only two of the old cottages remaining out of all those cottages Mr. Cooke had built. The cottage where we stayed was very rustic. We just slept there; we took our meals in the dining room used by the camp. One thing I especially remember was that the front porch of that cabin was covered with this big wisteria vine that was simply beautiful when it was in bloom. To me, looking at that rustic cabin with the blooming wisteria vine covering the old front porch was like looking at something out of a painting."

Nursing Home Opens

As soon as construction on the Cook Springs Nursing Home was completed in 1950, Mack and Grayce Roper and daughters Sarah and Martha moved into the nursing home. The family would live in the nursing home for several years.

Although newspaper articles sometimes would refer to this nursing home as the Home for the Aged, Sarah Roper Smith said the name she always heard for the facility was the Cook Springs Nursing Home. "All the time that Daddy and Mother were associated with the nursing home, I heard it referred to as Cook Springs Nursing Home," she said.

The nursing home was a U-shaped facility, much like a horseshoe-shape. It had a front porch. When the nursing home first opened, one wing of it was finished and ready for use, and a second wing was partly finished and would be completed as the need arose. As for furniture for the facility, "it just consisted of whatever Daddy and Mother could manage to come up with," said Martha Roper Saul. "I believe some of the furniture we used at the nursing home came from our home in Trussville. And some of it came out of the old hotel there in Cook Springs."

The very first people to move into the home were the four members of the Roper family.

"Mother and Daddy and Sarah and I lived in an apartment in the nursing home," said Martha. "At least, a kind of apartment was created for the four of us. Of course, the nursing home wasn't built as an apartment building. It was built as a nursing home. The rooms in which we lived had been constructed as rooms for four nursing home occupants — with two rooms with a bath in between, and two more rooms with a bath in between. When we moved into our family's little apartment in the nursing home after the nursing home first opened, this is how it was set up: The first room was our living room. It was fairly large. Then there was a bathroom, followed by Mother and Daddy's bedroom. Then there was Sarah's room, and another bathroom in between, and then my bedroom."

Sarah Roper would live in the nursing home for three years, until she married boyfriend Jerry Smith two months after she graduated from high school. Later Martha and her parents would move out of the nursing home into a home of their own. That move would come when the nursing home became so filled with patients that there was no longer room for the Roper family to live there.

For Mack Roper, it would be a happy time when he finally had a nursing home filled with patients.

The Nursing Home's First Years

The patients were slow in coming to the nursing home in the beginning. And, the Roper daughters said, from the start the patients who came were not the retired ministers and missionaries their father had envisioned.

"After the nursing home was completed and we moved in, at the beginning there were not any patients at all," said Martha.

"Not a soul," said Sarah.

However, it wasn't long before the nursing home's first patient arrived. The patient was an elderly woman. For a time, she was the only resident. She would live there several years, until she died.

"This woman was blind — had gone blind from glaucoma. She wasn't a

Ethel Cook, resident during early-day period of operation at Cook Springs Nursing Home, early 1950s.

minister. She wasn't a missionary," said Sarah.

The Ropers arranged some special services to help this woman enjoy life despite her loss of sight. "We ordered talking books for her — talking books for the blind that came on records that this lady could play on her record player," said Martha.

Also, as soon as teenager Sarah started driving, the woman was given some personal chauffeur services. "I would drive this lady up to see her sister, who lived up the mountain, not far from Cook Springs. This mountain location where this sister lived was really like way up in the boondocks!" said Sarah. "I had to drive up the mountain, with all these little pig-trails for roads, to get there. And that mountain fascinated me." Sarah believed this woman who was the nursing home's first patient likely had wanted to live in the new Cook Springs Nursing Home in order to be near her sister.

The weeks wore on before the nursing home's second patient arrived. This, too, was an elderly woman. She was not a minister, and she was not a missionary. However, she was very devoted to her religion. "I recall that this woman got up early every morning and had her own private devotional," said Martha.

The arrival of patients continued on a very gradual basis. "It was slow to fill up," said Martha.

"And it didn't take long for it to become apparent that they weren't going to fill up that nursing home with retired missionaries and ministers," said Sarah. "I think they (the trustees) just began changing the outlook about it and just said anyone could come. Now, they still really wanted to have Christian people there as patients."

Gradually more patients arrived.

"Within three to four years after it opened, the nursing home was pretty well full," said Martha. "One wing filled. The other wing was finished out, and it started filling up. As the nursing home got filled with patients, we moved our family apartment that we had there in the nursing home down to the end of that second wing."

The Whole Roper Family Pitching In

Running the nursing home was a family affair for the Ropers. Everyone in the family had a job — in fact, many jobs.

During the 1950s, Mack Roper was wearing two big hats at the faith-based American School of Evangelism in Cook Springs. He was running the nursing home. Also, he still was running the campground. With his time often spread thin, Mack Roper had to depend heavily on his wife, Grayce.

"During times when Daddy was so busy running the camp, particularly in the summer, Mother was basically running the nursing home. I mean, she was taking care of everything!" said Martha. "Mother really got close to the patients there. They loved her, and she loved them." Grayce was motherly to the patients. Even though most of the patients were quite a few years older than Grayce Roper, there was a tendency for some to refer to her as "Mama," said Sarah.

The nursing home tasks handled by Grayce Roper were diverse and many. From the outset, Grayce was handling the bookkeeping at the nursing home, just as she had done with her husband's businesses back in Trussville. In Grayce's initial years at the nursing home, she also was doing a lot of the cooking, laundry, and cleaning herself. "After we got in more residents, someone was hired to clean," said Martha. Already gifted at cooking, Grayce also took a college course in food preparation — a course at the University of Alabama geared specifically toward food preparation for nursing home residents. Even after she no longer was cooking all the meals, talented cook Grayce continued to oversee the cooking closely and frequently was there in the kitchen preparing food personally. Daughter Sarah recalled that when vendors would come calling, they seemed to like to come at mealtime. "Those salespeople who were selling various food items to the nursing home would try to schedule their sales visits for lunchtime, so they could eat some of Mother's delicious food."

Along the way, another relative of the Ropers moved into the nursing home and lived and worked there for a time. This was Grayce Roper's sister, Myrtle Stephens. "Aunt Myrtle was mother's sister who never married," said Martha. "It was after the nursing home started filling up when Aunt Myrtle moved in and worked there. By that time Sarah already had married, so Aunt Myrtle took one of the rooms in the second apartment we had there in the nursing home, down in the second wing."

The Roper daughters had a range of duties at the nursing home.

Sarah could remember all kinds of tasks, including tasks that helped to keep the nursing home looking pretty. "For example, I remember painting rooms in that nursing home," said Sarah.

Martha's talents as a pianist and organist were put to use at the nursing home. One of her jobs was playing the piano for daily devotional services. In addition to whatever private devotionals the patients might have in their rooms, the Roper family held a daily 10 a.m. devotional program that was open to all residents. Grayce Roper, with a clear alto voice, led the singing of three or four songs. Mack Roper would read scripture and give a short inspirational message. "When time came for the daily devotional, I would take my place at the piano in the dining room and just start playing a hymn," said Martha. "When the patients heard the piano start playing, that would be their signal that devotional services were about to start. The residents would all start coming to the dining room. I mean, everybody came! The nurses would roll some patients down in wheelchairs. They all just loved it!"

Becoming Attached to the Cook Springs Community

Just as the Roper family became close to the nursing home and its residents, the family members also became very attached to the Cook Springs community.

They became very active members of the Cook Springs Baptist Church. Martha Roper became first the church pianist and later its organist.

An already close friendship between the Ropers and Cook Springs residents Dempsey and Lizzie Moody deepened further. Even before the Roper family moved to Cook Springs, Mack and Grayce and their girls had been very fond of Mack Roper's fellow trustee, grocer/saw-miller Dempsey

Moody, and his wife, Cook Springs postmistress/grocer Lizzie. After the family moved to Cook Springs, the Ropers and Moodys saw more and more of one another.

"Oh, I can recall how much I enjoyed eating meals at the Moody home there in Cook Springs," said Sarah Roper Smith. "The Moodys' home was so neat and organized." She added with a laugh: "The neatness of their home was really a contrast to the fascinating clutter of the grocery and post office that Mr. and Mrs. Moody operated."

Sarah became quite close to Mrs. Moody. "I sometimes would go with Mrs. Moody to carry the mail to hang up on a hook by the railroad tracks, so the train-man could get it as the train passed by. Although the train no longer stopped in Cook Springs, a train-man would reach out and get that mail."

Fond memories of Mrs. Moody also would stick with Sarah regarding the period when Sarah was being courted by boyfriend Jerry Smith. "When Jerry went off in service with the Navy and was corresponding with me by mail, Mrs. Moody would get almost as excited as I would when those letters would arrive from him. I would go to check on my mail after I got home from school in the afternoon. And sometimes Mrs. Moody would be out in front of the post office calling to me excitedly, 'Oh, you just won't believe all this mail from Jerry that we've got for you here today!'"

A Lake and an Injury

After Mack Roper got the nursing home up and running, he added a lake out in front of the main entrance. Years later, after expansions and a new front entrance and new road were put in place at the nursing home, and after first the four-lane highway and later the interstate were built in the Cook Springs area, a smaller version of that lake would be located toward the back and side of the facility.

Through all the change and growth, the lake would endure as a source of beauty and entertainment for residents at the facility.

"When that lake was being built at the nursing home, Daddy sustained an injury to his shoulder," said daughter Martha Roper Saul. "It was a pretty big lake. And first they built a dam. One day before they had water in the lake, Daddy was out there walking across the top of that dam. He slipped and fell on the side of the dam, and caught himself with one arm. Now, the dam was not real, real high, but from where Daddy fell was as high off the ground as the roofs of some houses. It was a pretty bad fall and could have been much worse if Daddy had not caught himself. For the rest of his life, he had some arthritis in that injured shoulder."

"That lake at the nursing home always had been pretty and always had added a lot to the nursing home," said daughter Sarah Roper Smith. "I know that Daddy really liked lakes. But in addition to that, I always wondered if one of Daddy's reasons for building those lakes out there was that there seemed to be a lot of low-lying water in that area anyhow. In the back of my mind it seems perhaps Daddy had the lake dug as something of a concession. That was a low spot. Water might have been standing there. You know, there were all those mineral springs in the area. And any time you have a lot of springs, the water level can tend to be pretty close to the surface — a situation where you don't have to dig very far down below the ground surface to find water."

The lake that Mack Roper had built at the nursing home was fed by water from mineral springs in the area.

Dempsey Moody and the Nursing Home's Lake

Early on in the lake's existence, colorful Dempsey Moody made a mistake one day that resulted in his car rolling into the lake at the nursing home. That wasn't the first time one of Moody's vehicles had plunged into water. The first time had been years before, when Moody's truck (loaded with bricks) sank part of a ferry and ended up in the Coosa River — with Dempsey Moody and a passenger inside the truck.

This time, when Moody's car rolled into the lake in front of the Cook Springs Nursing Home, Moody was not inside the vehicle. Instead, he was standing nearby displaying his usual calm, unflappable attitude.

When the lake incident unfolded at the nursing home, Moody was up in years. Although he still was involved as a trustee for the faith-based operations in Cook Springs, he was not handling as many duties as in years gone by. The lead role was being taken by his fellow trustee, Mack Roper.

"I was on the front porch of the nursing home the day this happened," said Sarah Roper Smith. "Mr. Moody had arrived at the nursing home to deliver some newspapers. He got out of the car with his papers and left his car motor running and his car door open long enough to run in, so he could deliver those papers to us. The only thing was, he didn't put his car into park and the car started rolling toward the lake."

Teenager Sarah stood on the porch in horror and screamed out to Mr. Moody, "Mr. Moody! Mr. Moody! Your car is rolling into the lake!"

She recalled Dempsey Moody's reaction. "Why, Mr. Moody just stood there, calm as could be, and turned around and looked at his car as it headed toward the water and said very quietly, 'Well.'"

Suddenly someone appeared on the scene who was not calm and who did not stand still. It was Mack Roper.

"Daddy called out for help — called out to a man who worked there at the nursing home," recalled Sarah. "Real quickly Daddy managed to grab a chain from somewhere. By the time he got to Mr. Moody's car, it was already in the lake and sinking fast. Somehow Daddy managed to get a chain attached to the bumper of the car before it went completely under water. Between Daddy and that man he had called on for help, they were able to get the chain attached to a big vehicle nearby — I've forgotten if it was a truck or a tractor. They used that chain and the big vehicle to pull Mr. Moody's car out of the lake. To this day, I can still recall the expression on Mr. Moody's face. He was like, 'Oh well, so my car is going into the lake.' He wasn't one bit excited over it."

Nursing Home as a Spot for Courting

It proved to be an unusual but pleasant experience for Sarah Roper to live in a nursing home during the time she was being courted by her husband-to-be, Jerry Smith. Smith came to know and love some of the nursing home residents during the time he was dating Sarah. He would go out of his way to make pleasant conversation with them.

"Jerry teases me a bit now," Mrs. Smith said with a smile in a 2005 interview. "We now have been married 52 years. Jerry tells me that I have held up quite well considering that it has been more than 50 years since he got me out of a nursing home!"

Some Early Employees

During the tenure of Mack and Grayce Roper as operators of the Cook Springs Nursing Home, several individuals who already had close ties with the Cook Springs community became employees at the nursing home. Some of them would become longtime employees there.

In 2005, three of those former nursing home employees who still lived in Cook Springs recalled their earliest memories of working in the nursing home. In order of dates of employment, they were Dee Will Moss, Myrtis Ferguson, and Esta McLaughlin.

A Legendary Maintenance Man

Dee Will Moss was in his late teens when he worked for the contractor who built the nursing home for Mack Roper. When construction was completed on the nursing home project and the contractor moved on to his next job, Moss stayed at the nursing home and worked for Mack Roper. "I just stayed on!" said Moss.

Going to work in a maintenance job at the nursing home, Moss acquired a reputation as being someone who understood the nursing home physical plant and its grounds inside and out. Since he had been there when the foundation was laid and the walls, ceilings, floors, plumbing and electrical work were put in place, he had in his mind countless details about the structure and the terrain. Moss's term of employment at the nursing home would span several administrations and four and a half decades. He worked there from his late teens until his retirement at age 65.

"A lot of people have teased my brother about that," said his sister, Cook Springs resident Shirley Moss Wallace. They said things like, 'Well, Dee Will, you helped build the nursing home and then you just stayed with it.' "

Dee Will Moss himself became an inspiring story of drive and determination. Born with a form of severe arthritis that affected his arms, legs, and back, he pursued a career of hard labor despite his crippling, painful condition. As he got older, the condition just got worse. Big knots would develop around his joints.

"I've said for years that many people in Dee Will's condition would have just sat back and not worked and lived on disability if they could," said Mrs. Wallace. "Dee Will went on and did what he did with his work out of sheer will. He has been in pain all his life, but he just kept going with his work. Up at that nursing home he would do what had to be done, used a shovel and everything."

There was another character trait that accompanied his determination that pushed Dee Will Moss along, according to Mrs. Wallace and her sister, Sarah Moss Wells. That character trait was stubbornness.

"Oh yes, Dee Will was always stubborn, very stubborn," said Mrs. Wells with a laugh.

He was even stubborn about his name. His parents gave him one name. He didn't like it. So he changed it and made up an unusual name on his own — Dee Will.

"His name at birth was Dewey Douglas Moss, and they called him 'Doug' for short," said Mrs. Wallace. "Well, he hated that name. So he shortened Doug to 'Dee' and he added Will from our older brother's name. So there he had Dee Will. We had it changed on his birth certificate and everything. So he legally became Dee Will Moss."

After he retired from work, Moss continued to be plagued with health problems, often major ones. He continued to face those health problems with courage. At age 75, Dee Will Moss died on January 10, 2006.

An Early-day Nurse

Myrtis Ferguson became one of Cook Springs Nursing Home's early employees in nursing service. In a 2005 interview that came a year before her death, Mrs. Ferguson shared her memories.

She recalled that although she did not have formal training as a nurse, some at the nursing home in the early 1950s referred to her as a nurse.

Prior to Mack Roper hiring her to help care for patients at Cook Springs Nursing Home, Mrs. Ferguson had a background helping out many in the Cook Springs community with healthcare needs. She was most notably a lay-midwife who assisted physicians in home delivery of babies and delivered the babies by herself if need be. Her training had been on-the-job, having been taught by family physicians and by a former nurse-midwife in the Cook Springs community.

Mrs. Ferguson well recalled the first injection she ever gave — a number of years before she went to work at the nursing home. She was a very young woman at the time. The patient was a woman in the Cook Springs community who had just given birth, in her home, to a stillborn baby. The doctor knew ahead of time to expect a stillbirth. He had his hands full taking care of the woman, who was very emotional and who also was having a difficult time physically. In advance of the birth, the doctor asked Mrs. Ferguson, "Can you give a shot?" She told him, "I never have given one." He said, "Well, could you?" She said, "Yeah, if I have to." (Mrs. Ferguson said if she really had to do something, she usually could make herself do it.) "The minute that baby started coming, the doctor fixed the shot and he laid it down," recalled Mrs. Ferguson. "I was hoping and praying he'd get it and give it to her himself. I was just worried about it in my heart. Then the doctor said to me, 'Put that shot in her arm!' Well, this lady was hollering and calling out, 'I don't want Myrtis to give me a shot! I don't want Myrtis to give me a shot!' But I picked up that cotton sponge and the shot, and I gave her the shot. The doctor looked at me and said, 'You're like a pro.'"

After that experience, Myrtis was even calmer and more self-confident about taking on new tasks when people needed her help in times of health crises. Her good reputation as a caretaker in the community began to spread. Neighbors were asking her to help more and more — not just with delivery of babies, but in caring for local residents who had various health ailments or had suffered injuries in accidents.

When Mrs. Ferguson started working at the Cook Springs Nursing Home, she first worked 12-hour shifts. "Later, minimum wage came along and we got a raise and were working 8-hour shifts," she said. Mrs. Ferguson smiled and said that as time went along she was allowed to perform fewer types of clinical duties in the nursing home. As more formalized training and licensure and stricter oversight emerged for nursing staff, she said the rules would not allow her to perform tasks she had done when she first came — like giving injections. Myrtis Ferguson was a recurrent employee at the nursing home — working there awhile, then going home to be a full-time homemaker, then returning to the nursing home as an employee.

As the decades went by, the Cook Springs Nursing Home went through other administrations and was known by other names. During those years, Mrs. Ferguson was making her home just a short distance down the road from the long-term-care facility, which ultimately became the Village at Cook Springs. Then, in 2005, Myrtis Ferguson herself became a nursing home resident at the Village. On the evening of April 25, 2006, Mrs. Ferguson took front-and-center spotlight at the Village "queen pageant." She was one of the "queen" contestants who were competing for the title of Ms. Village at Cook Springs. Ironically, a bubbly and vibrant Mrs. Ferguson took part in this pageant only a short two months before her death. As Mrs. Ferguson took her turn to speak in front of a standing-room-only crowd on the evening of the pageant, she shared memories of days gone by when she helped give nursing care to some of the earliest residents at an early-day version of this very same nursing home. Looking many years younger than a woman in her mid-90s, the stunning Mrs. Ferguson wore a fashionable blue evening gown that evening — the evening she was crowned the 2006 Ms. Village at Cook Springs.

Fans of the Ropers

Esta McLaughlin went to work at the Cook Springs Nursing Home just a few weeks before the end of Mack Roper's tenure. She would work there for decades, through one administration after another.

Retired licensed practical nurse Esta McLaughlin, who went to work at Cook Springs Nursing Home in late 1950s and worked at the facility for four decades, into its eras as Baptist Home for Senior Citizens and Village at Cook Springs.

She began as a nursing assistant and then completed training that allowed her to become a licensed practical nurse at the nursing home.

Prior to going to work there, Mrs. McLaughlin already knew the Roper family. She and her husband, Ed, were fellow church members with the Ropers at Cook Springs Baptist Church. The McLaughlins were very impressed with the Ropers.

"Mack Roper was a fine man," said Mrs. McLaughlin. "And his wife, Grayce, was just as nice and sweet as was Mr. Roper."

Ed McLaughlin was favorably impressed with not only Mack Roper's character but also his very high energy level: "Mack Roper was one of the nicest fellows you ever met in your life! And that Mr. Roper was just a-going all the time!"

10

A Campground Moving Forward

"Daddy was so excited about the new four-lane highway coming through and being able to move the campground."—Sarah Roper Smith, daughter of trustee Mack F. Roper of the American School of Evangelism

The faith-based campground in Cook Springs that Mack Roper was leading grew into a booming operation, particularly in the summer months.

By the early 1950s, the campground was attracting not only Baptists but also Methodists and members of other denominations as well. The campground was flourishing, drawing children and teenagers and young adults who came for summer encampments and retreats. It also was a popular site for meetings of adult leaders in various religious organizations.

Although still relatively small as compared to some sprawling campgrounds, the Cook Springs facility was growing. In terms of popularity, the Cook Springs campground was making a positive mark alongside other nearby campgrounds such as Camp Winnataska and Camp Sumatanga. These were all camps that had found a home in this St. Clair County so known for its natural beauty.

Living at the Cook Springs Nursing Home next door to the campground, Mack Roper's two daughters continued to be familiar with the details of the religious and recreational programs for the campers.

Over the years, many new features had been added to these programs for campers. However, in many ways, the core format still resembled the earlier programs — programs held at the early-day Cook Springs campground in the 1930s and also programs to which the Roper girls had first been exposed in the 1940s.

Martha Roper Saul described typical Bible camps at the campground during the 1950s: "When the campers came for Bible Camp at Cook Springs, they usually would have a class in the morning and then there would be a morning worship service. After lunch, they were free to swim and hike. They'd go hiking up Bald Rock Mountain. They would play ping-pong and that sort of thing in the afternoon. And then there would be supper and an evening worship service after supper. I also can recall some campfires in the evening — really nice, with the campers gathered around the fire singing songs and enjoying themselves."

For the two Roper daughters, this campground provided continued interesting opportunities for work.

The Roper girls worked in the kitchen. There also were other chores. During some of the latter period she worked at the campground, Martha Roper would work in the snack bar, or canteen. "I sold snacks to the campers," said Martha. "I didn't have a cash register, but I had a little cardboard box I would use to keep the money and make my change." One of Sarah Roper's jobs at the campground was a true joy for a teenage girl who had been fascinated with the mountains from the time she first saw them as a young child. "I would lead hikes up the mountain for the campers," she recalled. "It was quite a ways up there, and I loved walking straight up that rock. It was gorgeous up there!"

A Bit of Difference in "The Rules"

As workers at the camps, the Roper girls had to adhere to whatever rules were put in place by the various sponsoring religious organizations.

In recalling those days of faith-based camping, both Martha Roper Saul and Sarah Roper Smith said they enjoyed the less-stringent rules of the Methodist camps as compared to the Baptist camps.

"You know, the Baptists would not allow the girls to wear shorts. And they wouldn't allow the boys and the girls to swim together in the pool at the same time," said Mrs. Saul.

"When the Methodists came with their camps, we could swim in the swimming pool with the boys," Mrs. Smith recalled. "And at Methodist camps we could wear shorts instead of skirts."

A Four-Lane Highway Signals Campground's Move

In the early 1950s, an announcement was made that a new four-lane highway soon would go under construction. That highway would cut straight through the Cook Springs campground.

Most folks around St. Clair County referred to the highway simply as the Birmingham-Pell City Highway. The stretch of that four-lane that cut through Cook Springs in the 1950s basically would take the same general route in that area as would the Interstate 20 that would replace it during the 1960s, explained Wayne Tucker of the St. Clair community of Springville. Prior to his retirement from a long career with the Alabama Department of Transportation (DOT), Tucker served as a division construction engineer for the DOT's third division, based in Birmingham. He noted that when the 1950s four-lane highway was built through Cook Springs, the highway did not have controlled access and there was no bridge, no overpass, at Cook Springs. In the 1960s, Tucker explained, a bridge was constructed at Cook Springs, and controlled access and other alterations were put in place, to convert the four-lane to interstate standards and to link it at either end to other I–20 segments.

Once the 1950s decision was made about the route for this four-lane, there was no doubt that the Cook Springs campground would have to move. Mack Roper got word of the highway route considerably prior to that information becoming widespread public knowledge. Instead of being unhappy about this development, Roper was delighted. He saw it as a chance to build an even bigger and better campground on a ridge slightly to the north of the existing location. He saw it as a chance to move the camp even further from the railroad, where the sounds were still sometimes quite loud from the passing trains. Roper saw the new four-lane as a great improvement in transportation that could do nothing but help Cook Springs and other areas of St. Clair County. He knew the development would give a boost to the campground and nursing home that he oversaw.

"Daddy was so excited about the new four-lane highway coming through and being able to move the campground," said Sarah Roper Smith. "You know, at that time there really were not that many four-lanes in existence. There in the Cook Springs area, the main road we had had for years was the old two-lane 78 Highway (also known as the Bankhead Highway). That was the road people had to use to get from Cook Springs to places such as Birmingham. Old Highway 78 was so narrow, so curvy. There was so much traffic on that two-lane highway that it was dangerous to pass anyone on it, and there had been so many terrible wrecks on it."

Mrs. Smith recalled one conversation in particular that her father had with a representative from the State Highway Department when the four-lane was about to go under construction. This man told Mack Roper there were many reasons they were pleased about the four-lane coming. He said one reason was a military issue. "This man told Daddy that once they got the four-lane in place, they could move military equipment about much more easily — including in time of war." The timing of his comments was when war-time concerns were paramount — just a few years after the end of World War II and while the Korean Conflict still was raging.

Mack Roper and His Water Projects

Mack Roper was in his element when he was planning and directing a new construction project. As soon as he got word about plans for the new four-lane highway, he started making plans for a new camp. As had always been the case with his camp developments, Roper wanted special touches for the new camp. Along the way, some of Roper's special touches had involved water.

Just as had been true of the nursing home project next door, Roper decided to include a big spring-fed lake at the new campground.

"Daddy definitely believed that a body of water enhanced the value of a property," said Martha Roper Saul.

From the time Roper became involved in developments at Cook Springs, he focused not just on buildings but also on water-related projects.

It had been important to Roper to preserve the mineral-springs water that had made the Cook Springs area famous. Back in the 1940s, he had made sure some of the old springs pumps had a cover erected over them and had a concrete slab poured at their base.

When he started building the 1940s version of the Cook Springs campground, Roper had an artesian well that provided water for a swimming pool. "Oh, was the water in that swimming pool ever cold! It was cold as ice!" said daughter Martha. At one point, daughter Sarah served as a lifeguard at that pool. She laughed and said she certainly could testify to the fact that the water this artesian well fed into that swimming pool was cold, cold, cold!

In keeping with his love of water projects, Mack Roper in the early 1950s had wasted little time adding a spring-fed lake to adorn the front entrance at the recently constructed Cook Springs Nursing Home.

Then, when he started planning for the new campground to replace the one disturbed by the four-lane highway, he embarked on his biggest Cook Springs water project to date.

"When Daddy started planning for a lake at the new campground, he had a lake designed that was even bigger than the one over at the nursing home," said Sarah Roper Smith. "Daddy had really gotten into this thing of building man-made lakes! The big new lake at the new campground was a truly beautiful lake." That lake ultimately would become a part of the campus of WorldSong, the Woman's Missionary Union (WMU) retreat that decades later would occupy that site.

A New Campground

The new campground that took shape in Cook Springs during the 1950s soon included several structures. There was a new dining hall. There was a chapel that also had space for classrooms. There was a dormitory for the girls and women and a dormitory for the boys and men. There was a new swimming pool. And, not long afterward, a recreation building would be added that included a snack bar.

An article that appeared in the *St. Clair News-Aegis* on August 6, 1953, told the story as the big project got under way. This is an excerpt from that article:

"More than 100 St. Clair County Baptists meeting this week at Cook's Springs were probably holding their final assembly at the present historical campsite.

"It is expected that by next summer they will be able to gather at improved facilities at an entirely new location on the 1,500-acre tract owned by the American School of Evangelism.

"The reason for moving is the new Birmingham-Pell City Highway, which will be cut across the center of the hilltop location, long used for church, school and other retreats. In fact, its right-of-way runs through three of the present buildings, according to Rev. Paul Mabe of Springville, longtime trustee of the property, and program director of The Baptist Assembly.

"He pointed out that the roadwork will also enable the campsite to be rebuilt under favorable conditions, since a number of concessions were gained from the State Highway Department in connection with granting the 58 acres of right-of-way required for construction of the new route."

The article noted that the trustees had gained even more financial concessions to help support the new campsite by granting additional right-of-way for natural gas lines.

Trustees' reactions to the campground move were described in the article as follows: "The Reverend Mr. Mabe, former county Baptist Association missionary and now pastor of Springville Baptist Church, said the trustees welcomed the chance to start afresh on a well-planned assembly-ground layout and to locate farther from the railroad as well as escape proximity to the new highway."

11

Founders' Administration
Draws to a Close

*"Daddy's idea was that the Baptists could take over the nursing home
and campground, but that he could still be the manager for a while."
—Martha Roper Saul, daughter of trustee Mack F. Roper of the American
School of Evangelism*

For a time during the mid-1950s, Mack and Grayce Roper enjoyed the
fruits of their labor with a thriving nursing home and well-received
new campsite.

The family no longer was living in the Cook Springs Nursing Home.
With the facility filled with patients, Mack Roper had purchased a farm in
the nearby Moody-Odenville area. He and wife Grayce and daughter Martha
were spending their nights in the farmhouse on the property. "We would
get up early in the mornings to go to the nursing home," recalled Martha.

Then a sad turn of events hit the Roper family. Grayce was stricken with
breast cancer. For as long as she could manage after she became ill, Grayce
Roper continued to handle the books for the nursing home. "Mother knew
she was quite sick. But she also was concerned about the nursing home,"
said Martha. "Mother said, 'If I can just keep doing these books as long as
I can . . .'"

The cancer spread rapidly, raging through her body. Grayce moved back

169

into the nursing home, ultimately as a patient. Mack Roper and daughter Martha were spending a lot of time there as well. "The nurses there cared so lovingly for Mother in her last days," said Martha. "And other patients in the nursing home who had become so attached to Mother were deeply concerned. They were always asking about her."

In December 1956, Grayce Stephens Roper died of the ravages of breast cancer. She was 63 years old.

There probably was no factor greater than the loss of Grayce that motivated Mack Roper to begin thinking about where to go next with the nursing home and the campground that he administered in Cook Springs.

He wasn't quite ready to retire. Mack already had retired twice. Now in his late 60s, he knew he wouldn't work a whole lot longer. Although he would remarry, he had lost his right-hand person in running the nursing home, Grayce. "Daddy's health was not as good as it had been either," said Martha.

"Daddy began to think about what would happen to the nursing home and the campground," said Sarah Roper Smith.

So he started shopping around for a competent religious group that could take it over and carry on a faith-based mission there. His fellow trustees in the American School of Evangelism shared his feelings that it was time to make this big change.

"First Daddy offered it to the United Methodists," said Mrs. Smith. She said the Methodists were known at that time for being a very progressive group with new ventures. She said the Methodists' lawyers looked at the possibilities. However, she said the lawyers were skittish about some of the strict specifications set out in 1930 by LaFayette Cooke when he donated his property for the Cook Springs faith-based mission.

Then Roper approached the Birmingham Baptist Association. They worked out a deal.

"Daddy's idea was that the Baptists could take over the nursing home and campground, but that he could still be the manager for a while," said Martha Roper Saul.

However, that was not to be.

"The Baptists told Daddy it was time for him to retire," said Mrs. Saul. "Daddy was really hurt by that. However, even though he was hurt, that's not to say that it wasn't time for him to retire. Daddy just did not have all that energy he had had in years past. And when they were working out that deal, he was right at 70 years of age."

Mrs. Saul said even though her father was disappointed that he could not stay on and work with the Baptists a while in Cook Springs, he did not seem to regret making a deal with the Baptists. "I do think Daddy had faith the Baptists would do a good job of running the nursing home and campground," she said. "I think Daddy was confident he had made a good decision in going to the Baptists."

Mack Roper did retire when the Baptists took over. About a year and a half later, in August 1960, he died of cancer at the age of 71.

In early 1959, when the Birmingham Baptist Association took over both the nursing home and campground, it was the start of a new era for the Cook Springs missions.

Mack and Grayce Roper left behind a legacy in the faith-based mission at Cook Springs. They also left behind a legacy with their three children. Their oldest, son Murray, reopened the family dairy, then later replaced the dairy by building a golf club on the site, and the site eventually became the site of the Trussville Country Club. Daughter Sarah followed the business leanings of both her parents by pursuing a career in accounting. And younger daughter Martha graduated from seminary, earned a master's degree in psychology, and entered a private psychology practice with a Christian-based therapists' group in San Francisco, California.

Section Four

~

Birmingham Baptist Association

A Second Husband-and-Wife Team

"I know that Guy and Elsie Jean Marlowe were very highly respected for what they accomplished in Cook Springs."—John M. Pruitt, successor to Guy Marlowe as administrator of Baptist Home for Senior Citizens (formerly known as Cook Springs Nursing Home)

Beginning in early 1959, a new Baptist administrative team began leading the nursing home in Cook Springs that had been built on property that once was part of LaFayette Cooke's mineral-springs resort.

Through efforts initiated by the nursing home's founding administrator, Mack Roper, operations of both the nursing home and its sister campground next door were transferred out of the control of the American School of Evangelism and into the control of the Birmingham Baptist Association.

When the new Baptist administration took over, the nursing home and the campground acquired new names. The nursing home no longer was the Cook Springs Nursing Home. Instead, the nursing home became known as the Baptist Home for Senior Citizens. The campground became known as the Birmingham Baptist Camp at Cook Springs.

Although the nursing home was in different hands and had a different name, the administrative structure under the Baptists bore a major similarity to the era of Mack Roper. That big similarity was that the nursing home continued to be administered by a strong husband-and-wife team.

Just as Mack Roper and his wife, Grayce, had been the nursing home's founding husband-and-wife administrative team, the Baptists placed the reins in the hands of their own husband-and-wife administrative team. The new team consisted of a Baptist minister, Guy H. Marlowe, and his wife, Elsie Jean. Prior to heading the administration of the Cook Springs operation, Marlowe had been pastor of the Eastmont Baptist Church in the eastern section of Birmingham.

The Marlowe leadership began when the Baptists took over the Cook Springs operation in 1959 and continued until Guy Marlowe's retirement in 1974. For the first several years of his tenure, Marlowe shouldered the same dual responsibilities that Mack Roper had handled, in that Marlowe, like Roper, was in charge of both the nursing home and the neighboring campground.

The Marlowe Period — at both the nursing home and the campground — would go down as a successful period of transition and growth.

Under Guy Marlowe's leadership, the campground continued to flourish, attracting increasing numbers of campers. By the late 1960s, the campground had grown to the point that the Baptists split off the campground administratively from the nursing home and appointed a full-time camp director. This released Marlowe from all responsibility for running the camp and made it possible for him to focus solely on running the nursing home during the latter years of his administration.

As for the nursing home, the Marlowes guided this facility successfully during a period when state, local, and national standards for healthcare facilities were tightening up. New staff members with higher levels of training began coming on board during the Marlowe years. Modest construction programs were launched to expand the nursing home. The 15 years of Marlowe administration were busy years, guided by the teamwork of Guy and Elsie Jean Marlowe.

"I know that Guy and Elsie Jean Marlowe were very highly respected for what they accomplished in Cook Springs," said John M. Pruitt, who in the mid-1970s succeeded Marlowe when the latter retired as administrator of Baptist Home for Senior Citizens.

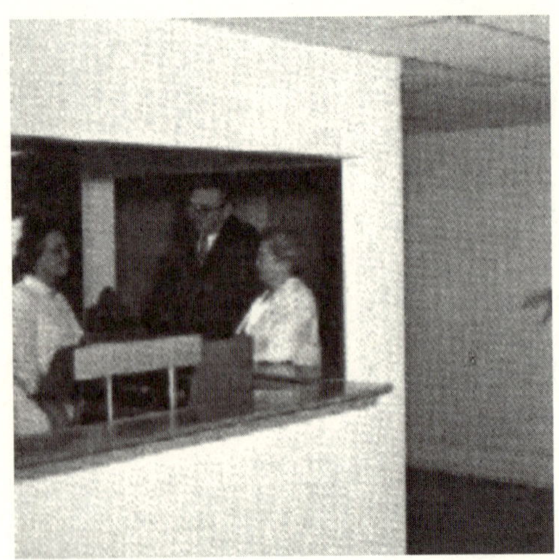

Administrator Guy H. Marlowe and his wife, Elsie Jean, stop by nurses' station at Baptist Home for Senior Citizens that the Marlowes led from 1959 until 1974.

Pruitt came to know Marlowe well, and in fact trained closely under Marlowe's direction. He recalled Guy Marlowe's personality and style: "Guy Marlowe was a combination of two things. Mr. Marlowe had a way about him that was very gentle and kind. Mr. Marlowe also had a way about him that could be on the tough side."

Pruitt said that Marlowe's wife, Elsie Jean, had great skills for interacting with people — skills that served her well in helping her husband run the nursing home. As had been the case with Grayce Roper before her, Elsie Jean Marlowe took some college courses in how to oversee the preparation of food that was served to the senior citizens who resided in the nursing home. Mrs. Marlowe's official position at the nursing home was that of food service director. However, John Pruitt said there could be no doubt that Mrs. Marlowe also efficiently carried out a number of additional functions at the nursing home. "Mrs. Marlowe really was into much more than just food service there at the nursing home," said Pruitt. "She was sort of all around, everywhere in the nursing home, doing a lot of things in that nursing home." Pruitt said at the time the Marlowes came to the nursing home, the facility still was small enough that the administrative operation was not so spread out, and it was easier for Mrs. Marlowe to reach out and effectively work and oversee in a number of areas.

By the time the Marlowes were getting toward the end of their administration, there were occasions when Elsie Jean Marlowe was referred to in local newspaper articles not as the nursing home's food service director, but instead as the nursing home's assistant administrator.

Transfer from Evangelical Group to Baptist Association

From the time the Birmingham Baptist Association first seriously considered taking over the nursing home and campground in Cook Springs, Guy Marlowe was involved. It was at the Association's annual meeting in 1957 when a proposal initially was introduced concerning the possibility of the Association's taking over the Cook Springs-based nursing home and campground operations from the American School of Evangelism. When that proposal was introduced at the Association's 1957 meeting, it was formally presented by Guy Marlowe. Then, when the Association appointed a committee to study the proposal, Marlowe was one of the seven members named to the study committee. After the committee was a few months into its study of the proposal, Guy Marlowe became the committee's chairman.

The proposal this committee was studying was based on a plan Mack Roper had worked out for the Birmingham Baptist Association to continue to move forward with the nursing home and campground. These operations were dear to the heart of Roper on several fronts. He had been a lead trustee in the American School of Evangelism, under whose umbrella these operations were created. Mack Roper had been a key figure in expanding and operating the campground; he had been the founder and first operator of the nursing home.

When Roper took the idea to the Birmingham Baptist Association, it wasn't as though he was taking the proposal to complete strangers. There were strong ties between leaders of the Birmingham Baptist Association and the American School of Evangelism. The Evangelism group's campground at Cook Springs had been heavily used by the Baptists over the years. The Baptist faith was strongly represented among the Evangelism trustees who administered the Cook Springs operations — including trustee Mack Roper's devout Baptist convictions.

Even in light of those strong ties, members of the Birmingham Baptist Association engaged in several months of long, hard study of the Cook Springs proposal before making their decision to go forward. The Association's final deal was made with the American School of Evangelism in December 1958. Guy Marlowe officially took the helm of the Cook Springs nursing home and campground on February 1, 1959.

Under the agreement, the American School of Evangelism was not transferring ownership of the 1,600 acres of Cook Springs property into the hands of the Birmingham Baptist Association. Instead, the deal in late 1958 called for the Evangelism group to lease the Cook Springs property

to the Birmingham Baptist Association for a period of 99 years, with an option to renew.

Nursing Home Expansion Under Marlowe

Numbers varied a bit as to how much capacity was assigned to the nursing home around the time the Birmingham Baptist Association took it over from the American School of Evangelism. In some news media reports, the nursing home's capacity at that time was listed as being 32 residents. However, in some other reports, including Birmingham Baptist Association documents, the nursing home was listed as having a capacity for 50 residents when the Baptists took it over in the late 1950s.

One key reason for the varying capacity figures is believed to rest in how much double occupancy was associated with rooms in the nursing home. Martha Roper Saul, daughter of nursing home founder Mack Roper, recalled there being approximately 32 rooms in the nursing home at the time her father turned it over to the Baptists. She said at that time only a few of the rooms had double occupancy.

During the 15 years Guy Marlowe headed the administration, there were construction projects to expand the nursing home. However, these construction projects during Marlowe's administration were modest, not nearly as extensive as the construction and expansion that would follow under the administration of his successor, John M. Pruitt. By the time Marlowe retired in 1974, the Birmingham Baptist Association described the Baptist Home for Senior Citizens as having 65 skilled beds, 33 intermediate-care units, and eight apartments for independent living.

When Marlowe led the building of those eight apartments for use by senior citizens who could still function independently, he was pushing forth a new concept that was being undertaken in many parts of the nation. A typical dweller in one of these apartment units was envisioned as being a senior citizen in good enough health not to need ongoing nursing services, and also being someone who liked the convenience and/or reassurance of having the nursing home's support services nearby. Another theory behind the independent-living apartment concept was that such an apartment could become an ideal home for a healthy, still-independent spouse of someone who lived in the nursing home.

A Book Traces Success and Change

In 1984, the Birmingham Baptist Association published a book that chronicled the Association's 150-year history, from 1833 through 1983. A section of that book was devoted to the Association's experience with the Cook Springs nursing home and campground.

Entitled *Born for Missions*, the book was researched and written by well-known Birmingham-based historian Dr. Lee N. Allen, who for decades was a member of the history faculty at Samford University.

These are some highlights that Lee Allen recorded about the Birmingham Baptist Association's nursing home and campground missions under the leadership of Guy Marlowe:

• *About growth and change at the nursing home after Marlowe took over in 1959*: "Marlowe immediately began to upgrade the nursing home to meet standards of the State Board of Health. Within a year it was given its first license by the state and was accepted into membership of the Alabama Nursing Home Association. He also planned for a 20-bed expansion of the nursing home . . ."

• *About expansion at the campground after Marlowe's tenure began in 1959*: "During the first season, attendance at camp totaled 876, but in the next year jumped to 1,927, and in a decade exceeded 5,000. New construction and capital maintenance were constantly upgrading and enlarging the facilities of the camp."

• *About the success in managing finances at the Cook Springs-based nursing home and campground under Marlowe's leadership:* "He (Marlowe) developed both institutions (the nursing home and the campground) at no cost to the Association, although, as was true with many other associational projects, individual churches and members gave essential assistance. From the start, together the two operations at Cook Springs were self-supporting in their on-going operations. However, the nursing home subsidized the camp operations for a decade. Special contributions made possible major capital improvements."

• *A summary of Lee Allen's accounts of how operations of the nursing home and the campground were separated during the Marlowe administration:* Guy Marlowe did double-duty for several years managing both the Baptist Home for Senior Citizens and the Birmingham Baptist Camp at Cook Springs. The camp operation was getting so large that its operations were split off from the nursing home. A first big change came when Jim Partain became full-time camp director in 1968. It was in 1969 when the camp and the nursing home were legally separated. At that time, the Birmingham Baptist Association named one board to manage the camp, and it named another board to supervise the nursing home.

• *A summary of Lee Allen's accounts of how the camp continued to move forward as an independent operation:* The camp began moving to a more year-round operation (not just mainly summer camps). Day-camping was added to the residential-camping format. Catering was added; the camp began catering thousands of meals for large on-site affairs and for various churches. Too, additional camps were developed — such as a specialty camp for underprivileged children, a specialty camp for mentally retarded young people, and a large children's camp organized by a minister at Birmingham's Lakeview Baptist Church.

Sign at Baptist Home for Senior Citizens, with this commitment from the ministry of the Birmingham Baptist Association: "God cares . . . We care, too."

The Strict but Giving Guy Marlowe

Jerry Moss was a 16-year-old high-school student who was working part-time at a service station in Moody pumping gas when he first met Guy Marlowe. That was in 1968. "Mr. Marlowe and his wife came to buy gas at the service station where I worked," said Moss. "Mr. Marlowe talked to me a bit and then said, 'Why don't you come down to the nursing home and work with us?'" Moss, who grew up in Cook Springs and was familiar with the Baptist Home for Senior Citizens, did just that. He started out in housekeeping, doing a lot of floor-mopping. Several years and more schooling later, he would be inservice director and then assistant administrator at that facility and for a time would serve as the facility's administrator. He was among employees who had a number of family members who over the years had worked at what was first Cook Springs Nursing Home and then the Baptist Home for Senior Citizens. (His uncle was longtime maintenance technician Dee Will Moss.)

Grateful to Marlowe for the interest he took in him, Jerry Moss said his experience with Guy Marlowe was that "he was always very kind to me."

However, he said there could be no doubt that Marlowe wanted employees to toe the line in doing their jobs. "I thought Mr. Marlowe was a fantastic person," said Moss. "He also was a gentleman of few words — a stern person. Mr. Marlowe was the type of person who went out of his way to help those who wanted to be helped. But if you didn't want to be helped, he didn't want to waste time with you."

Administrator Guy Marlowe earned a reputation as someone who was fair to his employees but who expected topnotch work from them — topnotch work that met his rigid standards.

"Mr. Marlowe wanted everything to be just so. He wanted everything to be just right," said Esta McLaughlin, who worked under Marlowe's administration first as a nursing assistant and later as a licensed practical nurse. "But he was a very nice man."

Leola Kelly agreed. She came to work at the Marlowe-led nursing home in housekeeping and laundry positions. "Mr. Marlowe was a real good, down-to-earth person who would really just sit down and talk to you. But, now, you didn't slack up on Mr. Marlowe's work! He wanted his work done. Mr. Marlowe was serious about that!"

Guy Marlowe demonstrated his concern about the well-being of his employees, said Mrs. Kelly. "There were some employees who came in real early who reported for work without having had any breakfast," said Mrs. Kelly. "And Mr. Marlowe made sure we all ate breakfast, and also that we ate lunch. There was no charge to us for that."

Marlowe also was an administrator who worked out solutions for employees' problems, said Mrs. Kelly. She recalled a problem he solved that had to do with the nursing home's laundry.

When Mrs. Kelly went to work in 1969, the nursing home was using hard-to-handle laundry equipment typical of some other institutions of the day. It was laundry equipment that later would be viewed as quite primitive compared to washing-and-ironing improvements that would come down the pike. Back at that time, the nursing home residents' clothing and the heavy linens were washed in washing machines that were not effective in spinning out the water. After clothes and linens were washed and before they were placed in a dryer, an extra step had to be taken to spin out the water. "What we would do back then is to take the clothes and linens out of the washer and put them down in this thing called 'the extractor,' and the extractor would spin all the water out of the clothes before we put them in the dryer," said Mrs. Kelly.

Lifting those heavy water-logged clothes was physically very difficult for some of the women who worked in the laundry. "I remember how tough it was to tug on those heavy bedspreads, blankets, and sheets when they were still so full of water," said Mrs. Kelly. "Now, I had been brought up on a farm and was accustomed to doing hard, heavy work. Even though I weighed only 105 pounds at the time I went to work at the nursing home, my experience working on a farm helped me when I was tugging on those heavy, wet clothes." However, she said that for some of the women the tugging and lifting and pulling just became too much after a time, and someone brought this problem to the attention of administrator Guy Marlowe. The administrator was quick with a solution, said Mrs. Kelly: "Mr. Marlowe said, 'What I'll do is to get a man to do all that heavy pulling for you ladies.'" And he did.

Helpmate Elsie Jean Marlowe

Elsie Jean Marlowe was a tremendous help to her husband in making it possible for him to handle the administration of both the camp and nursing home, said Esta McLaughlin.

Since Cook Springs resident Mrs. McLaughlin was an employee of the nursing home, she came to know Mrs. Marlowe as a supervisor there. Also, Mrs. McLaughlin came to know the personal side of Mrs. Marlowe. "Elsie Jean and I developed a friendship," said Mrs. McLaughlin, who could recall details and milestones about the Marlowe family. She could remember, for example, when Guy and Elsie Jean Marlowe's son went off to college and when the Marlowes' daughter got married.

She also could remember the important role that Elise Jean Marlowe played in the nursing home operation. "Elsie Jean had a lot of input into how that nursing home was run," said Mrs. McLaughlin. "Elsie Jean didn't just help out at the nursing home. She also helped over at the campground when Mr. Marlowe was in charge of the campground. I can remember Elsie Jean working some in the camp in the food-preparation area."

Mrs. McLaughlin said she believed that Elsie Jean Marlowe's past experiences as a minister's wife, including her leadership in organizing church activities, had given her a taste of organization and management. Also, she said Mrs. Marlowe had a natural knack for getting along well with people. "Elsie Jean was just a fine person who had this wonderful personality. She was real friendly and outgoing with everybody, and everybody who knew her loved her. Elsie Jean Marlowe just never seemed to meet a stranger!"

Longtime employee Estell Robbins was among those who kept in touch with Elsie Jean Marlowe after the Marlowes retired. Mrs. Robbins recalled these memories in 2005: "Mrs. Marlowe and I would call one another on the phone after they retired and she was living down in Florida," said Mrs. Robbins, who worked in laundry and housekeeping and ultimately became director of housekeeping at the Baptist Home for Senior Citizens. "I know that after Mrs. Marlowe retired she wrote me a letter telling me how much she appreciated how I kept things clean."

One Family Member Follows Another

The close-knit family atmosphere that existed at the Baptist Home for Senior Citizens was a drawing card for employees. Employees came and stayed. Often they had family members who also sought and obtained employment there.

Leola Kelly and her family became early examples of this trend. When Leola Kelly came to work for Guy Marlowe in 1969, it was clear that this friendly, comfortable environment at the nursing home was attractive to her. As she spoke in a 2005 interview, she had worked continuously at the nursing home for 36 years. "I love it!" she said. "My husband tells me that he knows me well enough that if I weren't still working there, I would miss my work and miss the employees and miss the patients. He's right. I would."

When she first came, she was 22 years old and still single. Her name in those days was Leola Williamson. She came via a route that many other new employees traveled — a referral from others. Her brother already worked there, and her good friend was the daughter of the nursing home's highly respected director of housekeeping, Estell Robbins.

Leola Kelly and her family became an example of multiple family members being drawn to work in this nursing home that had a close, homey, family atmosphere.

At the time Mrs. Kelly was interviewed in 2005, there already had been six members of Mrs. Kelly's family, besides herself, who had worked at various times on the senior-living campus where Mrs. Kelly went to work in 1969.

• Her brother, Henry Williamson, came to the Baptist Home for Senior Citizens at age 19, as an orderly working with male residents. He stayed three years, preceding sister Leola and influencing her to seek a job there.

• Leola's mother, Ruby Williamson, worked for a few years in the nursing home's laundry.

• Her sister, Diane Hilliard, worked for a short time in the laundry.

• Another sister, Lizzie Jones, in 2005 was working in the senior-citizen complex as a cook.

• Another sister, Leola's youngest, Wanda Miles, also was working there as a cook — her second time to work at the facility.

• And still another sister, Josephine Moore, as of 2005 had been working at the facility 32 years. She was working in the laundry area with sister Leola.

As one family member after another from Mrs. Kelly's family went to work in the nursing home at Cook Springs, the trend was indicative of a pattern that literally had started when the nursing home was built. The trend started when the nursing home was staffed with the help (sometimes paid help, sometimes volunteer help) of several members of the family of founding administrator Mack Roper — Roper; his wife, Grayce; his two daughters, Sarah and Martha; and his sister-in-law, Myrtle. The trend continued under the administration of Guy Marlowe, when it was not unusual to hire more than one member of a family. And the trend would continue into subsequent administrations.

Trying To Get That Sidewalk Perfect

If there was any single trait of Guy Marlowe's that seemed to stand out, it was his preciseness, his sense of being a perfectionist.

Esta McLaughlin's husband, Ed, was aware of that Marlowe streak of perfectionism.

One day Ed got a taste of how Guy Marlowe's perfectionism could intimidate employees when he was assisting Dee Will Moss, a maintenance technician at the nursing home.

Even though Dee Will Moss himself was known for his own high standards of doing things correctly, McLaughlin described how Moss drove himself the extra mile and beyond to make sure he pleased his boss, Guy Marlowe.

"I was at the nursing home this particular day helping Dee Will pour a concrete sidewalk that Mr. Marlowe wanted up there at the nursing home," said McLaughlin.

He said he began to think he and Moss would never finish the job, because Moss kept referring to the exact specifications set forth by Guy Marlowe.

"One of the things that Mr. Marlowe wanted where that sidewalk was concerned was for the ground under the concrete to be real slick. Now, I mean real, real slick. Mr. Marlowe wanted the ground underneath the cement to be as slick as the concrete that was laid to cover that ground!" said McLaughlin.

McLaughlin recalled that Moss kept fiddling with the ground that would be under the concrete — fiddling and fiddling and fiddling. "Dee Will told me, 'Ed, I just don't think this ground is smooth enough yet to suit the boss. I don't think the boss would like this.'"

In Ed McLaughlin's view, Dee Will Moss was just nervous because he was intimidated by Guy Marlowe's everything-must-be-perfect standards. "That ground was fine to pour the cement for that sidewalk, and I told Dee Will the ground was fine," said McLaughlin. "Finally I said, 'Dee Will, let's pour this sidewalk!'"

Laughing as he recalled the incident, McLaughlin said, "I mean, I got to wondering if Dee Will thought Mr. Marlowe was going to come out and dig up the concrete in order to check and make sure the ground underneath it was slick enough to suit him!"

Knowing about Family and Perfectionism

Estell Robbins was among those working at the Baptist Home for Senior Citizens during the Marlowe administration. She knew about family working there. And she knew about Guy Marlowe's streak of perfectionism.

Mrs. Robbins, who died in 2006, was interviewed in 2005 about her memories working at the nursing home in Cook Springs. When asked how many of her family members worked at the nursing home over the years, Mrs. Robbins laughed and said, "It seems like all of them did!" Estell Robbins herself came to work there when the nursing home was still in its original form, as the Cook Springs Nursing Home led by Mack and Grayce Roper. She came when she was still in her 20s. At the time, her mother had a job in the nursing home's laundry. Her mother got sick, and young Estell came to fill in. The nursing home kept her on. She stayed 43 years, rising to the position of director of housekeeping. As for members of her family who worked there, in addition to her and her mother, there were "my sister, my son, and two grandchildren." A nephew worked at the adjacent campground. Mrs. Robbins and her sister both worked at the campground. Mrs. Robbins worked some up at the administrator's house for administrator Guy Marlowe and his wife Elsie Jean.

It was when she was working for the Marlowes that she learned about Guy Marlowe's streak of perfectionism. "When I was ironing his shirt collars, I mean they had to be right. I had to get those wrinkles out of those collars. I can remember Mrs. Marlowe bringing me back Mr. Marlowe's shirts that I already had ironed and putting them down on the ironing board and saying those collars had to be ironed again." As she recalled those days, Estell Robbins spoke with gratitude. She learned to be a perfectionist herself. She was proud of what Guy Marlowe taught her. "Now, when you have to do things over, you get to where you pay attention to things!" she said. "Mr. Marlowe would call me in and tell me I was doing a good job and give me a raise when he was handing out raises. When I look back, one of the things I remember most about Mr. Marlowe was that strong voice of his. Now, when he was telling you to do something he had this strong voice that could make you take notice. I mean, he could roar like a lion. But inside he was really a nice person."

Esta Goes Back to School

Guy Marlowe was looking around for ways to bring on board well-trained health workers. And he was using every workable approach he could find.

When he took over administration of the nursing home in 1959, there was a severe general shortage of well-trained health workers. That shortage of healthcare workers extended throughout Alabama and across the nation. The problem in the 1950s and 1960s was that the nation's post-war healthcare industry was expanding much faster than the supply of workers to staff the industry. In light of a low supply of health workers, the newer licensing requirements were setting forth staffing standards that were hard to meet. On top of that, Marlowe faced the problem that even though he ran a nursing home that was located in beautiful surroundings, the rural location was considered remote at the time and made it difficult to recruit workers from urban areas such as Birmingham.

One of Marlowe's solutions was to train and promote from within. If he spotted an ambitious employee in the Baptist Home for Senior Citizens who was doing an especially good job, he sometimes would encourage that employee to go to school to train for a more skilled position in the nursing home.

He found such an employee in Esta McLaughlin. Before Marlowe took over as administrator, Mrs. McLaughlin already was working for Mack Roper as a nursing assistant at Cook Springs Nursing Home. After the changeover to the Marlowe administration, Esta McLaughlin was among those who remained in the employment of this nursing home that came to be known as the Baptist Home for Senior Citizens.

Mrs. McLaughlin was ideal for internal promotion. She already was familiar with the nursing home. She and her husband made their home in Cook Springs. She was a good employee.

So Marlowe approached her with the idea that she go to school to become a licensed practical nurse. To do that, she would need to commute — to a trade school in Gadsden in adjacent Etowah County for her classroom courses, and to a hospital in Anniston in adjacent Calhoun County for her clinical training. Mrs. McLaughlin and her husband had children ages 6, 12 and 16. Since Mrs. McLaughlin already was working, she had childcare arrangements in place. However, if she started commuting to school, she would face some transportation obstacles.

"When Mr. Marlowe approached me with this idea, he was trying to get the nursing home up to the standards of the times. Things were getting stricter and stricter in that regard," said Mrs. McLaughlin. "When Mr. Marlowe first took over, they didn't have any licensed nurses on the work force. Mr. Marlowe knew there was a time coming when he must have a registered nurse (RN) as director of nursing and also have so many licensed practical nurses, or LPNs, per patient.

"Now, Mr. Marlowe knew I was ambitious. When he told me his idea, I was interested in going to school and becoming a licensed practical nurse. But the transportation was a real issue. Ed and I had only one vehicle, a Dodge pickup truck. Well, it was so important to Mr. Marlowe that I go to nursing school that he offered to sell me an automobile and for me to have no payments on that automobile until I finished my schooling. But I didn't accept. I never even asked Mr. Marlowe the price of the car he was offering to sell me. The reason was that I didn't want to be obligated. I knew that one reason that Mr. Marlowe was making such a generous offer was that he didn't just want me to go to school to become a licensed practical nurse; he also wanted to make sure that after I finished school I came back there to work at the Baptist Home for Senior Citizens. I mean, that was the reason he wanted me to go to school. Now, I loved working there at the nursing home, I planned to come back there if I did decide to go to school, and as it turned out I did go to school and I did come back there to work.

But when I was trying to figure out transportation to go to school and Mr. Marlowe was talking to me about that deal with the car, I just didn't want to have that obligation."

While she was going to school, Mrs. McLaughlin managed transportation through a combination of ways, including driving that Dodge pickup and riding a school bus. When she took a hiatus from the nursing home in 1959 to go to school, she was a nursing assistant. When she returned a year later, she was a licensed practical nurse who was placed in a supervisory position. She worked at the nursing home in Cook Springs almost 40 years. "I loved my work as a licensed practical nurse. Why, in not too long a period of time after I finished school, between the upgrading of my position and pay raises that came along I was making as much in a hour working as a licensed practical nurse in a supervisory position as I formerly had made in an entire day working as a nursing assistant! Over the years, I have been so grateful for the pushing and encouraging that I received from Guy Marlowe."

13

A Third Husband-and-Wife Team

"I recall those years in Cook Springs as some of the best times I have ever experienced."–John M. Pruitt, administrator, Baptist Home for Senior Citizens, 1974–1986

Guy Marlowe was getting ready to retire as the administrator of the Baptist Home for Senior Citizens in the early 1970s. As he made his plans, Marlowe worked with the Birmingham Baptist Association to put in place an organized system to prepare for his successor.

Since Marlowe had been the first and only administrator the Birmingham Baptist Association had had since taking over the nursing home facility from the American School of Evangelism, Marlowe and Association leaders wanted to proceed with caution. They wanted to make sure there was a smooth transition at the end of Marlowe's decade and a half of leadership.

This preparation for transition produced somewhat of an understudy system. Well in advance of Marlowe's retirement, the Association would appoint someone to succeed him. This understudy would have plenty of time to work under Marlowe's direction at the nursing home before assuming the leadership post.

In 1973, a full year before Marlowe's retirement, the Association announced its choice to be Marlowe's successor. The appointment went to John M. Pruitt, who, like Marlowe, was a Baptist minister.

191

The Teamwork of John and Libba Pruitt

As had been the case with the Marlowe administration, the succeeding administration would bring in a husband-and-wife team. In addition to John Pruitt coming as administrator, Pruitt's wife also would assume a position of employment at the nursing home.

There were threads of similarity in the backgrounds of John Pruitt and his wife, Elizabeth, better known as Libba. Both John and Libba Pruitt had similar roots in the south Alabama county of Sumter — Libba having moved as a teenager from nearby Pickens County to Sumter's largest town of Demopolis, and John having grown up in the rural hamlet of Short Leaf near Demopolis. Both of the Pruitts obtained a Baptist seminary education in Fort Worth, Texas. John Pruitt earned a master's degree in religious education, while Libba Pruitt earned an associate degree in religious education and child development.

Prior to John Pruitt's appointment as administrator of the Baptist Home for Senior Citizens in Cook Springs, both the Pruitts served on the staff of Woodlawn Baptist Church in the eastern section of Birmingham. John Pruitt was minister of education and administration at the church,

John M. Pruitt, administrator of Baptist Home for Senior Citizens, 1974–86, and his wife, Elizabeth "Libba" Pruitt. As the food-service director, Mrs. Pruitt followed in the footsteps of the wives of the two previous administrators.

and Libba Pruitt was in charge of running the church's child development (daycare) center.

At the Baptist Home for Senior Citizens, Libba Pruitt took on the same job of food service director that had been held by the two administrators' wives who preceded her — Grayce Roper and Elsie Jean Marlowe. Like Mrs. Roper and Mrs. Marlowe before her, Mrs. Pruitt completed a college course in food preparation for nursing home patients. However, unlike Mrs. Roper and Mrs. Marlowe, Libba Pruitt did not assume a strong role in helping to administer the overall nursing home. In the Pruitt administration, the nursing home at Cook Springs underwent a considerable growth spurt. John Pruitt had others under his employment to help him with administration.

A Year of Understudy

When John Pruitt arrived at the Baptist Home for Senior Citizens in 1973 to begin his understudy year, he knew he had one mission for a year — to learn everything he could about the job of running the nursing home.

"The first year I was there, I was called 'administrator-elect,'" said Pruitt. "During that year, Guy Marlowe was still in charge, complete charge. I just observed Mr. Marlowe and what he did for a whole year. I never made any suggestions about the operation in any way or fashion. During that year I was there just to learn and observe and decide what I wanted to do when I became administrator."

A Long Tenure

John Pruitt would be at the helm of the Baptist Home for Senior Citizens until 1986 — a period of 12 years following his year of understudy.

"Mr. Pruitt put a lot of pride and time in the Baptist Home for Senior Citizens," said Jerry Moss, who became the nursing home's inservice director and later assistant administrator and then, during a transitional period, served as administrator. "Mr. Pruitt showed great leadership. He really strived to make the facility bigger and better."

An Administration of Expansion

During the dozen years that John Pruitt led the nursing home, a key feature of his administration that stood out was expansion. As the nursing home took on considerable growth, there were frequent meetings with architects, engineers, and builders as construction projects were being planned or carried out.

John Pruitt said one of his great joys as administrator was seeing these construction projects come together.

Preliminary planning for the first expansion under Pruitt's administration was initiated in 1974, the year Pruitt became administrator. Actual construction got under way the following year. In the spring of 1975, official details about the expansion were released to the news media.

"Baptist Home for Senior Citizens Announces $1.5 Million Expansion," was a headline in *The Alabama Baptist* publication on April 10, 1975. This is an excerpt from the article that accompanied the headline, detailing plans for additions to the Baptist-run nursing home in Cook Springs:

"A wing of 28 skilled beds plus attending medical and nursing services, a new kitchen and dining room complex, a needed modernized laundry operation, a warehouse, plus a chapel with a sitting capacity of 80 compose the new construction. Also included are renovations in the present structure for an enlarged program of patient activities, other paramedical services and an office suite.

"John M. Pruitt, former minister of education at Woodlawn Church, Birmingham, is the present administrator. Rev. George H. Jackson, director of the Extension Department of Samford University, is chairman of the Board of Trustees. According to these two men, the Board of Trustees is planning for the day when the facilities will be a total retirement center for senior citizens.

"Ground breaking ceremonies are scheduled for Sunday, April 13, at 3:00 p.m. at the Cook Springs site. The public is invited."

Pruitt said when this first expansion was finished, the design of the nursing home was more like "a completed square."

"When we completed this 1970s expansion, the facility was just a beautiful

Late 1970s view of Baptist Home for Senior Citizens following expansion, under leadership of administrator John M. Pruitt.

place to come up to," Pruitt reflected in his 2005 interview. "We even had this nice fountain at the nursing home, given to us by one of the members of our board. To see the expansion all come together, and then to enjoy the day that we opened it . . . That was a great day."

Funding, Corporate Structure, and Property Ownership

When the Birmingham Baptist Association was putting together the funding for this first expansion during the Pruitt administration, the Association made use of a state law that made it possible to use tax-free revenue bonds for health-related construction undertaken by a not-for-profit organization. To do this, authorization had to come from a locally based Medical Clinic Board.

In the case of the mid-1970s construction at the Baptist Home for Senior Citizens, this authorization for use of tax-free revenue bonds came through the Medical Clinic Board of Pell City-Cook Springs, Alabama.

When plans were being put in place to use this funding mechanism, the Birmingham Baptist Association had the nursing home officially incorporated as a not-for-profit corporation. From a corporate view, the nursing home became the Baptist Home for Senior Citizens, Inc. This meant that John Pruitt would wear two hats: In day-to-day operations, he would be the nursing home's administrator. From a corporate view, he would be executive vice president and secretary-treasurer of the Baptist Home for Senior Citizens, Inc.

Around the time these funding and corporate mechanisms were in play, the American School of Evangelism deeded some 300 previously leased acres to the nursing home. (The Evangelism group also later would deed several hundred acres to the campground next door.)

The Administrator's Home

Back in 1950 when Mack Roper founded the nursing home, he had moved himself, his wife, and his two daughters into the new nursing home facility. The Roper family had lived in the nursing home for several years, until it became filled with patients. Then Roper had bought his own residence a few miles away in the Moody-Odenville area.

One of the steps the Birmingham Baptist Association made after taking over the nursing home was to add an administrator's residence in Cook Springs — a home where the administrator and his family could live. The house was located very near the nursing home, at the edge of the campground property next door. Guy Marlowe and his wife, Elsie, were the first to live in that administrator's house.

"After Libba and I came to Cook Springs, the Marlowes moved out of the administrator's house and moved into the independent-living-apartments facility there at the Baptist Home for Senior Citizens," said John Pruitt. Then the Pruitts moved into the administrator's house. That transition took place while Guy Marlowe was still administrator, during the year that John Pruitt was serving in his understudy role.

"That administrator's house was a real convenience," said Pruitt. "It was located so close to the nursing home — just on the opposite side of Interstate 20 from the nursing home."

While the administrator's house was convenient for John and Libba Pruitt from a standpoint of being so close to work, the house proved to be rather isolated from any neighbors and also a considerable distance from the many friends they still had in Birmingham.

Libba Pruitt said that although she and her administrator husband lived in that house for almost 13 years, they still kept close ties with Birmingham. "John had many of his meetings with the Association in Birmingham, and we continued to go to Birmingham to attend church," she said.

The Intruder

Libba and John Pruitt always were very aware of the remote location of the administrator's house that became their home in Cook Springs. "It was up in the woods, by itself," said John Pruitt.

They became especially conscious of the remote location after a disturbing event that occurred shortly after they moved in. On that day, Mrs. Pruitt was at home alone when an intruder confronted her.

Libba Pruitt recalled that day:

"The day this happened, I was busy going up and down the stairs in the house getting some Christmas decorations out to prepare the house for a board meeting and Christmas party. I heard our dog start barking. The dog was in a fenced-in area in the back yard, and I just thought he was barking at birds. But then I heard this knock on our front door — a strong knock. Then another strong knock. I looked out into the yard and saw a car. It looked kind of strange, because it was not pulled in like you usually would pull in. It was backed in, backed in toward our house. I didn't think much about it though. I just thought it was probably somebody selling something. Since I was there by myself, I decided not to answer the knock on the door."

As she heard a third loud knock at the door, Mrs. Pruitt stuck with her decision to ignore the knocking and let the visitor go away. She wanted to continue without interruption in getting the house ready for the board meeting and Christmas party. However, the man who was on her front porch had other ideas. When Mrs. Pruitt didn't answer, the man took a tool in hand and pried open the front door.

As Libba Pruitt recalled the incident in a 2005 interview, the details were still very vivid in her mind even though more than 30 years had passed since the scary intrusion had occurred:

"When that man pushed open the front door of our house, I was standing in the middle of the living room. And there this man stood, facing me, with something stuck down in his shirt. I still don't know if it was the tool he used to break in with, or a gun, or what. Anyhow, I lunged toward him and screamed, 'What are you doing breaking into my house??!!' "

Fortunately for Mrs. Pruitt, the intruder chose not to be aggressive. Despite the fact he had just broken in and had done enough damage that the door and door facing would have to be replaced, he made a feeble excuse and left abruptly. He told Mrs. Pruitt he had the wrong house, that he was looking for someone else.

The intruder was never located and arrested for this break-in by law enforcement officials. In the meantime, John Pruitt and leaders of the nursing home's board took steps to ensure that security was strengthened at the administrator's house.

"Boy, did we get strong security after that!" said John Pruitt. "A double fence was built around the house, and we had seven German shepherd dogs patrolling the area around that fence. Also, at the entrance to the fence, there was a gate equipped with an intercom system. If you were a visitor driving up to our gate, you had to identify yourself through the intercom system before you could get in. And we could open the gate from the inside of the house. Why, after that intruder came in on Libba, we would have people come visit who would tease us and say that going to visit the Pruitts in Cook Springs was like trying to pay a visit to the Mafia!"

The Vegetable Garden

The spacious, rural location of the administrator's house carried a big bonus for John Pruitt. It made an area available for him to have a vegetable garden he thoroughly enjoyed.

Having been reared in the small south Alabama hamlet of Short Leaf in Sumter County, John Pruitt was a farmboy by nature. He felt comfortable tilling the soil.

"In my growing-up years in Short Leaf, our family raised all that we had to eat," he said. "After Libba and I moved to Cook Springs, I decided to start a big garden at our house. Our sons were in a fraternity at Samford (Samford University in Birmingham). A bunch of the fraternity boys came out to Cook Springs one Saturday, and we cut down trees and pulled stumps and cleared off a nice big area for a garden."

The garden Pruitt planted near the administrator's house was not a small garden. It was big enough to grow far more than enough vegetables for the Pruitt household. The garden also produced vegetables for some good home cooking at the Baptist Home for Senior Citizens.

John Pruitt recalled his garden with pride: "I didn't plant just one or two tomato plants. I planted a whole row of tomato plants about a hundred feet long. We had green beans and butterbeans, corn, okra, Irish potatoes. You name it, we grew it there. We had a place big enough to grow everything! We would pick fresh tomatoes and take them down and serve them in the dining room at the nursing home. We would do the same with other things. And my advisor for this gardening project was Dee Will Moss, who worked in maintenance at the nursing home."

Taking Care of Business

In addition to launching new construction projects, John Pruitt became very focused on several other areas at the nursing home that he felt were important.

One was continuing to recruit topnotch employees.

Another was addressing some ongoing problems — such as the nursing home's outdated water supply.

And still another was making sure there was a strong program of faith and spirituality in place for nursing home residents.

Recruiting and Retaining Employees

Recruiting employee candidates and selecting good ones was a task that Pruitt very much enjoyed. "Oh, we were able to recruit some very great, dedicated workers," he said. Pruitt also was proud of being able to retain some employees who had gone to work during the Roper and Marlowe administrations that preceded his own administration.

One employee who was recruited early in Pruitt's administration was licensed practical nurse Betty Chapman. When interviewed in 2005, Mrs. Chapman still worked at the facility. "When I came in 1975 under the Baptists, I was impressed that the nursing home was such a friendly place.

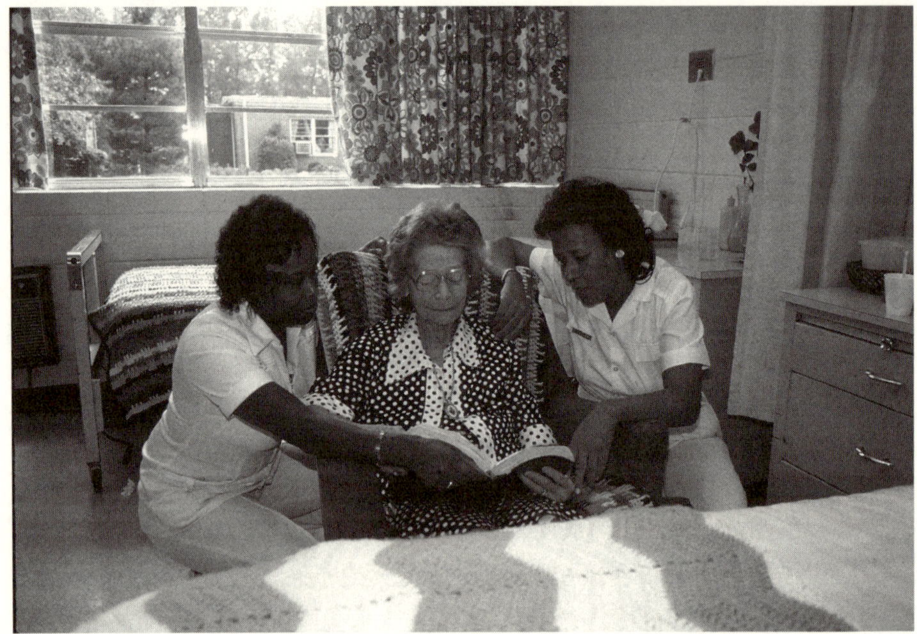

I really liked that friendliness," said Mrs. Chapman. "As I stayed through the years, the nursing home got much bigger. Even with the growth, the friendly part didn't change."

Among employees Pruitt was able to retain who would go on to stay at the facility for decades were Dee Will Moss, who played such a strong role in maintenance at the facility, and Estell Robbins, who became housekeeping director. Both had come to work during the years when Mack Roper was running the nursing home. Pruitt praised the work of both Mrs. Robbins and Moss.

When asked in a 2005 interview about the praise she received over the decades for her housekeeping leadership, Estell Robbins said that she did things the way she did because "I just cared about my work and wanted everything to be nice and clean!" Even after she was a supervisor, Mrs. Robbins had a reputation for coming to work early and getting a head start on the work to be done by the housekeepers under her direction. She would open windows and air out areas, use spray and disinfectant, and run right and left gathering up linen. "I just didn't like odors. By the time those administrators got in, everything was smelling great!"

As for Dee Will Moss, administrator John Pruitt said that "Dee Will could do everything, I mean everything!" Pruitt said that it was a plus that Dee Will Moss had been with the nursing home since it was built; in fact, he worked for the contractor that built the nursing home for Mack Roper. "And I can tell you that Dee Will knew where every single pipe was in that facility," said Pruitt. "He knew about anything and everything that could conceivably go wrong with the building, and he knew where and how to go and fix it." Libba Pruitt agreed: "I thought Dee Will was a lifesaver!"

Upgrading the Water Supply

When Pruitt took over as administrator, the nursing home's water supply came from a well system. He said the system was very high-maintenance. Also, it had limited capacity. Pruitt felt it was time to solve the problem.

"When I first went to Cook Springs, there were seven wells involved with that water system. And Dee Will Moss was maintaining those wells, in addition to everything else he was doing," said Pruitt. "On occasion, Dee Will and I would work together in pulling the pumps out of the wells and installing new pumps. Now, we were enlarging out at the nursing home.

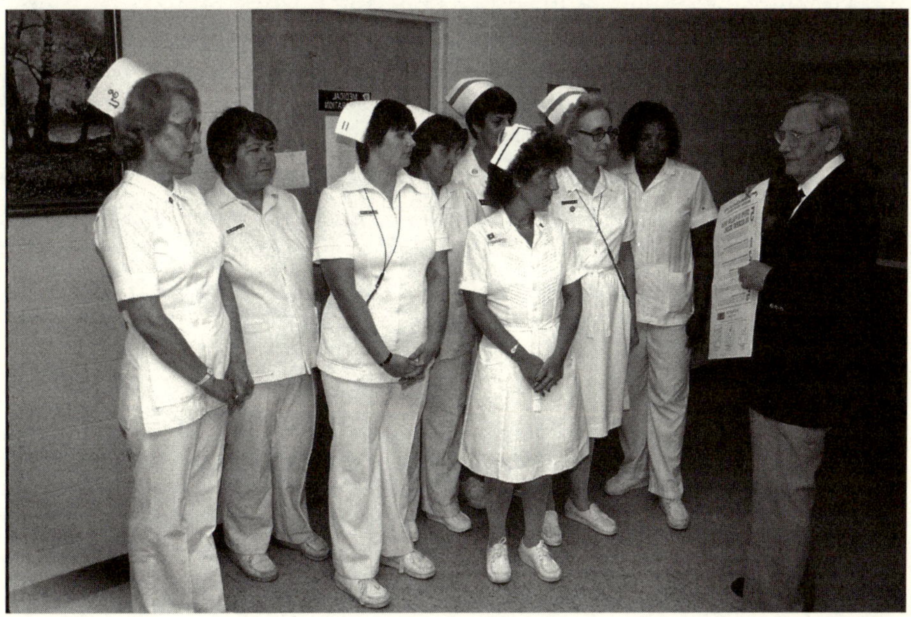

In freshly starched caps, nursing staff receives instructions at Baptist Home for Senior Citizens, late 1970s.

We were expanding. We couldn't expand efficiently with that kind of water system."

Pruitt launched a quest for funding to upgrade the nursing home's outdated water supply.

"I went and talked with Governor George Wallace about this need we had," Pruitt said. "The governor was able to get us some funding help to start what became the waterworks down there at Cook Springs. It wasn't necessary anymore to depend on those wells."

Ministering to the Spiritual Side

The nursing home's programs of faith and spirituality were given a real boost through the construction program that was launched the year after Pruitt became administrator.

One addition that made a difference was the new chapel that was included in that construction. Pruitt said the chapel was much-welcomed at the nursing home, which had daily devotional programs and an attentive chaplain (the pastor of Cook Springs Baptist Church).

Another addition that came with the 1970s construction was a closed-circuit television system. With this system, the nursing home's devotional services were televised and could be seen on television sets in the residents' rooms. "This was to accommodate our residents who were bedridden and couldn't get to chapel service," said Pruitt. "There were residents who could not get to the chapel service who really enjoyed having the devotional programs turned on for them to see on televisions in their rooms."

An Art Gallery, Some Dead Fish, and a Wedding

As soon as John Pruitt became entrenched in his job, he and his staff started taking time to try their hand at a few "extras" at the nursing home.

One extra that was a real success was an art gallery that Pruitt had put in place in the nursing home. Pruitt got this started during an era when it was becoming popular for hospitals and nursing homes to feature exhibits of local artists' paintings. Such exhibits offered a double benefit of providing a facility with an attractive artistic display and affording artists an outlet for

First class of certified nursing assistants (CNAs) at Baptist Home for Senior Citizens, 1980s.

showing and selling their artwork. "In setting up our art gallery, we had help from a well-known local artist, Evelyn Matthews. Libba and I had come to know Mrs. Matthews as a fellow member of Woodlawn Baptist Church," said Pruitt. "We named the nursing home's new art gallery for Mrs. Matthews. One of Mrs. Matthews' paintings always was on display along with other artists' exhibits that we changed out on a regular basis. When we started the art gallery, Mrs. Matthews still was in good health and still painting. As time went on, her health and that of her husband deteriorated, and they both became residents at the Baptist Home for Senior Citizens. That art gallery she helped us get under way was a very popular feature at our nursing home."

Another "extra" at the nursing home that was not quite as big a success had to do with dead fish. John Pruitt smiled as he recalled the ill-fated venture: "Well, we had this lake at the nursing home — this pond. So, since we

Activity director Bobbie Hobson, right, leads group of hula dancers at 1988 social event at Village's Springs Manor assisted-living facility.

had the pond there, we decided we would try to grow fish. We fashioned all these things to put the fish in — sort of like cages — and we put the fish in the cages and placed the cages down in the pond. This was while Guy Marlowe was still there, and Mr. Marlowe really liked this project. Now, these were little bitty fish. After we put them in these cages and began feeding them, we thought we were going to harvest a big crop of fish — that we were going to have fish in abundance. And then it came time to pull out all our fish. When we pulled the cages out of the pond, we had only one fish left. Just one fish! And that one fish was still little bitty; it was still about the same size as when we put it in." That was the end of the fish project.

Still another "extra" at the nursing home was a happy event — a wedding. The bride was one of the nursing home's dietary employees who worked under the supervision of Libba Pruitt. This lady worked in the dining room and kitchen and had a range of duties from dishwasher to serving residents in the dining room. The groom was a senior citizen who resided in one of the eight independent-living apartments adjacent to the nursing home. After the marriage, the newlyweds made their home in that apartment. "Oh, their wedding was quite an affair," said Mrs. Pruitt. "The bride and groom invited their families and also people from the Baptist Home for Senior Citizens who were able to come." John Pruitt said the whole event created a lot of positive excitement in the nursing home. "We really were thrilled with this wedding. It was such a great occasion for all of us."

A Construction Crisis

In the early 1980s, leaders of the Baptist Home for Senior Citizens began planning for a construction project to add an "assisted-living" facility. That lovely facility would become a reality and would be known as Springs Manor. In years to come, the facility would be a popular showplace filled with happy residents — a facility that would be known for its spacious design and its beautiful rustic wooded setting.

However, during the construction of this building in the 1980s, there were major problems — problems having to do with foundation issues. Springs Manor would turn out to have the benefit of an extra-strong foundation beneath the building — a foundation that actually had to be created, and that some would describe as being as strong as the Rock of Gibraltar. However, having to build that extra-strong reinforced foundation was not expected; it was not in the original building plans, and it was not in the budget. The rock-solid foundation came at a considerable unexpected cost of time and money.

The problem, said Pruitt, was that when workers started doing work on the building's foundation, they encountered a huge deep hole below the ground surface. The hole was there, said Pruitt, as a leftover from days gone by when the lake at the nursing home apparently had been a much bigger lake. "The people working on our building project discovered that there was not sufficient foundation to support a building. We were told we were going to have to build up a foundation."

Pruitt said the discovery of that huge hole came as a jolting surprise. He said he had no idea that the small lake that was adjacent to the nursing home — the lake he often referred to as "a pond" — once had been so extensive. He had no idea that, in years gone by, part of the original lake had extended into the area that now was the building site for the assisted-living facility.

"That lake apparently had been really very large in its original form. We just didn't know the lake had been that big!" said Pruitt. "Before we started work on the foundation, if you were just standing there looking at that building site for the assisted-living facility, you couldn't see a problem." He said the surface of the ground in that area looked normal. "It was a good many feet down where the people doing the foundation work discovered the problem," said Pruitt.

The hole was not a minor dilemma — far from it. "That hole went down very, very deep — believe me!!" said Pruitt. "I was there, and I saw it!"

What workers found was a complex, messy situation — not only a hole that seemed to go down forever, but also a hole that contained various kinds of soft debris. "Apparently at some point there had been people who were trying to fill in at least part of that hole, and they had dumped all kinds of things into it — loose stuff, just junk," said Pruitt.

As information was pieced together, it became clear that a major role in this unexpected big hole had been played by construction of the interstate roadway through Cook Springs a number of years previously, and likely also by the construction of the four-lane highway that preceded the interstate a number of years before that. (Since the four-lane and the subsequent interstate followed much the same path in the Cook Springs area, there were some who would link the impact of the two roadways, although they were built years apart.)

Cook Springs' rich history in having an abundance of naturally occurring mineral springs also figured into the story of this big hole that presented such a problem with the assisted-living building's foundation.

"Now, this lake that had been built out at the nursing home had been built as a spring-fed lake. And, when they built Interstate 20, there were springs that ended up being under that interstate," said Pruitt. "So, when the interstate was built, workers put in these big culvert-type things under the interstate, so the springs could be preserved and still feed the lake. At the same time, the interstate construction apparently covered up a big part of the lake."

In terms of the impact all this had on the construction project for the assisted-living facility, there was a delay of several months in completing the project and there also was a considerable increase in cost of construction.

"In order to build up a really strong foundation to support the assisted-living building, we had to have all kinds of rock and other strong materials poured in there," said Pruitt. "When you start a project like that, and then you make such a discovery, it's really a very bad discovery. It cost us a lot of time and a lot of money." Pruitt recalled that period as a very, very stressful one.

A Marketing Challenge

After the foundation problems were dealt with and the Springs Manor assisted-living facility was completed, the building was every bit as beautiful as had been anticipated by Pruitt, board members, and leaders of the Birmingham Baptist Association.

"When we opened that (assisted-living) building, it was really something!" Pruitt said with pride.

However, once the Springs Manor building opened, there were still more problems — in the area of marketing. The building was slow to fill up with residents.

To much of the public at the time, the concept of assisted living was quite new. As years went by, the assisted-living model would grow in popularity. More and more people would be drawn to this living arrangement designed for the senior citizen who did not need around-the-clock nursing care but who could use the "assistance" of certain support services. A big drawing card would be the support services — including meals, housekeeping, security, on-site planned activities, off-site activities complete with transportation, and the availability of various other types of professional help in time of need.

"When we first opened the assisted-living facility, we undertook some rather extensive marketing — such as through mailings, presentations, and a video we had done," said Pruitt. However, he said the slowness in filling the facility persisted.

Back in that difficult period, Mary Ferguson was one of those who could

Late-1970s photo in Baptist Home for Senior Citizens brochure showed residents relaxing on nursing home back porch and administrator John Pruitt talking on telephone.

see the situation both from her view then as an employee of the Baptist Home for Senior Citizens and also from her view as one who lived in the Cook Springs community. (Mary Ferguson came to work as a nursing assistant at the Baptist Home for Senior Citizens in 1978, and in subsequent administrations at that facility she would rise through the ranks to become a department head. Mary Ferguson was a relative by marriage of Myrtis Ferguson, who had come to work in the nursing home's era as Cook Springs Nursing Home.)

As Mary Ferguson reflected in a 2005 interview, she explained how she could see that an assisted-living facility in the 1980s could have been a bit ahead of its time for Cook Springs and nearby communities. She said in terms of senior-citizen residential living at that time, most people she knew were mainly familiar with the idea of 24-hour-a-day skilled nursing care for nursing home patients who were chronically sick or disabled, often bedridden. "During that era, when many people thought of anything related to senior-living facilities, what they tended to think of was a patient being in one room and staff members coming into that one room to take care of the person," said Mrs. Ferguson. "Back 20 years ago, people around here just were not accustomed to this whole assisted-living concept. At the time the assisted-living facility was built at what then was the Baptist Home for Senior Citizens, it was a totally new idea for this area."

Another Phase of Church-Related Work for the Pruitts

John and Libba Pruitt left the Baptist Home for Senior Citizens in 1986. They accepted positions that once again involved them in church-related work — the same type of work they had done prior to going to the Baptist Home for Senior Citizens.

The Pruitts moved to Wilmington, North Carolina. There John Pruitt became a church minister of education and administration. Libba Pruitt helped to start a child-development center in the Wilmington community and then taught in a church-based child-development center there. The Pruitts lived in Wilmington for 13 years, until their retirement. After they retired, they returned to Alabama and made their home in Leeds, not too far from the Cook Springs community where they had spent a long career period during the 1970s and 1980s.

The years in Wilmington were good years, said John Pruitt. He said he was doing work there that he really wanted to do at that time in his life. "I just had this feeling that I would like to be in the service of a church during my last years of working," he said.

All in all, the years in Cook Springs also were very good years, said Pruitt. As he spoke in 2005 of his days at the Baptist Home for Senior Citizens, he said he had had time to reflect on his overall experience there. He noted while his last days there were impacted by stresses related to the assisted-living facility and accompanying financial challenges, he was extremely proud of the considerable progress that was made during the years he was administrator at the Baptist Home for Senior Citizens. He expressed pride in the employees who worked for him and in what they accomplished. John Pruitt said he had balanced the memories of the good times and the difficult times. "I recall those years in Cook Springs as some of the best times I have ever experienced."

14

A Financially Troubled Baptist Mission

"There were times out there at the Baptist Home for Senior Citizens when we were scrambling."–The Reverend L. Earl Tew, executive director, Birmingham Baptist Association, 1985–1987

When the Birmingham Baptist Association took over the Baptist Home for Senior Citizens in December 1958, the move was very much in keeping with the Association's long history of being involved in missions to help others.

After all, this was the same Birmingham Baptist Association that during the 1920s had founded a hospital operation that grew into the large, diverse Baptist Medical Centers (later known as Baptist Health System). It was the same Association that had cooperated with Baptist-linked, Birmingham-based Samford University in many successful projects, including those having to do with the education of ministers. It was the same Association that had partnered with various groups for programs to help enrich the lives of young people, aid the bonding of families, and reach out to the needy, the immigrants, and other groups that could use a helping hand.

So, when the opportunity presented itself for the Birmingham Baptist Association to be the umbrella agency to operate a nursing home in Cook Springs, it was a natural fit — to reach out to the elderly. From the late 1950s on through the 1960s and 1970s and into the 1980s, the Association took great pride in the service rendered at the nursing home facility in Cook Springs.

210

The Money Woes Begin

When financial troubles came calling at the nursing home facility in the 1980s and seemed to get progressively worse, Association leaders were drawn into years of stressful times trying to find a solution. For several years, these financially linked stresses would take a front seat on the agenda.

"The Baptist Home for Senior Citizens was generating enough money until they built that assisted-living facility," said the Reverend L. Earl Tew, who from 1985 until 1987 served as the Association's director of missions, a position equivalent to being the organization's executive director, or chief executive officer. "When that assisted-living facility was built out at the Baptist Home for Senior Citizens, they ran into those foundation problems with the construction and had to spend a lot more money than anticipated to build it. The assisted-living building was a rather large facility. Then they couldn't fill it up (with residents). And the indebtedness was overwhelming."

Tew said the financial problems the Cook Springs senior-living complex encountered in the 1980s represented quite a contrast to the smooth financial status the facility had experienced under Baptist administration in times past. "Actually, years back when the nursing home operation still was linked to the campground operation next door, there had been a time when the nursing home was sort of carrying the camp financially," said Tew.

Marketing Issues a Factor

As he looked back on that trying period during a 2005 interview, Tew said he agreed with those who felt that "back in the 1980s, perhaps that assisted-living facility was a little ahead of its time."

Tew was very familiar with the Birmingham area and surrounding counties, having served as a minister at Birmingham's Lakeside Baptist Church for 21 years of his career prior to heading up the Birmingham Baptist Association. Tew said from a marketing perspective it was his feeling that the assisted-living addition likely was ahead of its time in two ways. One was the newness of the assisted-living concept itself. Another was what Tew viewed as the lack of a target market population that was large enough and receptive enough at that time.

A view of grounds of Baptist Home for Senior Citizens, looking out through nursing home's activity-room windows, late 1970s.

"When that assisted-living facility first was built, the Cook Springs location still was viewed by many as being a bit remote from the highly populated Birmingham area," said Tew. "However, the way commercial and residential development has expanded and spread from Birmingham out toward Cook Springs since that time, it's certainly no longer the case that Cook Springs seems remote."

Since the 1980s, Tew said there had been tremendous development in suburbs to the east of Birmingham. He said that suburban expansion easily could motivate senior citizens from those areas to be much more likely than in the past to select Cook Springs as a place for an assisted-living residence. Also, he said the Cook Springs of the 21st century was helped along by big population growth in St. Clair County and other neighboring counties.

"All those factors have changed so much in recent years, to the benefit of the Cook Springs facility," said Tew.

An Attorney Is Asked To Help

As the financial problems deepened at the Cook Springs operation in the 1980s, a well-known Birmingham attorney and Baptist leader was asked to become a member of the board that was directly in charge of running the Baptist Home for Senior Citizens.

That attorney, Chriss H. Doss, had a diverse background and a broad range of experiences. He was not only an attorney; he also was an ordained Baptist minister. He had served for 12 years as a member of the Jefferson County Commission, including five years as the Commission's president. In the mid-1980s, he also would become director of the Center for the Study of Law and the Church at Samford University's Cumberland School of Law.

Doss was approached about serving on the Baptist Home for Senior Citizens board more than once, and by several different Baptist leaders who either held key positions in the Association or on the nursing home board itself. Among those who came to him for help was Oley C. Kidd, who had been executive director of the Association in a period prior to Earl Tew. Another was Hudson Baggett, long known as editor of *The Alabama Baptist* publication. Another who called on Doss for help was George H. Jackson, who had long been a board leader at the Baptist Home for Senior Citizens, including serving as board chairman as far back as in the 1970s.

"When these fine men approached me, they came with the feeling that the board out there in Cook Springs really needed additional legal advice," said Doss. "They told me that the Baptist Home for Senior Citizens was having some real grave financial problems. They said they really were afraid the facility was going to go belly-up financially."

When Doss was asked to help out in Cook Springs, he already had a full plate of activities. But then, as his Baptist colleagues kept asking, he said yes. He believed the service on that board would be time-consuming and stressful. And it was.

More than One Problem

As Doss became deeply involved with the board at Cook Springs, he was increasingly convinced that the assisted-living facility was not the only factor in the financial problems there.

"Oh, the issues with that assisted-living facility were a big, big part of the overall financial crisis. There's no question about that," said Doss. "But in my view, the financial problems went beyond assisted living and had started prior to assisted living."

He described one key ongoing problem as being the generous, good-hearted mission nature of the Baptists. In Doss's view, the Baptists had been giving away too much at the Cook Springs facility and had not been running it in as businesslike a manner as they should.

"My impression really was that some of the problems were primarily due to a lack of being as businesslike as was needed — and instead taking approaches in which the heart tended to overrule the head," said Doss. Noting that he was a Baptist minister, Doss said he believed strongly in the mission spirit of the Baptists. At the same time, he said he had come face-to-face over the years with the realities of management. He said some of the harshest realities came home to him during his service on the Jefferson County Commission. During his Commission service, he saw what he described as the extensive needs of many citizens. At the same time, he said he saw that it was impossible to meet all those needs with a budget that had its limitations. "There just has to be a realistic side to management," said Doss. "You can't let your heart just take over. Your head has to exercise some strong control."

Earl Tew said there was no question in his mind that there were times when administrators at the Baptist Home for Senior Citizens had a tendency to be extremely generous to those in need. After all, he noted that helping the needy was in keeping with the goals of Baptist missions. Tew said he could feel for Baptist administrators who had to weigh human-need issues against making businesslike decisions in running a nursing home: "I mean, it's tough on some families who are trying to see to it that their loved ones are properly cared for in a good nursing home. On the other hand, if you are a nursing home administrator who is running an institution that requires X amount of money, you also have financial demands laid on you. That's not easy at all," said Tew. "There

A cold winter brings ice to fountain in front of Baptist Home for Senior Citizens, 1980s.

were times out there at the Baptist Home for Senior Citizens when we were scrambling. And I personally feel there were exceptions made (when people were not pushed to pay all their bills, or not pushed to pay their bills on time). There were people who were unable to pay. We kept working with many of them . . . It's just difficult."

The Meetings at Denny's

As the 1980s wore on, the financial problems got worse instead of better at the Baptist Home for Senior Citizens. The way the Birmingham Baptist Association was set up with its missions, the Association generally did not involve itself in ongoing financing and subsidizing of the missions. The Association was an umbrella organization, a facilitator. The idea was that the Association had appointed a board to run the Baptist Home for Senior Citizens, and that the nursing home was supposed to be financially self-sustaining.

"At the same time, with these financial problems out there at the Baptist Home for Senior Citizens, the Birmingham Baptist Association felt some moral kind of obligation to come to the rescue of this entity that was affiliated with us," said Tew.

In terms of coming to the rescue, Tew was not referring to the Birmingham Baptist Association somehow coming up with the very large sums of money it would take to bail out the struggling nursing home in Cook Springs. He was talking instead of Association leaders trying to find some kind of ongoing solution — including perhaps finding a new operator for the nursing home.

Tew said a lot of people stood to be adversely affected by these financial problems. "For example, bonds had been sold to fund construction out there at Cook Springs," said Tew. "During this difficult period, we at the Association worked long and hard to try to do everything we could to protect those who had invested there so that they didn't lose money."

On a number of occasions, said Tew, Baptist leaders who were grappling with the Cook Springs financial crisis gathered for breakfast meetings at Denny's Restaurant near Eastwood Mall. "Denny's just seemed to be a convenient place to meet and address these financial problems," he said.

Chriss Doss said the situation got so bad that a real possibility loomed that the Cook Springs facility could be closed, and that a bankruptcy could occur that would result in creditors and bondholders not being paid. "This came very close to resulting in a very serious, very embarrassing situation," said Doss.

"Our World Was Being Torn Apart"

During some of the worst financial times at the Baptist Home for Senior Citizens, the facility's board had a management contract with Northport Health Services to try to keep the facility going. Working for Northport as the administrator for the Baptist Home during this period was Jerry Moss. Moss had worked for years at the Baptist Home for Senior Citizens; he had experience as inservice director and as assistant administrator.

Moss said the word "terrible" was the best description he could think of for how bad the financial problems became. "It was like our world was being torn apart," he said. "The financial situation became so difficult that if the facility was going to survive, something positive had to happen fast."

An Eleventh-Hour Solution

In 1990, when it appeared that a final blow was about to be dealt to the Baptist Home for Senior Citizens, a solution was worked out.

The solution came in the form of three individuals. One was named George Smith. Another was named Max Huie. And the third was Dale Sasser.

Yet another era was about to dawn for the senior-citizen facility in Cook Springs.

Section Five

~

The Smith-Huie-Sasser Era

15

Three Men Take On a Challenge

"The Baptists approached me. I approached Max Huie. And Max Huie approached Dale Sasser. Together the three of us became the board that took over the Baptist Home for Senior Citizens and changed its name to The Village at Cook Springs."–George H. Smith, chairman of three-member board that assumed responsibility for The Village at Cook Springs, 1990

Transition time loomed in the late 1980s for the Cook Springs property once owned by LaFayette Cooke. In fact, the property was on the verge of the third major transition since the days when Cooke had used it as the site for a mineral-springs resort centered by a grand hotel.

In the two previous transitions, men in power had a vision for the on-going use of the property, and they identified leaders they knew to follow them and carry out that vision.

However, when time came for this third transition, a tremendous cloud of pressure existed that had not plagued the first two transition periods.

With the first transition, in 1930, LaFayette Cooke made an arrangement through Mississippi evangelist T.T. Martin of the American School of Evangelism. Cooke trusted Martin to get a faith-based mission started. That mission would use Cooke's property for good deeds. Cooke's agreement with anti-evolution proponent Martin was that his Cook Springs property could be used to promote various good deeds and religious teachings and that it would not be used to teach the controversial theory of evolution.

When the second transition occurred, in the late 1950s, the American School of Evangelism's head trustee, Mack Roper, contacted leaders of the Birmingham Baptist Association whom he personally knew and trusted. Roper felt comfortable in entrusting the Baptists with the continuing operation of the nursing home and the faith-based campground that had been founded on Cooke's property under the auspices of the American School of Evangelism.

As it became clear that it was time for a third transition, leaders of the Birmingham Baptist Association found themselves with two facilities that had very different situations — one situation good, the other quite bad.

In the case of the Baptist-operated campground in Cook Springs, the campground was faring well. The Baptists would turn to a trusted, long-established fellow Baptist organization, the Woman's Missionary Union (WMU). The WMU would take it over and develop it into a mission retreat called WorldSong.

However, in the case of the other Cook Springs operation, the Baptist Home for Senior Citizens, the financial situation at that institution was such a troubling one that time was running out for a solution.

On the one hand, on a positive note, the long-term-care facility had expanded under the Baptist leadership to a point where in many ways it had increased potential. It no longer was just a nursing home. It was a senior-living campus consisting of a nursing home, plus eight apartments for independent living, plus a large assisted-living facility that was just a few years old.

Yet, despite its increased services and increased potential, the Baptist Home for Senior Citizens was in such deep financial trouble that anyone taking it over would be shouldering a risky undertaking. The financial situation was so grave that the senior-living campus was millions of dollars in debt and in danger of having to close its doors to senior care. In order to save the facility and pave the way for it to continue serving senior citizens, the Baptists very quickly had to find a risk-taking successor to operate it — a successor they could convince to step up to the helm during stressful times, and also a successor they could trust to do a good job. Working against the clock, the Baptists indeed were searching for a trustworthy successor who

The three board members who operated The Village at Cook Springs, beginning in 1990. From left, George Smith (board chairman), Max Huie, and Dale Sasser.

could be the rescuer of the Baptist Home for Senior Citizens.

In Quest of New Leadership

Even after wrestling for several years with financial problems of the Baptist Home for Senior Citizens, a number of Baptist leaders still believed in the Cook Springs facility. They believed the right leadership could come in and make a go of it.

As they looked around, the mission-focused Baptists were looking for a new leader who fit three main criteria:

They wanted someone they could trust as a humanitarian, someone who cared for people and had good ethics. The Baptists had put a lot of love and caring into the institution. It was important to them that whoever took it over carry forward that love and caring.

Secondly, the Baptists wanted someone who had experience in the nursing home business. It was a business that was getting more and more complex.

And thirdly, they had to find someone who was willing to take a risk — who was willing to take on a financially ailing senior-citizen facility.

In addition to those three main characteristics, the Baptist Home for

Senior Citizens also was in need of someone with a couple of other characteristics.

The Cook Springs senior-care facility was in desperate need of creative leadership in marketing and public relations. One of the big financial problems at the facility was the marketing challenge of filling up the new assisted-living building — a building that had run over budget in the construction phase and then had experienced low occupancy.

The Cook Springs senior-care facility also needed leadership that strongly believed in the pluses and potential of the Baptist Home for Senior Citizens. One of those outstanding pluses was the facility's location in a peaceful, rustic Cook Springs setting surrounded by grassy fields, stately trees, a lake, and stunning mountains.

In 1989, as they searched under pressure, the Baptists had their eyes on George H. Smith.

George H. Smith

On every front, George H. Smith fit the qualifications of being the leader for whom the Baptists were searching.

"Everything that we knew about George H. Smith was commendable and good," said the Reverend L. Earl Tew, who had served as president of the Birmingham Baptist Association for a period during the mid-1980s.

George H. Smith was well known to several of the leaders of the Birmingham Baptist Association. He also was well known to several of the leaders of the Association-appointed board that ran the day-to-day operations of the Baptist Home for Senior Citizens.

Some of those Baptist leaders had known Smith for decades, dating back to the years when Smith was director of public relations for the Birmingham-based, Baptist-linked Howard College, which became Samford University.

Smith had a strong and successful marketing and public-relations background. After a decade of success as a college public-relations director, he became vice president for marketing for Birmingham's Exchange Security Bank (later known as First Alabama Bank and then as Regions Bank). While at Exchange Security, Smith played a key role in spearheading the new Second Century program aimed at attracting young banking clients. After his stint at Exchange Security, Smith became senior vice president for marketing at the Bank of the Southeast.

George Smith also knew the long-term-care industry — as a result of having already been a successful leader in the industry. Beginning in the late 1970s, Smith had embarked upon a business venture involving long-term care. Smith and his partners developed a long-term-care company known as Southern Medical Services, Inc. Then they bought a Pennsylvania long-term-care company that became Northern Medical Services. Smith was founder, chief executive officer, and president of Southern Medical Services and Northern Medical Services. Along the way, George Smith pioneered nationally in setting up an Employee Stock Ownership Program (ESOP). Employees of Southern Medical Services and Northern Medical Services held 100 percent company ownership — a structure that Smith said contributed heavily to success. In 1984, Smith and his partners sold out their long-term-care holdings to Beverly Enterprises, owner of the Beverly Healthcare long-term-care enterprise. By the time Smith and his partners sold, their operation had grown to comprise 41 nursing homes, two assisted-living facilities, and two pharmacies.

At the time Smith and his partners sold out in 1984, George Smith was still in the prime of his working career. Baptist leaders who approached him in the late 1980s were very aware of additional business and marketing leadership Smith had provided since he and his partners sold their long-term-care company. Beginning in the mid-1980s, Smith scored a marketing success as an airline-recruitment consultant in the Birmingham area. Working with the city of Birmingham and other groups to attract more airlines to Birmingham's airport, Smith had helped bring in Air New Orleans, Piedmont, and, a particularly big coup at the time, Southwest Airlines. Too, George Smith had become fascinated with the long-term-care business. Even after he and his partners sold their long-term-care company, Smith remained active in the 1980s as part owner of a nursing home in North Alabama, in the town of Crossville.

As Baptist leaders talked to Smith in the late 1980s, they pointed out pluses of the financially troubled long-term-care facility in Cook Springs. Among pluses that excited Smith was the facility's beautiful location. George Smith had a great appreciation for the beauty of the outdoors and for the rural-setting appeal of a facility such as Cook Springs. Although he had forged his career in the city, Smith was born and reared in the small town of Cleveland, Alabama, in Blount County. He had retained a love for trees, mountains, lakes, and clean air. "When I was growing up, the main businesses in our little town were a general store and a hot-dog stand," Smith recalled with a smile. "And my family lived in such a rural spot that we were a couple of miles from either the general store or the hot-dog stand."

George Smith was the Baptists' number-one choice for taking over the troubled Cook Springs long-term-care operation — that is, if Smith could see fit to take on the challenge.

George Smith Brings in Max Huie

As George Smith looked at the situation at the Baptist Home for Senior Citizens in the late 1980s, he was seeing two things. He saw tremendous potential at the facility — potential that really attracted him. He also saw a formidable financial challenge.

Before Smith gave the Baptists an answer, he wanted to see if he could convince a colleague in the nursing home business to partner with him. The colleague's name was H. Max Huie. He was an accountant based in the Alabama town of Oneonta, in Blount County. As a part of his accounting business, Huie had developed a large clientele of nursing home owners and had become a leader in nursing home accounting. Too, Huie himself had gone into the nursing home business, as owner or part-owner of several nursing homes.

"I had known Max Huie for a long time. I really respected him, as did so many others in the nursing home industry," said Smith. "During that era, Max probably had been handling accounting for more nursing homes than any other accounting firm in Alabama. He also had done accounting work for nursing homes in several states besides Alabama — Georgia, Florida, Tennessee, other states as well."

Max Huie knew finances of nursing homes from many perspectives, said George Smith: "Max handled cost reports for nursing homes. He was a real guru in nursing home reimbursement — in Medicaid and Medicare reimbursement for skilled-care nursing homes. Max also was an expert on tax-free municipal bonds, and he helped nursing homes with bond issues. I knew that Max Huie was brilliant!"

Smith said he felt it would be a real asset if Max could come into a project with him to assume responsibility for operating the Baptists' financially troubled nursing home in Cook Springs. "So I contacted Max," he said. "I asked Max if he and I could get together and look at this financial dilemma at the Baptist Home for Senior Citizens in Cook Springs — to see if he felt there was any way we could make a go of this together, if there was any way he felt we could pay off that tremendous debt."

Max Huie Brings in Dale Sasser

As was the case with George Smith, Max Huie felt drawn to the potential he felt existed with the Baptist Home for Senior Citizens in Cook Springs. Also, like George Smith, Max Huie believed that the huge task of leading this project out of troubled waters would require a broad array of leadership skills.

Huie's mind turned immediately to a man from the South Alabama town of Andalusia who was knowledgeable in nursing home operations. His name was G. Dale Sasser. Huie and Sasser owned some nursing homes together. Sasser was a licensed nursing home administrator, and he had modern-day approaches to nursing home development and administration. Too, he had a good business head on his shoulders. In addition to running nursing homes, Sasser also was in the chicken-raising business and had enjoyed success in that business as well.

Max Huie told George Smith that he felt they should bring Dale Sasser on board to go into the Cook Springs project with them.

Registered nurse Sandy Everson had worked for Max Huie and Dale Sasser in nursing homes that Huie and Sasser jointly owned in the South Alabama towns of Andalusia and Hartford. Ms. Everson had seen the strengths of

Huie and Sasser firsthand. She said there was no doubt that Max Huie pioneered in the state in terms of Medicaid cost reports relevant to long-term care. And she said Dale Sasser was very forward-thinking in understanding how nursing homes were changing in the late 1980s. "Dale could really see ahead as to how the nursing home industry was going to be so very different as a result of new changes in federal laws governing nursing home care," she said. "Dale knew, for example, the big impact of stricter government regulations requiring that nursing homes have more registered nurses and more credentialed social workers, dietitians, and so forth. I think Dale and Max both saw that, with these new laws, it was going to be virtually impossible for nursing home operators to own just one nursing home. They could see that in most cases the old Mom-and-Pop nursing homes just weren't going to be able to withstand all these federal changes."

When Max Huie suggested Dale Sassser as a third partner for the Cook Springs project, George Smith agreed readily.

"So that is how it went in getting together a new board," said George Smith. "The Baptists approached me. I approached Max Huie. And Max Huie approached Dale Sasser. Together the three of us became the board that took over the Baptist Home for Senior Citizens and changed its name to The Village at Cook Springs."

Transition Occurs

As the Baptists went forward in releasing the reins of the Baptist Home for Senior Citizens, the process was gradual rather than all at once.

The first step came in 1989, when George Smith and Max Huie entered into a management contract with the Baptists to operate the Baptist Home for Senior Citizens. Prior to entering into that agreement, the Baptists already had had some experience operating the facility under a management contract. Their first such contract had been with Northport Health Services, based in Tuscaloosa.

After Smith and Huie ran the facility for several months under the management contract agreement, Sasser officially joined the group. Together, the three became board members who in 1990 assumed full responsibility for

*Sign at The
Village at Cook
Springs, put in
place in 1990s.*

operating the long-term-care facility in Cook Springs — a facility that since December 1958 had been under the umbrella operation of the Birmingham Baptist Association.

To make this transition complete, a board reorganization took place. All board members of the Baptist Home for Senior Citizens resigned. The resigning board elected a new board to succeed them. That new board was made up of George H. Smith, H. Max Huie, and G. Dale Sasser. Smith became board chairman.

The board's structure as a not-for-profit long-term-care operation had not changed. That structure would continue, with new board members in place.

However, with the departure of the Baptists from the helm, the name of the facility did change. The Baptist Home for Senior Citizens was renamed as The Village at Cook Springs. As time went on, many would refer to the institution simply as "the Village."

It was George Smith who selected the facility's new name. Throughout his career, Smith had placed a great deal of importance on names and the images that were conveyed by names. "I wanted Cook Springs in the facility's name. As for 'the Village,' to me 'the Village' says, 'This is a place where people live. This is their home.'"

Starting an Uphill Financial Climb

When the Baptist Home for Senior Citizens passed into the hands of the Smith-Huie-Sasser group in 1990, the facility was about $7 million in debt. By far the majority of the debt involved payments owed to bondholders who had purchased tax-free revenue bonds to fund expansion projects at the Baptist Home for Senior Citizens. There were some debts owed to banks. There was money owed for various services provided by the Birmingham-based Baptist Medical Centers, later known as the Baptist Health System. And there were outstanding debts to other vendors who provided various types of supplies and services.

"We knew this was going to be a tremendous challenge," said Smith.

At the beginning, before the Smith-Huie-Sasser group took over, a voluntary bankruptcy structure was worked out for the entity known as the Baptist Home for Senior Citizens, Inc. It was worked out with the cooperation of the Birmingham Baptist Association and the Association-appointed board charged with ongoing operation of the Baptist Home for Senior Citizens. This voluntary bankruptcy structure provided the new Smith-Huie-Sasser leadership board with a workable timetable to start digging the facility out of its deep financial hole.

George Smith noted that even though creditors often lose out in these kinds of voluntary bankruptcy deals, the Smith-Huie-Sasser group made a commitment that the creditors would be paid. "We told the Baptists that we would pay everybody. They believed us. And we kept our commitment," said George Smith. He said that by the early 1990s, all of that huge debt was paid off. "We paid every penny that was owed," said Smith.

The digging out was accomplished in a variety of ways — upgrading and further expanding the facility to bring in more occupants, using varied mechanisms to generate funds, and traveling the creative route in marketing and public relations. These are examples of some of the approaches taken by the three new leaders:

• Making significant progress in filling up the assisted-living facility with happy residents. This was a key goal when the Smith-Huie-Sasser group took charge. It was a goal that had to be met — and it was met.

• Carrying out needed maintenance, repair and facelift work, plus some modest new expansion as well, to attract more residents into all sections of the senior-living campus.

• Using funding mechanisms such as bond issues and various borrowings.

• Generating funds by selling off some property near The Village at Cook Springs — property that was included in the acreage that the Smith-Huie-Sasser group took over. One parcel of property was sold to the Boy Scouts of America, which operated a camp in the area. A smaller parcel of property, sold to the Woman's Missionary Union (WMU), included several acres and the house that had been used by the Birmingham Baptist Association as the home for the administrator of the Baptist Home for Senior Citizens. "This property was located on the same side of the interstate as the campground that was conveyed to the WMU by the Birmingham Baptist Association," said George Smith. "It just made sense that the WMU would have this property and thus have better control of their land."

Village residents Mamie Speaks and Gene Harris picking blueberries, 1990s.

A Cooke Family Signoff

When LaFayette Cooke conveyed his large tract of Cook Springs acreage to the American School of Evangelism in 1930, he included a number of strict restrictions, or covenants, about how the property should be managed. Among those covenants were directions that in some cases would prevent cutting of timber and also prevent the mortgage or sale of property.

Once these limitations were put into place in 1930,

the only way they could be removed was through a revised directive from the persons signing the 1930 agreement — LaFayette Cooke and his wife, Eliza — or, in the event of their deaths, a release order signed by their direct heirs.

With the Baptist Home for Senior Citizens in grave financial condition in the late 1980s, a successful effort was made to contact the heirs of LaFayette and Eliza Cooke and seek a cancellation of those 1930 covenants.

Such a release was obtained on September 20, 1990.

Taking the lead in efforts that led to this Cooke family-members' agreement was John Frank Cooke, of Ormond Beach, Florida, a grandson of LaFayette and Eliza Cooke. In helping to pave the way for the cancellation-of-covenants agreement, Cooke aided in the contacting of 12 other Cooke grandchildren and one great-grandson. At the time, these descendants were residing in a wide range of locales — in Florida, California, Alabama, Georgia, Louisiana, Michigan, and Washington, D.C.

Feeling for the Past and Present

The attorney who handled the interaction with the Cooke family in the signoff agreement was H. Hampton "Hamp" Boles of the Birmingham-based law firm of Balch & Bingham.

During the time this process was unfolding, Boles became familiar with documents signed 60 years in the past by LaFayette and Eliza Cooke. He also became familiar with missions carried out at the Baptist Home for Senior Citizens and with that institution's evolvement into The Village at Cook Springs.

There was no doubt the Cooke family cancellation-of-covenants agreement helped elevate chances that the Cook Springs long-term-care facility could continue as a viable operation, said Boles. "The facility in Cook Springs could have continued to operate on a not-for-profit basis even if those covenants had remained in place. However, with the covenants in place, the use of that land would have been highly restricted," he said.

Boles praised John Frank Cooke, of Ormond Beach, Florida, for being willing to spend so much time aiding in the contact of his relatives. "He did a lot of phoning and legwork in tracking down his relatives, in explaining that the cancellation of these covenants would be useful and appropriate," said Boles.

As Boles learned more about LaFayette and Eliza Cooke, he came to deeply respect them. "When you read about the generosity of LaFayette and Eliza Cooke, you have to believe that they were people who really cared for their church, their spiritual life, and for other people," said Boles.

Based on what he had learned about LaFayette and Eliza Cooke's dedication to helping others, Boles believed the couple would have been pleased that a long-term-care facility would continue to operate in Cook Springs: "If Mr. and Mrs. Cooke had been alive in 1990, I believe they would have been happy that people would continue to be cared for in that facility in Cook Springs."

16

A Workable Formula

"After Carol Moseley became the administrator at The Village at Cook Springs, she told all of us who worked there, 'You take care of our residents here, and I'll take care of you.'"—Leola Kelly, longtime employee, The Village at Cook Springs

There was a new name. There was a new board. And soon there was a new plan of operations and marketing in place. To push forward this facility that now was known as The Village at Cook Springs, the three-man board had a simple yet far-reaching formula.

First they would recruit a top administrator as the facility's executive director. Then, joining with this administrator, they would make sure the standards of care remained high and that new programs were added. And, all along the way, they would keep chiseling away at the financial problems.

A New Executive Director

A top priority of the Smith-Huie-Sasser team was to recruit the ideal executive director to serve as the top administrator of The Village at Cook Springs. They found this top administrator in Carol Moseley. She came on board in 1990, just a few months after the Smith-Huie-Sasser group assumed the leadership. Ms. Moseley remained for eight years in the position of executive director of The Village at Cook Springs.

Ms. Moseley had come into the nursing home industry through her

Judge Bill Hereford and Carol Moseley, Village at Cook Springs' executive director, at "duck pond" during Village's Halloween Carnival, 1990s.

knowledge and training in food service, or dietetics. She had a college degree in dietetics and obtained employment in the nursing home field. She found she had an interest not only in the food-service end of nursing homes, but also in nursing care for the nursing home residents and in activities for the residents. So she took more training and became a licensed nursing home administrator.

"When I first started working in the nursing home field, I thought, 'Well, I'll just do this temporarily.' But then as I really got into it, I just fell in love with the long-term-care business," Ms. Moseley said in a 2005 interview. "To me, working in a long-term-care facility in a sense is like being called to preach. If you find you have a true love for taking care of senior citizens, it really does become like a calling. I think that can be true for any employee working in the nursing home field — regardless of what position he or she holds."

From the time she arrived at The Village at Cook Springs, Carol Moseley made a major positive impression on staff, residents, and families.

When Carol Moseley came to the Village, Leola Kelly already had been working at the institution for 21 years — dating back to its days as the Cook Springs Nursing Home and then during the time it was the Baptist Home for Senior Citizens. Mrs. Kelly knew how to spot an administrator who was both caring and competent. She said that Carol Moseley clearly was both. "I was so glad they put Carol in there as administrator at the Village.

I thought she was the nicest person, and so smart," said Mrs. Kelly. "After Carol Moseley became the administrator at The Village at Cook Springs, she told all of us who worked there, 'You take care of our residents here, and I'll take care of you.' Carol met with the employees and she talked to us and let us know where she stood from the beginning. She told us, 'Now, my first priority is our residents here at the Village. My next priority is you all — the employees — because you all are the ones who have got to take care of our residents. If you do your job in taking care of our residents, then we will get along. If you run into a problem, come talk to me and I'll try to straighten it out.'"

When Carol Moseley went to work for the Smith-Huie-Sasser team to administer The Village at Cook Springs, the team member who knew her professional track record best was Max Huie. Ms. Moseley and Huie were both from the same Alabama hometown, Oneonta.

George Smith said that Huie's high recommendation of Carol Moseley proved to be correct. Smith said Ms. Moseley was the perfect executive director for the Village. "I think Carol Moseley is due a lot of credit for what was accomplished at the Village during the 1990s," said Smith. "She truly is an outstanding administrator. She knows quality, she knows nursing homes, she knows employees, and she knows residents and their families."

Sprucing Up the Village

Financial problems that plagued the Baptist Home for Senior Citizens during the 1980s took a toll on the appearance of some of the older areas of the institution. As the institution's financial problems deepened, funds simply were not available to pay for the upkeep the Baptists would have liked to have accomplished. By the time the Smith-Huie-Sasser group became the operators, a major facelift was in order for The Village at Cook Springs.

Longtime employee Mary Ferguson said the group wasted no time in making that facelift happen. She said those taking the lead in hands-on supervision were George Smith and Carol Moseley. "Between the two of them, they tore this place apart and improved it!" said Mrs. Ferguson. "They made

Village pageant winners: Left, board chairman George Smith with Marjorie Moore, 1997 pageant winner in Village's nursing home section. Right, Maggie Clement, winner of first pageant at Village's Springs Manor (assisted-living), 1990.

sure that needed painting was done and that chipped tiles were patched in our hallways. They had new carpeting put in. They replaced some of the older furniture."

Mrs. Ferguson said the facelift also extended to beautifying the outdoors. "And I will tell you that Carol Moseley herself spent time outside working. Carol worked in the yards, in the gardens. She planted flowers. She was right there."

Expanding the Residents' Activities

By the 1990s, those who were forward thinkers in long-term care were turning their attention more and more to activities for residents of long-term-care facilities.

The basic concept was that just giving residents good care and a pleasant living environment was not enough. Interesting, stimulating daily activities were needed to enrich their lives.

Carol Moseley strongly subscribed to that line of thinking. "For the residents, planned activities are such a wonderful way to keep them involved and occupied," said Ms. Moseley. "I firmly believe that when we have residents who are happy and involved, they are less likely to be depressed and they are likely to need less medication and less medical treatment."

Beginning soon after she arrived at the Village, Ms. Moseley led the staff in greatly expanding the activities for residents at The Village at Cook Springs. When she came to the Village, the facility already had in place a strong program of devotional activities. She and her staff kept those devotional programs in place and added many other activities.

A large program of arts and crafts soon was in place, complete with a gift shop where residents' arts and crafts creations could be sold. More church and civic groups started coming into the Village — including church choirs that would sing and civic groups that would conduct some type of volunteer program to interact with residents. When election-time rolled around, political candidates came in and spoke to residents. When Christmas-time came, some of the Village's residents boarded a bus to ride in community Christmas parades in nearby towns of Pell City and Leeds. The year 1990 marked the first year for the Ms. Springs Manor pageant in the Village's assisted-living facility. Bingo games became a real drawing card for residents. There were more special events at the Village, involving residents, their family members, employees, and people from out in the community — including many who had never before visited the facility. The Village became a scene of activities that attracted many visitors from St. Clair County communities such as Cook Springs, Moody, Pell City, Leeds and Odenville.

"Through our expanded activities programs for our residents, the Village became more a part of surrounding communities, and surrounding communities became more a part of the Village," said Ms. Moseley. "We had so many community citizens coming in to share events with us, and in so doing the visitors had a chance to see that our nursing home and our assisted-living facility really were great places."

One of the most popular activities at the Village during that period was an annual fishing tournament that was named for State Senator Jack Biddle, III. For the event, the lake at the Village was stocked with fish. As those who enjoyed fishing took their places at the lake with fishing gear in hand, residents of the Village were among the excited fishermen and fisherwomen taking part. "This fishing tournament was a way for us to honor Jack

Biddle. We respected Jack Biddle as a state senator whose district included our home county of St. Clair. We also respected him as a member of the State Legislature who was doing a lot for healthcare in the state," said Ms. Moseley. "Too, the fishing tournament was just an enjoyable affair. People from surrounding communities came. We fished. We gave prizes. We had a cookout. We were doing something fun, and our residents were so deeply involved in every bit of it."

Judge Bill Hereford of Pell City was among those who enjoyed attending the fishing tournaments honoring Jack Biddle. Well-known as a circuit judge and later as a senior circuit judge, Hereford and his wife, Paula, would volunteer their time at the Village in a number of ways. They also had family members who were residents at the Village. "Oh, my wife and I have had such good times at the Village over the years!" Hereford said in a 2005 interview. "And I can tell you that those fishing tournaments were among the really good times!"

In a 2005 interview, that 1990s period of growth in activities was recalled by Bobbie Hobson, longtime activity director for the assisted-living side of the Village. By the time the Smith-Huie-Sasser administration got into full swing in 1990, Ms. Hobson already had been working for six years at the Cook Springs facility. In fact, when the facility was still under Baptist leadership, she had been one of the first employees on the assisted-living side. Ms. Hobson recalled the 1990s as a period of exciting growth in activities. "I remember well one of the additions that made it possible for us to expand programs to take our residents out into the community. That addition came when George Smith authorized us to get a bus. Up until then, all we had for use in transporting our residents was a passenger van. That was really great for our activity programs when we got that bus," she said. Ms. Hobson had positive memories of programs beginning in the 1990s that took residents outside the Village and also of programs during that period that brought the community into the Village. "One of the enjoyable things I recall during the 1990s was our Senior Celebration Days," said Ms. Hobson. "We had senior groups who would visit our facility, and we took them on tours of The Village at Cook Springs."

Offering Options in Food Service

It was Carol Moseley's knowledge about food service that first brought her into the nursing home industry. As she moved from being a dietitian to being a nursing home administrator, she retained the value she placed on high-quality food service.

Thus, one of the projects that pleased her most at the Village was the move there in the 1990s to put in place expanded food-service options. She expressed pride in the work accomplished by Village employees in that area.

"Often when people think of food in a nursing home or an assisted-living facility, all they picture is an institutional-type menu," said Ms. Moseley. "What we did out at the Village in the 1990s was to add some special food-service features." She said those types of menu options later would become more commonplace in long-term-care facilities. But she said at the time the Village instituted the changes, the features were still a bit ahead of the curve in long-term-care trends.

"We knew there were options we could offer and still serve a well-balanced diet," said Ms. Moseley. "So we started having meetings with our residents to see what they would like to see on the menu. And we met with our employees to get their ideas. We included all our residents in this planning — in the nursing home and in assisted living. We looked at what we needed to add to the menus and what we needed to take off."

When it came to residents who were not well enough to speak for themselves, questions about their food were posed to those who cared for them.

To generate additional ideas, some of the dietary staff were treated to meals in restaurants out in the community. "Our dietary staff looked at possibilities for buffet-style meals and also for very nice sit-down meals," said Ms. Moseley.

These are some of the results:

Cafeteria lines were put in place, with increased choices. "Residents had a choice of more than one kind of meat, choices of multiple kinds of vegetables," said Ms. Moseley. Salad and soup bars were added. "If a resident didn't feel up to a heavy meal, he or she could just have soup, or soup and a salad."

Continental breakfasts were added. "This meant that if a resident wanted to have breakfast a little bit later in the morning, he or she could do so, and just have a continental breakfast," said Ms. Moseley.

Self-serve machines and cappuccino also were offered.

As for how these options were received by residents, Carol Moseley and her staff found out once again what they already knew — that food service very much matters in a residential facility. "Oh, these options we offered were so very well received by our residents," said Ms. Moseley. "Our residents absolutely loved this!"

The Three-Man Board Hums

As the Smith-Huie-Sasser management team became entrenched in operating The Village at Cook Springs, each team member worked closely with Carol Moseley in bringing about a smooth operation.

Hamp Boles, Birmingham attorney who did legal work for the three, was in admiration of the leadership demonstrated by the Smith-Huie-Sasser trio: "I would put great stock in the management of this facility by these three. They worked together to change that facility from one that was close to being insolvent to one that was solvent and was able to borrow money and change and renovate the place."

To do this, the three members of the Village's board blended their respective talents:

George Smith took the lead and spent more time at the facility with a hands-on presence than did the other two. In fact, for a decade Smith focused his energies on the Village full-time — concentrating on marketing, rebuilding and renovation, and debt reduction.

Max Huie was the numbers man — the one who took a lead in guiding the Village out of its deep financial problems. He particularly took the financial-guidance lead on the nursing home side of the Village operation. It was in regard to nursing homes that Huie had the most experience. Much of the challenge on the assisted-living side was a marketing challenge — a challenge that rested much on the shoulders of George Smith.

Of the three, the one who was most knowledgeable about nursing home operations was Dale Sasser — the only licensed nursing home administrator among the three.

George Smith quickly bonded with employees, residents, and families. "George has always been a real people-person," said Hamp Boles. During visits Boles made to the Village, he observed the friendliness, warmth and caring that George Smith showed to those he encountered at the Village. "George was so loved out there at the Village that when he walked down the halls it seemed like everybody in the place knew him," said Boles. "People would stop George in the hallways and want to talk to him. And George was just as interested in stopping and talking with those residents, their families, and the employees. You see, George really got to know the people associated with the Village!"

Carol Moseley said that the Village greatly benefited from the vision of George Smith. "I felt that George was far ahead with his vision. And I believe that one of the things that made us successful at the Village in the 1990s was the vision of George Smith. I know that George himself was coming up with new ideas. Too, George was letting others at the Village come up with new ideas. These ideas we implemented at the Village were some of the same types of concepts that nursing home leaders at a national level later would point to in talking about what led to a positive national culture change in nursing homes. George had been leading the way in letting us do those things years before many other people. George was the type of person who would listen to your ideas and would let you try new things — including some approaches that at the time were not typical for nursing homes and assisted living."

When it came to Max Huie, he had the reputation of being a mixture of a kind, personable man and a brilliant man. The Village's executive director, Carol Moseley, said that

Board member Max Huie at a Christmas-time social event at the Village, 1990s.

One of Village's cats, whose name was Baby, tries hand at playing "telephone operator."

reputation for brilliance followed Max Huie all his working years, dating back to his accounting work in Oneonta. "Max was so, so smart!" she said. "If you were around Max Huie, you didn't need a calculator. Max could add numbers in the thousands in his head quicker than many people could put them into a calculator!"

Max Huie loved to work. He thrived on crunching numbers. He wasn't much into hobbies — except for cars, that is (especially his Corvette). "My dad loved accounting so much that accounting really was like a hobby to him," said John Huie, the middle of the three sons born to Max and Grace Huie. "My dad's heart was much more into crunching numbers and putting deals together than it was in day-to-day running of operations. My dad just loved those challenges that involved managing finances. Actually, with this debt-ridden situation that he and George and Dale took over at The Village at Cook Springs, I believe my dad probably saw that as a challenge he really wanted to tackle. He was the kind of person who would see the overcoming of a financial problem as a positive challenge, whereas someone else might look at confronting something like that as a burden. Dad just loved accounting so much that he would look at it from a positive view that could be a completely different angle from what most people typically would view it."

In terms of Max's kindness to others, he didn't talk about performing those kindnesses. He just quietly performed good deeds. John Huie said that his father did many kind things for people that members of the Huie family didn't even hear about until years later. He said the family was very touched when they would hear how Max had reached out to help someone.

"I know that I found out years after the fact about a number of good deeds my dad had done in which he helped people who didn't even realize at the time that Dad was the one who had done something for them. Someone would tell Dad about something that needed to be done — like, for example, tell him about an old cemetery that really needing fixing up

— and Dad would just quietly have it done."

As for Dale Sasser, he could be a no-nonsense businessman and administrator and he could also be a very disarming man who could crack one joke after another.

John Huie said he saw both sides of his dad's friend and business partner. On the business side, John Huie felt that his father and Sasser had business traits that complemented and balanced one another. "When Dad and Dale would buy nursing homes together, my dad tended to be conservative and Dale was more likely to take risks in business actions. Dale was much more a risk-taker than was my dad." Then, on the personal side, John Huie saw Dale Sasser as a man filled with charm and laughter. "Dale could be really funny. He could get on a streak when he was like continuously telling jokes! I mean, Dale just never met a stranger. He was a very outgoing person."

Having observed Dale Sasser as he functioned as a nursing home owner and administrator, registered nurse Sandy Everson said there was no doubt in her mind that Sasser's charming personality contributed to his business success. "I do think Dale Sasser was good in operations not only because he knew operations but also because he was so good with people," said Ms. Everson, who worked in South Alabama nursing homes operated by Dale Sasser and Max Huie prior to coming to work at The Village at Cook Springs in 1992. "Dale Sasser was really the charming Dale Carnegie type. He had the gift of gab, a winning smile, and people skills. I've always said that I thought Dale could have sold ice cubes to Eskimos!"

Jerry Moss, who worked for years in administration at the Village, said that Sasser brought with him knowledge about operations and about getting along with other people in the nursing home industry. "Dale worked well with Alabama's Nursing Home Association. Also, Dale was always venturing out, wanting to know more about long-term care and how to better run a facility. Dale had good long-term strategies."

A Double Blow

Within a few weeks of one another in late 1992, two tragedies occurred that deeply impacted the Smith-Huie-Sasser group.

Village residents on an outing at Birmingham Zoo, 1990s. At left, Village group embarks on a fun day. At right, Village resident John Martin visits with a llama at the zoo.

Both tragedies involved car accidents. And both involved fatalities.

The first car accident claimed the life of the eldest son of Max and Grace Huie — Howard Max Huie, Jr. Better known as Hal Huie, this Huie son ran a medical-supply business owned by the Huie family.

The second car accident claimed the life of Dale Sasser. People at the Village were still reeling from the death of Hal Huie when word came that Dale Sasser had been killed in a one-car accident.

A notice about Sasser's death appeared in the November 1992 edition of *The Village Press*, the newsletter of The Village at Cook Springs. The headline indicated that the Village had lost both a co-operator and a friend. This is an excerpt: "Sasser, 41, was killed in an auto accident during the early morning hours of Oct. 21. He had served on the Village's Board of Directors for three years. Sasser also served as administrator and owner of several other health care facilities . . ."

Several hours before Sasser's death, nurse Sandy Everson had been on the phone with Sasser, discussing his latest nursing home venture and a nursing-care role she would take on with that project. Then she received word he had been killed. "It's one of those things that just happens so quickly!" said Ms. Everson. "One afternoon I was on the phone talking with Dale, and he was telling me that he and Max had just signed the papers that day to buy still another nursing home, in Phenix City, Alabama. And then that night he was killed in the accident."

These tragedies of Dale Sasser's death and Hal Huie's death created a cloud of sadness at The Village at Cook Springs. No one at the Village suffered more than did Max Huie.

"That was a really, really bad time," said John Huie. "For my dad, he lost a son, and then shortly thereafter he lost someone who was both a business partner and a very good friend."

John Huie Takes on a Role

After the death of Dale Sasser, the board vacancy that Sasser left behind at the Village was filled by John Huie. Thus, the Village's three-man board that had taken the helm as Smith-Huie-Sasser became Smith-Huie-Huie.

As time went on, the younger Huie would become more and more deeply immersed in the Huie family's involvement in the nursing home business. A young man whose theatrical interests had led him to be a film major in college, John Huie became a licensed nursing home administrator. His involvement in the nursing home business would become even deeper several years later after his father, Max, succumbed to cancer.

Vivian Moves In

One of those greatly affected by the sadnesses of 1992 was Max Huie's mother, Vivian Huie.

A widow, Mrs. Huie was devastated by the loss of her grandson, Hal. Not long after his death, she moved from her own home into the assisted-living facility at The Village at Cook Springs.

"I've always thought that move was such a good thing for my grandmother," said John Huie. "Ever since my grandfather's death, my grandmother had not been getting out much. She pretty much had stayed at home. Also, a number of her friends had died. So, after the sudden death of my brother, I thought it was good for her to move to the Village, to kind of re-immerse herself in being around other people."

In Carol Moseley's years as a nursing home administrator, she had seen many senior men and women go through the transition of moving from their homes into a nursing home or assisted-living facility following a major change in their lives — a change such as deteriorating health or the loss of a loved one. She also had seen many cases in which individuals benefited from such a move. She felt that Vivian Huie was one of those individuals who benefited.

Once Mrs. Huie moved to the Village, she stayed there and made it her home for years, for the rest of her life. She lived first in the Village's assisted-living side. Later, as her healthcare needs increased, she moved to the Village's nursing home.

However, when Mrs. Huie first came, it was her plan to pass through briefly.

"Mrs. Huie came to live with us at a point when it was such a difficult time for the Huie family," said Ms. Moseley. "It was her intention to stay with us a very short period of time." She said Vivian Huie actually planned to stay only a few weeks, until the period passed following the initial shock of grandson Hal Huie's death.

"Mrs. Huie would tell people, 'Now, I'm just here for a short period of time.'" said Ms. Moseley.

But soon it became apparent that Mrs. Huie was feeling comfortable in the facility, said Ms. Moseley. If Mrs. Huie ventured outside the Village for a visit, sometimes she would want to make sure she returned to the Village in time to take part in some special activity that interested her. "Mrs. Huie really came to enjoy being in the middle of all the entertainment that was going on at the Village," said Ms. Moseley.

John Huie said he saw positive changes in his grandmother after she moved to the Village. "When our family would visit my grandmother, she would tell us all about what was going on out there at the Village!" he said.

As time went by, Ms. Moseley said that when Mrs. Huie's friends would ask her when she planned to leave, she would say, "Well, I think I need to stay on here just a few more weeks."

Touching the Staff

During the eight years she was executive director of the Village during the 1990s, Carol Moseley built a legacy of touching employees' lives in positive ways.

"I just cannot express strongly enough what a great mentor Carol Moseley was for me," said Sandy Everson. When registered nurse Everson was offered a job at the Village as admissions director, she wanted the position but was nervous about whether she would be able to handle it. "Carol said to me, 'Sandy, don't worry. I'll teach you.'" Ms. Everson believed that, and the teaching did take place as promised. Ms. Everson, who herself would later go on to be a teacher of others, said that Carol Moseley was always teaching her. "Carol added so, so much to my bank of knowledge," said Ms. Everson. "She taught me things I didn't know. Also, there were things I already knew something about that Carol polished and helped me understand better. With some of the new nursing home regulations that were going into effect, even when I knew what the regulations were it was often Carol who taught me the 'why' behind these new rules."

Another staff member who said Carol Moseley touched her deeply was Mary Ferguson. At the time Mrs. Ferguson was interviewed in 2005, she had been at the Village for 27 years, having started in 1978 when the institution was the Baptist Home for Senior Citizens. Mrs. Ferguson started as a nursing assistant on the third shift, back in the days before the nursing assistants had to go through a certification process. She worked her way up the ladder to become a department head at the Village. At the time she was interviewed, Mrs. Ferguson held a department-head post that placed her in charge of coordinating purchasing and medical records for the Village.

Independent-living Village resident Laura Mitchell takes a bike ride to have lunch in the dining room on the Village campus, 1990s.

She credited Carol Moseley with supporting her in her professional rise. She said Ms. Moseley believed in her ability and encouraged her to learn and move up. "Carol was willing to teach you. Now, she was firm. You knew when she meant business, when you had to walk the line," said Mrs. Ferguson. "But Carol was a people-person, and a person I felt was there for me."

Mrs. Ferguson said that Carol Moseley's support of her extended to times of personal crisis. The example that came immediately to her mind was the time when Mrs. Ferguson's two sons were injured in a truck accident and one son had to undergo surgery. "Carol came to Birmingham right after that accident occurred, in the middle of the night, to be with me at UAB Medical Center when my son underwent surgery. Carol Moseley treated me like a sister!"

17

A Home in the Country

"The goats would follow the horse around little trails at the Village. The goats and the horse would walk up and down those little trails — up and down, up and down."—George H. Smith, chairman of the board, The Village at Cook Springs, 1990–2001

The peaceful "country-style" atmosphere that for decades had been a trademark of the facility that was to become The Village at Cook Springs took on an even more "farm-like" ambience in the 1990s. Ever since the first component had been built in 1950, this long-term-care facility had possessed a special attraction associated with the natural beauty of its location — a wooded location with mountains in the background. When a lake was added to the site in the 1950s, the location became more of a pastoral showplace.

Then, during the 1990s, the Village's setting became even more compelling. In addition to work in replacing and renovating buildings at the Village, there were also "country-style" changes that included the on-site addition of animals, new landscaping and fences, and even a pretty red barn.

Adding to that aura was a network of names. During the 1990s, various units within the Village were given names that matched the Village's rural location.

It was the making of a long-term-care facility that truly stood apart from most senior-citizen residences. The Village developed into a sprawling

senior-living campus that for its residents became more like their home in the country.

A Tale of Goats, Horses, Cats and Ducks

Board chairman George Smith led the way in bringing to the Village an assortment of four-legged, winged, and aquatic additions that he affectionately called "critters."

Before Smith came to the Village, a few animals had been at the facility during its era as the Baptist Home for Senior Citizens — but nothing like the volume that came in the 1990s.

In a 2005 interview, Smith recalled the fun that the critters brought to the Village in the 1990s — and the many purposes they served.

"Well, part of this started with a need we had to do something to control all the extra growth around the Village — all those honeysuckle vines, kudzu, what have you," said Smith. "We had all this growth of kudzu and vines and saplings at the edge of the road. This growth actually was creeping up to the edge of the Village's buildings on three sides! So I thought, 'You know, goats are so funny. Also, goats will eat anything. What if I go get some nanny goats and a billy goat to put at the Village? They will eat up all this extra growth. Also, our residents will love watching them, because they are so funny!' So that's what we did. It worked, on both counts. Those goats started eating up the kudzu and the honeysuckles and vines and so forth. And the residents did love watching the goats! Why, the goats were so popular with folks at the Village that I even built a 'performing stand' for the goats. The Goat Performing Stand was about six feet tall. There were boards going up to the stand — so the goats could walk up there and perform on that stand. The goats would butt each other. They would stand up on their hind legs. The residents would watch them and watch them. And, we kept getting more goats, and more goats. I started out in 1990 with four nanny goats and one billy goat. New baby goats were born at the Village, including twin baby goats and triplet baby goats. Pretty soon, we had 23 goats at the Village! My wife, Jan, and I spent many night-time hours out at the Village taking care of these baby goats. They became very special pets."

Then there were the horses at the Village. "The first horse we had out at the Village was named Sara Lee," said Smith. "Now, Sara Lee the horse and the goats made a great pairing. The goats would follow the horse around little trails at the Village. The goats and the horse would walk up and down those little trails — up and down, up and down. Then we added a second horse — Gayla's Delight. We fixed up a pasture out there at the Village, located so that the residents in both the nursing home area and the assisted-living area could look out the windows and watch the goats and horses."

Then there were the ducks at the Village. "I went to a little place in Blount County that has all these different kinds of birds and ducks," said Smith. "There I found five little brown South American ducks for the Village — really small, miniature ducks. We nursed them at the Village. They grew. They had babies. You could look out at the lake at the Village and see all these little ducks swimming across our lake. Oh, did our residents love that! And then we had some mallard ducks who came in. And they mated with the little South American ducks. That of course started a whole new different-looking duck population for the Village — ducks that had the brown

Residents wait in Village's Jolly Trolley while resident Dorothy Carlson feeds horses on Village campus, late 1990s. Horses, from left, Gayla's Delight and Sara Lee.

coloring of the miniature ducks we had gotten in Blount County and the beautiful green head and neck of the mallard ducks."

On top of that, there also were fish and turtles at the Village's lake.

And here and there someone could spot a cat on the Village's premises. George Smith recalled that the Village's executive director, Carol Moseley, enjoyed the feline addition.

"Oh, I'm a real cat lover, and I really participated in the 'cat part' out at the Village," said Ms. Moseley. She said time and again she saw resident-and-cat bonding. She recalled an example of a resident who was facing some grave health problems, and a particular cat became such a source of comfort to the resident. "This was a solid white Persian cat — so, so pretty," she said. "That cat would be right there with the resident. It was as though the cat could sense what was going on with this lady. Oh, that resident did enjoy that cat. To her, the cat was so, so special."

The concept of bringing in animals at the Village was an example of George Smith's vision in connecting with senior citizens and helping them to live happier lives, said Carol Moseley. "You know, not too long after George began bringing in the horses and goats and ducks to the Village, we started hearing a lot nationally in the long-term-care field concerning the value of pet therapy with older people. Experts started talking about how seniors tended to connect with animals, to enjoy interacting with them." She said George Smith was bringing in animals as just a natural part of his understanding of seniors, prior to pet therapy really being spotlighted as having so much value as a formalized therapeutic approach. "George just had that vision for working with seniors," said Ms. Moseley. "The pet therapy was just one example of his vision."

A Goat Named Miss Dee Dee

One of the goats born at the Village stood a bit apart from the others. She was an individualist.

"I actually don't think this goat realized she was a goat!" said George Smith with a laugh. He explained that the goat behaved more like a little human. "She was very different, very regal. Why, she wouldn't even eat with the other goats. She went off and ate by herself."

The goat made a wonderful pet, said Smith. "She was a real favorite with my wife, Jan."

This little goat was named for a man to whom she owed her very life. She was given the name of Miss Dee Dee — named in honor of Dee Will Moss, longtime maintenance technician at the Village.

"The reason we named her for Dee Will is what Dee Will did for this little goat," said Smith. "Miss Dee Dee was born down in our pasture at the Village on a very cold night — when the temperature dropped down to between 15 and 20 degrees. Dee Will found the newborn goat just wandering around out in the cold. If he had not found her, she could not have withstood those cold temperatures. She surely would have died. It was Dee

The Red Barn, built at the Village in 1990s, with screened porch added later.

Will who brought her to our barn, got her settled down with her mother. Pretty soon we just started calling her Miss Dee Dee."

The Names

As the Village itself took on more and more of a rustic aura that matched the woods, mountains, and lake where it was located, some name-changing took place.

This had to do with naming the various sections of the Village. With the aid of staff members who worked at the Village, lovely "outdoorsy" names were selected that matched the Village's setting. Various sections of the Village in which residents resided came to be known by names such as Dogwood Way and Camellia Trace.

"Thus, instead of having institutional-sounding names such as Hall A or Hall B, we had names that actually sounded like names of some street on which an individual would live," said Carol Moseley.

Again, she said visionary George Smith led the way in the name-giving.

"I've just always felt that names should paint pictures," explained Smith. "And if you're living in a long-term-care facility, that is your home and you need to be living in a place that has a name you enjoy. I tried to put myself in the place of a person who was living in a nursing home. I mean, would you rather be there living on Station 2, or would you rather be living on Dogwood Way?"

Completing the Picture

As more animals moved onto the Village grounds, workmen got busy adding to an outdoors environment that matched and accommodated them.

One major 1990s addition was the big Red Barn — a barn that was highly visible when driving onto the grounds of the Village. The barn became a popular attraction for residents and visitors. It also served practical purposes for the animals and for storage.

Then there was a carefully designed rural-theme facelift for the grounds — including a rustic entrance and a quaint wooden pastoral sign. George Smith said it was a joy to see all this take shape. "We put up fences, had rockwork put in place, had grass planted, had plants set out, and installed some new outdoor lighting."

It was indeed a partnership that created this cozy, quaint setting. It was a partnership between the natural surroundings that had been such a gift to the Village and some special touches put in place by the facility's operators during the 1990s.

18

Source of Pride

"When you look at the size of The Village at Cook Springs during the time I served as a board member there, it really had grown into a very large facility. But still it kept the atmosphere of a much smaller facility – a feeling much like that of a small town. That's one of the things I've always liked about it so much."–John D. Huie, board member, The Village at Cook Springs, 1992–2001

As The Village at Cook Springs entered the 21st century, its report card was strong enough that others were taking notice. It wouldn't be long before a well-respected long-term-care company would express interest in the institution and become its fourth operator.

Among leading areas earning "good grades" on the Village's report card were quality of care, fiscal responsibility, and the overall "feel" of the institution.

Sandy Everson said that no greater indicator of the quality could come than through surveys conducted by Alabama's state inspectors on behalf of the federal government. She said that time and time again during the 1990s the Village emerged from those surveys as a star. She was seeing the meaning of that success through her view as a registered nurse who had worked at several long-term-care facilities. She saw it as one who became admissions director at the Village and later would serve for a time as director of nursing before going into a teaching position at the institution.

254

"This is something that during the 1990s made us real proud at The Village at Cook Springs: During that period, we had seven consecutive years of deficiency-free state surveys. That means in all the surveys during those years there were no deficiencies, across the board, that were noted for The Village at Cook Springs."

In terms of fiscal responsibility, this showed in several ways. George Smith recalled that the Village's three-man board during the 1990s took pride in being able to accomplish so much under such adverse financial circumstances. "We were of course proud that we were able to pay off that huge debt, that all the creditors got paid. We were proud that the facility was able to be preserved and that we went forward with it," he said. Too, he noted that board members were proud they managed to touch up, to renovate, and even to expand. "We were able to redo the old wing that the nursing home had started out in, which had such narrow halls," said Smith. "We also were able to build a new wing." He said at all times eyes were focused on a tight budget, on being able to stretch dollars as far as possible. "Even as we were doing that facelift on the outdoors in the 1990s — the landscaping, the rockwork, the fences — we were doing it as we could get the money. Money continued to be tight, and we did things only as we could afford to do them."

As progress took place in the 1990s, it did not do so at the expense of the close-knit "feel" of the Village at Cook Springs. After all, this was an institution where "the feel" was especially important — where employees and residents and families alike wanted to preserve and enhance the rustic, homelike setting and the matching warm, caring human spirit for which the Village traditionally was known. John Huie said he saw and admired how that feeling was preserved. He saw firsthand after he became a board member of the Village in the early 1990s — after he succeeded the late Dale Sasser and came in to serve on the Village's board along with his father (Max Huie) and George Smith. "When you look at the size of The Village at Cook Springs during the time I served as a board member there, it really had grown into a very large facility. But still it kept the atmosphere of a much smaller facility — a feeling much like that of a small town. That's one of the

Picket fences along lake at Village add another touch to a beautiful setting, 1990s. (Note edge of Village's assisted-living facility, in background at left.)

things I've always liked about it so much," said John Huie. He noted that at one time the Huie family was involved with 10 nursing homes and that The Village at Cook Springs was the largest among the 10. "Yet, as large as the Village became, I think that institution's really nice rural location and the personal attention that its staff brought to it made it possible for it to retain that small-town feeling."

Section Six

~

Modern-day Times of a County and a Community

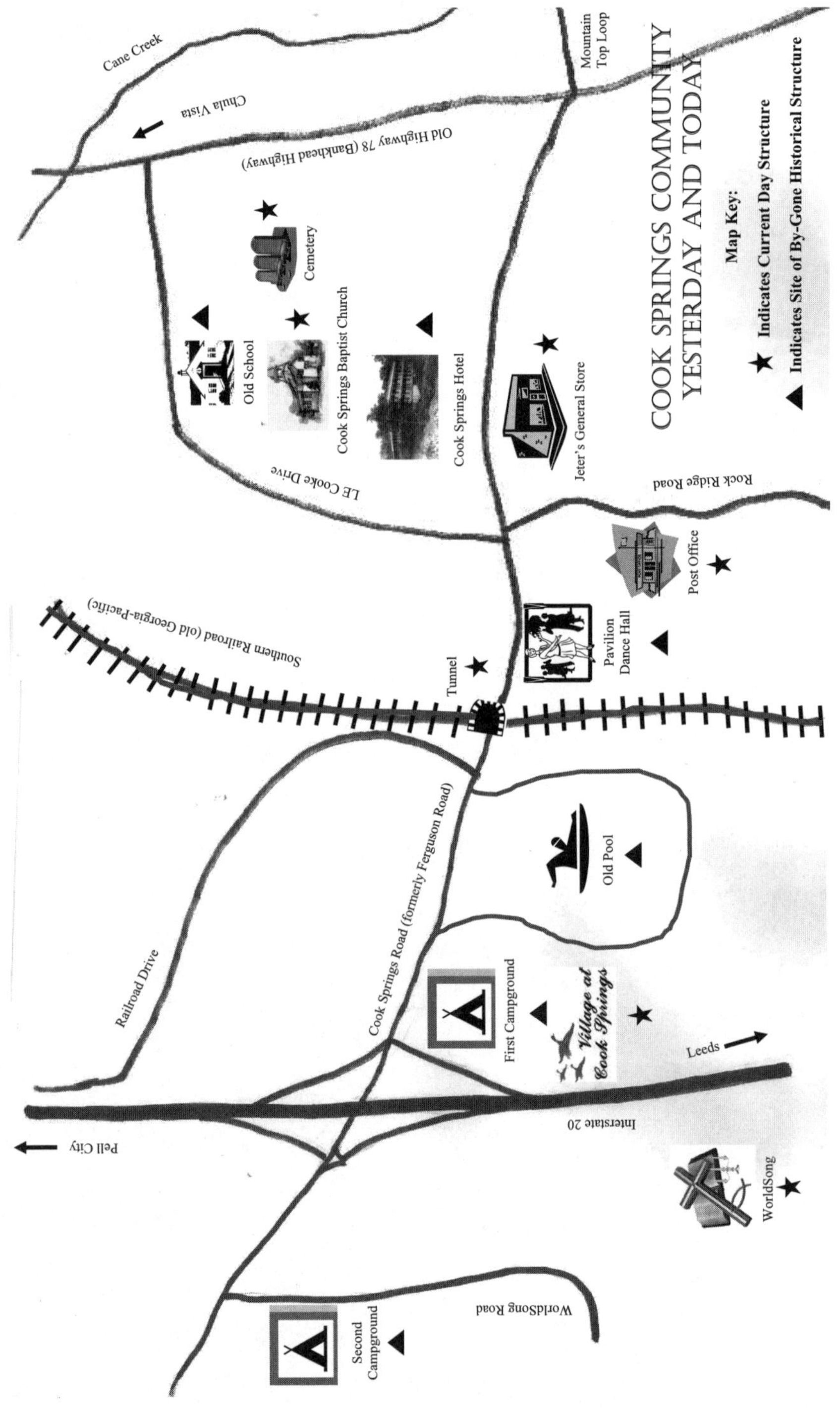

A 2006 map showing the Village at Cook Springs amid its immediate surroundings in the community of Cook Springs, Alabama.

258

19

A Booming County

"If the United States is a melting pot of cultures around the world, then St. Clair County is an Alabama melting pot of cultures."–Stanley Batemon, chairman, St. Clair County Commission

Just as the term "boom-town" was used to describe some of the 1800s fast-growth towns in what became the western United States, the term "boom-county" could well apply to St. Clair County from the latter part of the 1900s forward.

Leading factors that have fueled St. Clair County's growth include:

• Industries moving into St. Clair and surrounding counties.

• Ongoing development of properties on or near St. Clair's prized waterfront areas that have been opened up tremendously by the construction of Logan Martin Dam and Neely Henry Dam.

• St. Clair's escalating appeal as a residence for both retirees and still-employed individuals who have moved from the Birmingham area or other surrounding locales.

"Our growth rate in St. Clair County currently is in the neighborhood of between three to four percent a year," said Stanley Batemon, chairman of the St. Clair County Commission. "Just think about it — over a 10-year period adding 30 to 40 percent to your county's population!"

Speaking in a 2005 interview, Batemon said that St. Clair County's growth is bringing in people from far and wide, including from other nations. "If the United States is a melting pot of cultures around the world, then St. Clair County is an Alabama melting pot of cultures. It seems that people from just about everywhere now live in St. Clair County!"

Industries in St. Clair and surrounding counties have helped inject an international flavor into St. Clair County's growth. This includes Japanese-owned companies, such as the large Honda plant just across the Coosa River from St. Clair in neighboring Talladega County. French-owned industries have come to St. Clair. Also, industries with German and Swedish owner-ship have joined the mix.

There could be no doubt that the beautiful, bountiful natural water resources in St. Clair County continue to help fuel the county's growth. Batemon noted the generous miles of waterfront in the county, sprinkled with marinas, weekend lake homes, and full-time residences. "In some respects, St. Clair County is almost like a big resort community," said Batemon. He noted that since the early beginnings of St. Clair County, water has played an important role in the county's development. "Then along came Alabama Power Company and backed up the Coosa River into two major lakes — Logan Martin Lake, located south of Pell City, and Neely Henry Lake near Ragland." Those lakes have become great drawing cards for the county, said Batemon. "A lot of our development here is focused on those lakes."

Batemon said much of St. Clair's growth simply could not have occurred without the building of a very viable interstate system through the county. That system includes not just one major interstate; it consists of two — Interstate 20 and Interstate 59. "With the accessibility that's provided by these interstates, we have seen many commuters moving into communities that are bedroom communities of the Birmingham area," said Batemon. "There's quite a number of people who work in Birmingham and who have an accessible commute to reside here with us in St. Clair County."

A Blending of the Old and the New

With all the growth and change that have come its way, St. Clair County in the early 21st century has become a true blend of the old and the new. As one of the oldest counties in Alabama, St. Clair is rich in historical legacy

Picnic for Village assisted-living residents at Pell City Park.

and has many citizens who are interested in preserving historical structures and in commemorating the past. At the same time, there are many new residents moving in.

"We still have a lot of families in our county who have ties to the Indian backgrounds here," said Batemon.

In years before becoming St. Clair's first full-time County Commission chairman, Batemon was a longtime game warden in a section of Alabama that included St. Clair County. His work put him in close touch with changes that came to the area. He said that even with all the growth he believes the "feel" of the county had remained much the same. "In my mind, St. Clair County is still a rural county. It's not rural in the sense of having so much of its economy based on agriculture as was true in the past. But it is still rural in the sense that people around St. Clair still tend to enjoy a little more space for their lifestyles. They don't tend to like living in crowded subdivisions." Batemon said that St. Clair still has enough room to make that more-spacious living possible.

He said he is proud of how the old and the new have blended together. "It is my personal view that you are likely to find a little more tolerance in

St. Clair County than you will find in an average place," Batemon said with a grin. "You know, tolerance is something that's really going by the wayside in our society as a whole. But in my view St. Clair Countians have displayed a lot of patience and tolerance, because they have had to learn to live with neighbors with different ideas and opinions."

In the area of business development, the historical St. Clair town of Springville has become a good example of wisely and creatively blending the old and the new, Batemon said. When plans were being put together for a Wal-Mart Supercenter Mall in Springville, community leaders there worked with mall developers to make sure the mall had the quaint look of a small historical town. This included a building façade with the look of an older building, decorative lighting, and even sidewalks that were a step above the traditional poured concrete. That cost money, and Springville and St. Clair County helped the project along with a sales-tax rebate program that was an incentive to developers, said Batemon. "The City of Springville was saying, 'Hey, this new development needs to look like our historical town,'" said Batemon. "I think we are going to see a lot more of that kind of thing happening in St. Clair County."

Pulling Together to Manage the Growth

In 2005, St. Clair County Commissioner James S. "Jimmy" Roberts was living in the Eden section of the Pell City area, just a few blocks from where he grew up. He said he has seen his native county grow and thrive and that he is proud of the development. In most respects he feels the growth has been managed well, and he believes there are a couple of big reasons.

For one thing, Roberts said elected officials in the county have made a concerted effort to work together for the county as a whole. He said the St. Clair County Commission is a prime example of that — a commission headed by Batemon and also including district commissioners Jeff Brown, Mike Bowling, Paul Manning and Roberts. "With all this growth we've seen, we can't just think about our own respective districts. We have to think about this entire county, and we do!"

Another priority that is imperative, said Roberts, is to protect St. Clair's

20

'New Kids on the Block' in Cook Springs

"My wife and I met more people in Cook Springs the first year we lived here than you would meet in some places where you had been living for 10 years!"–Dewell Crumpton, Cook Springs resident beginning in 2001

Faye and Dewell Crumpton were excited as they looked around in the late 1990s for the ideal community where they would build a new home. For decades they had lived in Birmingham. There Dewell had taught school and coached football and track, and then, with Faye's assistance, he had been in the real-estate business and then in the insurance business before becoming a certified estate planner.

As the Crumptons looked around for the ideal location for their new home, they chose Cook Springs, Alabama. In 1997 they bought property there, and in 2001 they built their new home and moved in.

"One of our neighbors in the Birmingham area had described the beauty of Cook Springs. We also knew some people who had bought land there," said Faye Crumpton.

After they bought the property, Dewell Crumpton was in and out of Cook Springs a good bit, first planning for the building of their new home and then overseeing the building. The more he drove out to Cook Springs and spent time there, the more certain he was that he and Faye had made the right decision. The beauty of the surroundings captivated him. "I loved it!" he said.

269

View of modern-day Cook Springs Baptist Church.

After the Crumptons moved into their new Cook Springs home, they became captivated with another kind of beauty — the spirit of the people in the Cook Springs community.

Dewell and Faye began looking around for a church they would attend. One church they visited was the one that was most convenient, the only church in the Cook Springs community and one with a history dating back to the mid-1800s, the Cook Springs Baptist Church.

Among the church members the Crumptons met were a few people who, like themselves, had moved to the Cook Springs area in recent times. Also among the church members they met were quite a number of longtime local residents, whose ancestors had lived in or near Cook Springs for years and years.

"The people in that church were so warm and outgoing. We could feel their warmth," said Faye. "They were just wonderful to us."

It didn't take long before Dewell and Faye Crumpton were an integral part of the Cook Springs Baptist Church and of the entire Cook Springs community. In the church, the Crumptons became loyal members; Dewell Crumpton later would become the church's Sunday School director. In the community, the Crumptons accepted invitations to attend local social events sponsored by the Cook Springs Volunteer Fire Department. "We had fun attending a Thanksgiving supper, and a Christmas event, and a barbeque in the summer," said Faye.

"My wife and I met more people in Cook Springs the first year we lived here than you would meet in some places where you had been living for 10 years!" said Dewell.

Living in the serenity and beauty of Cook Springs was every bit as satisfying as the couple had thought it would be.

"I really enjoyed being so close to nature," said Faye. "Cook Springs is so pretty and a lot of its natural beauty still is untouched."

Dewell Crumpton described life in Cook Springs as "like getting lost in your own little world. In Cook Springs it is all about enjoying the big oak trees, looking up at Bald Rock Mountain, and watching the deer passing by. To me living in Cook Springs became like a treat, like living in a park."

As part of getting to know Cook Springs, the Crumptons learned the details of the rich history of the majestic Cook's Springs Hotel that LaFayette Cooke built. "Oh, you don't live in Cook Springs without learning that history. And it's a great history," said Dewell. "I got some firsthand details about the hotel's history from one of the older members of Cook Springs Baptist, one of the deacons who was in his 80s. One day when he was ill, not long before he died, I was visiting with him. And during that visit, he told me the whole history of Cook Springs and that great hotel. In his youth he had been in the hotel many times. He described it all to me. He said

A 2006 view of "downtown" Cook Springs – J's Retail at left, Post Office at right.

things like, 'Now the train pulled up right in front of the hotel, and there was this platform there.' He remembered it well. And I loved hearing the history straight from him."

The Cook Springs Baptist Church also became a supporter of a volunteer project that became close to the heart of Dewell Crumpton. Soon after the Crumptons moved to Cook Springs, Dewell began using his coaching ability to establish and coach a track program for children and teenagers who were being home-schooled in various parts of St. Clair County. "The church became a great supporter of this track program. We even have a course where the kids would run that included running around Cook Springs Baptist Church," he said.

Sports had been a big part of Dewell Crumpton's life. In the Birmingham area, he coached track and football at Phillips High School, then at Banks High School, and then at Ramsay High School. His final high-school coaching stint was at Huffman High School, where he became that school's first head football coach and also an assistant principal.

After the Crumptons moved to Cook Springs and were so warmly received, it was important to Dewell to make a successful contribution to community life in St. Clair County. Thus he was gratified when participation grew steadily in the track and field and cross-country running program that he founded. After getting started in 2001 with 6 participants, the program was serving 70 participants in 2005, when Dewell Crumpton was first interviewed for this book. A core sponsor of the track and field and cross-country running program was Crossroad Christian School, a home-school group based in the St. Clair community of Moody. This Crumpton-led track program had an affiliation with USA Track and Field. Although set up initially to serve home-schoolers, the program would accept other children and teens ages 5 to 19 who also wanted to participate. "We named our group the CC Flyers," said Dewell. "Now, that 'CC' part can stand for several things. It can stand for Crossroad Christian Flyers. Or it can stand for Cross Country Flyers. Or it can stand for Coach Crumpton's Flyers. Our goal has been to run and

Longtime Cook Springs resident Knox Wade in the back yard of his home with historical Cook Springs sign and some of old Cooke family farm equipment, given to him by his friend, Hubert Cooke, grandson of Cook's Springs Hotel founder LaFayette Cooke.

have fun, and people in the community have supported us."

As fate would have it, ultimately the CC Flyers and their families became powerful motivators for Coach Dewell Crumpton when he faced a major health challenge. Dewell was suffering from cancer, a soft-tissue sarcoma. For a time the cancer was in remission, but then symptoms returned. "I still coach the CC Flyers," he said in a December 2005 interview. "On days when I'm not feeling so well, the kids' parents carry me around in a golf cart."

As the months went by, the cancer worsened. As Dewell and wife Faye faced growing adversity and anxiety that accompanied his serious illness, they felt strong support from the people in Cook Springs who rallied to help them.

"The people of Cook Springs have been so incredibly supportive of Faye and me," said Dewell. "They have been so kind and generous that if they even think we need something they are there with it."

In mid-2006, the Crumptons made a heart-wrenching decision to move from Cook Springs — to move back to Birmingham, to be closer to family members and also closer to Dewell's cancer treatments at the University of Alabama at Birmingham (UAB).

Dewell Crumpton said he and his wife would continue to hold Cook Springs in their hearts and to visit whenever possible. He said that he and Faye would keep their church membership at Cook Springs Baptist. Also, he said they planned to continue to keep up with activities of the CC Flyers, who now were being coached by one of Dewell's former track students.

"We love Cook Springs. We love the people in Cook Springs. Living in Cook Springs has been beyond anything I could tell you," Dewell Crumpton said in an August 2006 interview. "I have a rare type of cancer, and doctors have told me it's very unusual for someone with what I have to live this long. I believe the prayers and the love and support of the people of Cook Springs have been great medicine for me!"

Section Seven

~

Noland Health Services, Inc.

21

Continuing a Legacy of Caring

"I believe that Dr. Lloyd Noland would take great pride in both the history and the present-day operation of the Village at Cook Springs."–Leon C. Hamrick, Sr., M.D., chairman of the board of directors, Noland Health Services, Inc.

Early in the 21st century, the rich history of the Village at Cook Springs became intertwined with the lasting legacy of a physician who made international healthcare history in the early 20th century.

The physician was Virginia-born Lloyd Noland. From the nation of Panama to the state of Alabama, Dr. Noland became known during his lifetime for establishing groundbreaking programs to address major health and social challenges.

Long after Dr. Noland's death, his progressive pioneering continues to live on through a Birmingham-based senior-care company that carries his name — Noland Health Services, Inc. In late 2001, that company became the new operator of the Village at Cook Springs.

"While there was reason to take considerable pride in how far the Village had come, by 2001 the time had arrived for a change in leadership," said George H. Smith, who along with his partners Max Huie and Dale Sasser had taken over running of the facility in 1990. Contributing to the timing of this changing of the guard in 2001 was the fact that Smith himself had become ready to enter what he termed "semi-retirement." At that point,

276

Smith was the last of the three original Smith-Huie-Sasser partners to be active in leadership at the Village. "While I loved the Village dearly and it was very difficult for me to turn loose, it was a comforting feeling to pass this wonderful facility into the capable, progressive leadership of an organization like Noland Health Services. I knew this company's record for progressive programs, high performance, and caring. I knew that the Village was being passed into great hands."

The Pioneering of Dr. Lloyd Noland

As a company that specializes in services for the elderly, Noland Health Services is following in the tradition of Dr. Lloyd Noland, who was known for using innovative approaches to address major needs of the time.

When Dr. Noland was a young surgeon, he became one of the leaders in medical forces that worked in the country of Panama to combat diseases such as yellow fever and malaria, making it possible for laborers to complete the building of the Panama Canal. As chief surgeon of a 600-bed hospital in Panama, Dr. Noland served on the staff of Dr. William Crawford Gorgas, the Alabama-born physician who was the Canal project's chief sanitation officer and whom history would remember as the father of sanitation. Dr. Gorgas selected Dr. Lloyd Noland as his executive officer and as head of a Panama hospital when Dr. Noland was in his mid-20s.

Drawing widespread attention for his leadership at such an early age, Dr. Noland was recruited in 1913 to Birmingham, Alabama, to tackle a grave and worsening health crisis. This crisis threatened the survival of an industry known as the Tennessee Coal, Iron and Railroad Company, or TCI, based in the Birmingham suburb of Fairfield. At the root of this crisis were the same types of crucial problems that Dr. Noland had fought in Panama — deplorable public health conditions, rampant spread of diseases, and inadequate health programs to prevent and treat illness and disease. At the time Dr. Noland was recruited to the Birmingham area, large numbers of TCI workers and their family members were falling sick and in many cases dying of diseases such as malaria and typhoid. These deadly disease outbreaks also were spilling over into the non-TCI population in the Birmingham

Lloyd Noland, M.D., whose pioneer programs in public health and industrial medicine laid the foundation for Noland Health Services, Inc., which in 2001 became the operator of Village at Cook Springs.

area. The spread of disease was so severe that TCI was in danger of closing its doors. Since the TCI work force was such a huge component of the Birmingham-area economy, TCI's closure could have meant devastation to the entire Birmingham area.

When he arrived in the Birmingham area to address this crisis, Dr. Noland was in his early 30s. He was recruited by the large steel company that owned TCI — the United States Steel Corporation.

Young Lloyd Noland did not disappoint U.S. Steel, TCI, and leaders of the Birmingham area. Using as a model the Gorgas system of public health and healthcare that had been so successful in Panama, Dr. Lloyd Noland established in the Birmingham area what came to be known as the first major experiment in industrial medicine in the United States. He established sanitation districts to address public health tasks such as human waste disposal and insect control. He set up a "district system" of outpatient clinics for TCI employees and their families that stressed not only disease treatment but also disease prevention (an outpatient system very similar to some of the 21st century trends in outpatient healthcare). He led in the building of a company hospital. The bottom line was that disease and death rates declined rapidly and significantly, and Dr. Lloyd Noland was credited with saving a company and likely with saving the Birmingham area.

Carrying on the Tradition of Dr. Lloyd Noland

In the early 20th century, Dr. Lloyd Noland focused on pressing issues of the times — such as reducing or eliminating public health hazards, preventing diseases, and creating a basic healthcare system. In the early 21st century, the company that bears his name also is focusing on some of the most pressing social and health challenges of current times. Noland Health Services is meeting the needs of elderly men and women, during an era when the numbers of senior citizens and their needs are skyrocketing.

"It's very fitting at this particular time that the focus of Noland Health Services would be in the field of aging, for the needs in that area are tremendous and will continue to rise," said Leon C. Hamrick, Sr., M.D., chairman of the board of directors of the not-for-profit company known as Noland Health Services, Inc. "It is my firm belief that Dr. Lloyd Noland would be proud of the senior-care facilities and programs that we are operating through Noland Health Services. I know that we at Noland Health Services were so very pleased in late 2001 to add the Village at Cook Springs to our growing array of senior-care facilities and programs. I believe that Dr. Lloyd Noland would take great pride in both the history and the present-day operation of the Village at Cook Springs."

Leon C. Hamrick, Sr., M.D., chairman of the board, Noland Health Services, Inc.

A Need for Innovative Approaches

As president and chief executive officer (CEO) of Noland Health Services, Gary M. Glasscock is keenly aware of the growing numbers of elderly men and women and of the pressing need to provide quality services for senior citizens.

"We are of course aware that there already is a very large senior-citizen population. Too, it's no secret that this population is expanding greatly, and will continue to expand, as the 'Baby-Boomer generation' even now is beginning to join the ranks of senior citizens," said Glasscock. "I really believe that from now on forward into decades to come, the scope of the needs of this senior generation is going to stagger society's ability to meet those needs."

Glasscock said it has become imperative that innovative programs be developed and operated to meet the needs of seniors on an individualized basis. On one end of the spectrum, he said that innovation means programs to take care of senior citizens who are bedridden and in need of around-the-clock care. On the other end of the spectrum, he said innovation calls for programs to address the lifestyles of still-active and relatively healthy senior

Gary M. Glasscock, president and chief executive officer, Noland Health Services, Inc.

citizens who want and/or need various types of support services to make their lives easier and more enjoyable.

"With the emphasis that our society has placed on wellness and prevention in recent decades, there are many men and women entering their senior years who still are vibrant and active and who need programs to address their wide variety of interests," said Glasscock. "The bigness and the diversity of this Baby-Boomer generation already has and will continue to challenge society's concepts of just what a 'senior' is. In years gone by, people who were entering their 60s traditionally were looked upon as being elderly. Now people in their 60s often are in the prime of their lives. Actually, someone who is 70 years old today can be in the prime of his or her life."

Understanding the broad spectrum of senior-citizen needs and addressing those needs is what Noland Health Services is all about, said Glasscock.

Comprehensive Services for Seniors

To address the diverse health and lifestyle needs of seniors, Noland Health Services is built on a platform of two divisions of services. Within those two divisions are many layers.

One division is the Hospital Division — through which senior citizens can receive services as hospital patients. Another division is the Senior Housing Division — providing facilities in which senior citizens can become residents on an ongoing basis.

Through its Hospital Division, Noland Health Services operates five facilities in five Alabama cities that are "hospitals within hospitals." In each location, Noland Health Services operates a facility that can provide patients with care in a hospital setting. Each of these facilities is called a "hospital within a hospital" because each is located in a larger hospital known as the "host hospital." In Montgomery, Noland Health Services has its Long Term Hospital of Montgomery at Jackson Hospital. In Dothan, Noland Health Services has its Long Term Hospital of Dothan at Southeast Alabama Medical

Center. In Anniston, Noland Health Services has its Long Term Hospital of Anniston at Northeast Alabama Regional Medical Center. In Tuscaloosa, Noland Health Services has its Long Term Hospital of Tuscaloosa at DCH Regional Medical Center. And, in Birmingham, Noland has its Long Term Hospital of Birmingham at Medical Center East. In all cases, these Noland "hospitals within hospitals" have their own separate licenses and separate staffs. Although most of the patients are in their 60s or above, there also are some younger adults in the patient mix.

Through its Senior Housing Division, Noland Health Services offers a variety of housing options for seniors — options that are, as CEO Glasscock emphasizes, tailored to individualized needs. Included in the housing options offered are 24-hour-a-day skilled nursing care, Alzheimer's care, rehabilitation services on both an inpatient and outpatient basis, and retirement-home accommodations for assisted living and independent living. Noland Health Services is operating four senior-living campuses. Three are in the Birmingham area — the Oaks on Parkwood, Greenbriar at the Altamont, and, the newest, the recently constructed East Glen Center for Nursing & Rehabilitation that is located on the campus of Medical Center East. (The new East Glen facility replaced Lakeview Nursing Home with additional capacity and services.) The fourth Noland senior-housing facility, the Village at Cook Springs, is located in St. Clair County, only a 20-minute drive from Birmingham.

Placing Value on What Had Come Before

Soon after Noland Health Services assumed operation of the Village at Cook Springs in late 2001, some of the residents were in a meeting with Noland CEO Gary Glasscock.

The residents had a question that was very important to them that they posed to him. "Mr. Glasscock, you're not going to change our name, are you? This is still going to be called the Village at Cook Springs?"

Glasscock assured them that indeed the name would not change.

Retaining the name of the facility was one of the steps that Noland Health Services took to hold on to the good that had been created at the Village over the years. "When the Village became a part of Noland Health Services, we were aware that this was a unique, wonderful facility — a great retirement community with a great staff," said Glasscock. He said it was important to retain and honor those components that had made it so special. "We are grateful to operators of the Village over the years who are responsible for tremendous contributions that have made the Village what it is today. It is with much pride that we continue to refer to this fine institution as the Village at Cook Springs."

In taking over the Village at Cook Springs, Noland became the operator of a long-term-care campus that has a work force of more than 200 and is one of the leading employers in St. Clair County.

Noland Health Services' approach was to retain the best of the Village's past programs, and to add new programs and facilities as needed. When Noland initially took over, some "face-lift" work was carried out to refurbish and upgrade existing facilities. In addition, a major new facility was added — the Cornerstone Rehabilitation Center, that provides inpatient and out-patient rehabilitation services.

Another example of retaining parts of the Village's past is that animals have continued to thrive at the Village since Noland Health Services took the leadership reins. "For years the Village has been known for having all kinds of critters," Glasscock said with a smile. "The Village continues to have critters, and we enjoy having critters. In fact, the operators just prior to us were real pioneers in the therapeutic uses of animals in senior care."

Noland's board chairman Dr. Leon C. Hamrick, Sr., called attention to two key components of the Village that are a blend of the past and the present. "I'm referring to our residents and to our employees," said Dr. Hamrick. "We have some wonderful residents who have been at the Village for years, blended with new residents who have come to live there recently. With our employees, there's a blend of the longtime employees with the newer additions, to make up what I really think of as our 'trademark' at Noland Health Services — our caring Noland employees."

Changing a Capital Letter in a Name

Although the wording of the Village's name has not been changed, in 2005 a minor change was made in the capitalization of the name.

Instead of listing the name as The Village at Cook Springs (with a capital "T" in The), Noland administration began listing the name without a capital "T" — the Village at Cook Springs. This book reflects that slight difference in how the name is listed from one era to another.

Still a Community Made Up of Neighborhoods

Since Noland became the Village's operator in 2001, the Village has continued to be a campus made up of "neighborhoods." Those neighborhoods are reflective of the different levels of care that are available for senior residents.

The neighborhoods include a 168-bed skilled nursing home, the Springs Manor assisted-living neighborhood, a cluster of apartments for independent living, a rehabilitation center, and specialized neighborhoods for providing dementia-care, including for Alzheimer's disease.

Visits From a Special Good Will Ambassador

Even though the Village at Cook Springs changed hands in late 2001, there is still a much-welcomed presence on the Village grounds that is a symbol of a previous administration. That presence is in the form of George H. Smith, who served as chairman of the three-man board that ran the Village during the 1990s. George Smith is the sole surviving member of the trio of 1990s leaders that had included Smith, Max Huie, and Dale Sasser. Dale Sasser lost his life in a car accident in the early 1990s, and Max Huie died of cancer several years later.

George Smith is semi-retired, but he is still involved in senior care, including at the Village at Cook Springs. His role at the Village is not a formal one. He is a frequent visitor to this facility that he has helped develop and that he still admires and loves. George Smith comes to the Village to see the residents, the employees, and the animals. "I guess you could say I'm kind of a good will ambassador at the Village at Cook Springs," said Smith.

In addition to his informal volunteer role in senior care at the Village, Smith continues to be in the long-term-care business in more formal ways through St. Clair Services, Inc., a small long-term-care company that he co-owns with a partner. Through this company, Smith participates in the operation of a long-term-care facility in the northwest Alabama town of Winfield. He also works on computer projects to aid programs for the elderly. Some of those programs are aimed at making it easier for senior citizens to surf the Internet and use e-mail services. Too, he maintains a website to aid in locating volunteers and entertainers to assist activity directors in long-term-care facilities.

When asked how he could do all this and still consider himself not working full-time, Smith laughed and said, "Because now I make sure I leave some time for my race car and for driving my race car in competition." George Smith travels frequently to compete in vintage-sports-car racing events. He has become a well-known racing figure in those racing circles and has made it to the winner's circle with his sleek yellow British racing machine, a race car known as the Elva Courier.

Spreading the Word about the Village's History

During the time that George Smith led the Village at Cook Springs, he became very adept in describing the Village's rich history to others.

Among those who heard Smith relate that history was Pam Nichols, marketing officer for Noland Health Services' senior-housing division. Mrs. Nichols first heard Smith's historical account when she met with him during the period that led up to the Village coming under the umbrella of Noland Health Services.

"I was fascinated as I listened to George tell about the old mineral-springs hotel at Cook Springs and about the hotel's founder, LaFayette Cooke," Mrs. Nichols recalled in a 2006 interview. "From that day forward, I could see such a tremendous value in the colorful history of the Village at Cook Springs. George Smith is so gifted at communication, and he has had such strong ties with the Village, that the entire history made a really vivid impression on me."

Mrs. Nichols said she currently is excited that, through the publication of this book about the Village's history, and through events surrounding the book's release, the Village's history will be spotlighted in a major way.

In her role with Noland, Mrs. Nichols has seen firsthand the positive community impact that can be made by historical preservation. She has been involved with initiatives of Noland Health Services to preserve another historically rich legacy — that of the late public health and sanitation pioneer Dr. Lloyd Noland.

Just as is true of the history of the Village at Cook Springs, the legacy of Dr. Noland was recorded in a book project and also in displays of photographs and other memorabilia. The Noland historical photographs and memorabilia for years have been on display at Noland Hall, on the campus of the Oaks on Parkwood, a Noland senior-housing facility in the Birmingham area. In recent months, a Noland historical display has been put in place at Noland Health Services' new corporate headquarters in Birmingham.

This preservation of the Noland history has a personal meaning to Mrs. Nichols, who for more than 20 years has been employed in programs that had their beginnings with Dr. Lloyd Noland.

"I see the impact of how much it means to individuals and to entire communities to be able to celebrate the Dr. Lloyd Noland legacy," and Mrs. Nichols. "I foresee a similar experience for the Village at Cook Springs, through our recording the Village's history in book form and also establishing displays of photographs and other memorabilia."

She predicted an impact on the short-term and also for decades to come.

"I believe the celebration of the Village's history will have great meaning immediately to honoring the legacy of our residents and our employees, and in honoring the history of the community of Cook Springs and its neighboring communities. Down through the years, this preservation also can have ongoing meaning to future descendants of those involved in the Village's history. Too, we have an opportunity to make a contribution to historical preservation in a county, St. Clair, that long has been known for its strong commitment to historical preservation. An example of that commitment is a book, *Sparkling Waters*, that was published several years ago by the St. Clair Historical Society to focus on the history of Cook Springs."

Mrs. Nichols predicted that through the showcasing of the history of the Village at Cook Springs, many a person will be able to relive his or her memories. She described a recent touching scene of reliving memories from the Dr. Lloyd Noland era.

The occasion was a senior-citizen focus group at the Oaks on Parkwood. Mrs. Nichols had invited a group of seniors to participate in this session at Noland Hall on the Oaks' campus. As seniors took part in the focus group, they were in a setting filled with archival materials commemorating the contributions of Dr. Lloyd Noland, and others who followed him, through programs he founded.

Among those participating in this focus group at Noland Hall was Dr. Leroy Holt, a well-known physician who for decades practiced medicine in the town of Bessemer, just west of Birmingham. Dr. Holt had reason to know the Lloyd Noland era well, for Dr. Holt was a part of that era. Beginning in 1947, two years before Dr. Noland's death, Dr. Holt took medical training first in an internship and then in a surgery residency that had been founded by Dr. Noland.

"After we finished our focus-group meeting, Dr. Holt escorted his wife on a tour of the Dr. Lloyd Noland memorabilia," said Mrs. Nichols. "I could see the Holt couple moving about from photograph to photograph, as Dr. Holt described to his wife the history of that era. As I watched that scene unfold, I could see how meaningful it was for Dr. Holt to be able to recall and describe those famous Noland medical programs that helped mold his life, that helped mold what he became as a physician. I thought, 'This is important. This is what historical preservation is all about.' My thoughts turned to the excitement we feel about the historical preservation project on which we're now embarking to showcase the history of the Village at Cook Springs. Just as has been accomplished through showcasing the Lloyd Noland legacy, we'll now be able to spread far and wide the history of the Village at Cook Springs."

Recognizing the Village's Network of Support

Time and again, Glenn Brewer has been taken aback in a positive way by the tremendous network of support that reaches out to the Village at Cook Springs.

The support network became evident to Brewer from the time he became the Village's new executive director in December 2005.

Brewer came to the Village from Florida, where he had been administrator of the Emerald Coast Center, a long-term-care facility in Fort Walton Beach.

Living in Alabama is not new to Glenn Brewer. During his high school days, he lived in the Birmingham area, one of several cities or towns where his family lived as part of his dad's mobile Coast Guard career.

However, it is new to Brewer to head up a long-term-care facility that has a decades-old support network like the one that benefits the Village at Cook Springs. Brewer said that this support network is wonderful for the Village's residents and their families.

"I've just never seen anything like this support!" said Brewer. "It's also

Glenn Brewer, executive director of Village at Cook Springs, shown with Village assisted-living resident Patsy Lewis Carter (who is featured in Chapters 1 and 2 of this book).

great that this support comes from so many directions." These are some directions he listed:

• "Some of the support comes from the Village's rich heritage, the fact that the Village has been here a long time and is so well thought of, and also that the community of Cook Springs has such a fascinating history. All that is combined with a history of prideful operation of the Village. Every operator of the Village has taken pride in this institution. That pride shows in what the Village is today.

• "Incredible support comes from the staff at the Village, who render such unsurpassed quality care to the residents. The Village staff has a special way of reaching out to people, whether it be a new resident, a new staff member, or whomever. As a newcomer, I have felt that personally in recent months, as staff members have reached out to welcome me to the Village family.

• "The support comes from the community of Cook Springs and from other surrounding communities in this area. I have never ever witnessed such caring community support for a long-term-care facility as the Village receives!

• "And the support comes from the Village's operator, from Noland Health Services. The residents and their families very much benefit from Noland's attitude of quality care and quality growth. From my view, I hear this Noland attitude of support as basically 'Glenn, just tell us what you need at the Village in order to render excellent care to the Village's residents.' That feels good."

Coming Full Circle

On a sunny day in May 2006, a long-term-care executive was paying a visit to the Village at Cook Springs.

As she drove her car through the entrance, a feeling of almost overwhelming nostalgia engulfed her. She had made the turn into this entrance many times.

"I looked at the rustic entrance sign that depicted a scene of birds flying, and I thought, 'Oh, I remember when we put that sign up! It still looks great!'" she said.

She passed through the entrance, arrived at the buildings that made up the Village campus, and soon was looking at some of the landscaping.

"I literally ran over to some of the shrubs and felt like giving them a hug! I recalled, 'Oh, I planted this shrub myself. And I planted that one, and that one!'"

It was, by all standards, the grandest of homecomings for a woman who from 1990 until 1998 had served as the executive director of the Village at Cook Springs.

She had left the Village to take a position of broader responsibility with Northport Health Services, Inc., later known as NHS Management, LLC, a long-term-care company based in Tuscaloosa, Alabama. She served first as NHS's director of operations for its Alabama long-term-care facilities, and then for several years was the company's director of quality assurance for 40 long-term-care facilities scattered in four states.

Carol Moseley Knight, former executive director of Village at Cook Springs. In 2006, she became vice president for senior housing for Noland Health Services.

Over the years, her personal life has changed as well. When she left the Village in 1998, she was Carol Moseley. When she drove through the gates for her emotional homecoming in May 2006, she was Carol Moseley Knight. In November 2005, she married real-estate developer Al Knight, a former member of the House of Representatives of the Alabama Legislature.

"What made it especially meaningful for me to return to the Village in May 2006 was that I had not been there one single time in the eight years since I had left my position there as executive director in 1998," said Mrs. Knight. "When I left, it was to take an upward step in my career and certainly not because I wanted to leave the Village. It was so difficult for me to leave the Village. In fact, I left crying. The reason I had not returned in all those years is that I believe it's best after you leave a position like that to let the new administrators do their jobs and not go

back and interfere in any way with their leadership."

Ironically, what brought Mrs. Knight back to the Village in May 2006 was an invitation from the same leader in long-term care who had hired her for her job at the Village back in 1990, former Village operator George H. Smith. In his semi-retirement, Smith continued to be involved in long-term-care innovations. He and his partner in current long-term-care projects, Cherri Harris, were demonstrating a project at the Village called Touchdown Television (a project that later won an award). They wanted Mrs. Knight to see it.

"I was impressed with the project that George and Cherri showed me," said Mrs. Knight. "I also was very impressed with seeing the Village at Cook Springs in its current state. It was so good to see that the Village had been able to retain its wonderful uniqueness while at the same time embrace the progress made since Noland Health Services took it over."

As fate would have it, the visit that Carol Moseley Knight made to the Village that day was a prologue to an unexpected development that would come into her life only a few weeks later. She would be offered, and would accept, the position of vice president for senior housing for Noland Health Services. Accepting this position meant that, beginning July 3, 2006, she would oversee the operations of all of Noland's senior-housing facilities — the Oaks on Parkwood, Greenbriar at the Altamont, the Village at Cook Springs, and, the last few months of operation of Lakeview Nursing Home and then the opening of Lakeview's modern-day successor, East Glen Center for Nursing & Rehabilitation on the campus of Medical Center East.

"It's very meaningful to me that, just prior to being offered this new position by Noland, I experienced that incredible homecoming visit at the Village at Cook Springs, an institution that is so dear to my heart from years past and is so reflective today of what Noland Health Services stands for," said Mrs. Knight.

Mrs. Knight shared her feelings in an interview in June 2006, as she prepared to start her new position with Noland. She spoke of how that visit to the Village in May had served as a connecting bridge to link her past and her future.

"I can remember one thought after another that went through my mind that day I visited at the Village, never having any idea that I soon would be overseeing operations for the Village and all its sister Noland senior-housing facilities," she said.

"The Village is such a warm place that stirs up feelings of family — a place where you tend to recall people and events from your personal life at the same time you think of people and events in your professional life.

"I sat there that day and looked at the beautiful fountain in the lake at the Village, and I recalled an earlier version of a Village fountain for which we raised money. Some of the first donations to that first fountain were in memory of my sister, Dorothy Ragsdale Gilliland.

"I thought of a cookbook project we had when I was at the Village. Now, this was a cookbook to which staff and residents and families contributed recipes and also personal family stories. One of my own family's recipes for the cookbook was for 'Shoebox Candy,' a nickname my late brother Joe Ragsdale gave to this candy my sister would prepare, wrap in special wrappings, and then place in a shoebox at Christmas-time.

"I thought of my new husband, Al Knight, and his track record when he was a state legislator in sponsoring legislation that benefited quality long-term care in Alabama.

Left, Gary M. Glasscock, Noland Health Services' president/CEO, joining in work to build screened-porch addition for the Village's Red Barn. Above, Noland Health Services' board chairman, Leon C. Hamrick, Sr., M.D., and his wife, Bunny, doing a little gardening at their home, circa 1987.

"Memories of Al's late mother and father also came to my mind. When I was still at the Village, I came to know his parents when they were residents of the Village — his mom, Kathryn, in the Village's skilled nursing home, and his dad, Buford, in the Village's Springs Manor assisted-living facility. I still have such lovely, vivid images of Kathryn and Buford at the Village. At least three times a day Buford would make his way through the halls and offices at the Village, exchanging hugs and handshakes with those he encountered, as he made his way back and forth from assisted living to the nursing home to visit his wife Kathryn.

"My husband still talks of the loving touches extended to his parents at the Village. Even after Al's mother was bedridden and so fragile, the Village staff made sure that life's extra touches were there for her. Al told the activity staff that his mother's favorite singer was Andy Williams. When Al came to visit her, he often would hear familiar music from the tapes that the activity staff had placed in her room. Know who would be singing on those tapes to his mom? You guessed it. Andy Williams."

22

'Home Sweet Home' at the Village

*"I really didn't know anybody here when I first moved in — not anybody.
But then I just started right off making friends."–Herbert McKay, resident,
Village at Cook Springs*

The senior-age men and women who are becoming residents of the
Village at Cook Springs increasingly represent a diversity that can
be compared to a "melting pot" pattern.

It is clear that residents who are coming together to make the Village
their home in the first decade of the 21st century indeed are a blend of
longtime area residents and also newcomers moving in from other locales.
In fact, residents of the Village at Cook Springs represent a blending that
fast is becoming a trademark of growing-and-changing St. Clair County as
a whole.

Among the Village's residents are those who have arrived in recent years
as total strangers — strangers to the community of Cook Springs and to St.
Clair County as a whole. On the other hand, there are those who long have
been familiar with the area, who have connections (often family ties) that
run deep to Cook Springs and/or other parts of St. Clair County.

This smorgasbord of senior residents and their family members have
varied, interesting backgrounds that attract and entertain one another and
form the basis for lasting friendships. Residents are drawn together by their
sharing of both common ground and new experiences.

A Stranger Not for Long

When Herbert McKay moved to the Village at Cook Springs in January 2003, he was, as the old saying goes, the new guy in the community. He was 88 years old at the time.

"I really didn't know anybody here when I first moved in — not anybody," he said. "But then I just started right off making friends."

A native of Marion County in northwest Alabama, McKay spent most of his adult life living in Jefferson County — in or near the western Jefferson County towns of Hueytown and Jonesboro. Prior to moving to the Village, he had little knowledge of St. Clair County or of the St. Clair community of Cook Springs. It was his son's ties that brought him to the Village. His son (and only child), John McKay, and his wife Brenda, lived in one of St. Clair's larger towns, Pell City.

"I lived alone in Jonesboro for a few years after the death of my wife, Mary Helen. We had been married for 52 years," he said.

After McKay moved into the skilled-nursing home section of the Village, he came to value his association with fellow residents and with employees. He began regarding his newfound friends as a part of his extended family.

As time passed, McKay's own biological family became smaller. He also lost his son, John. Herbert McKay was glad he was living close to the home

Below, miniature horse Jellybean pays Easter visit to Village residents. Below right, Village assisted-living resident Marie Mezick gets a feel of being aboard a motorcycle.

of his daughter-in-law, Brenda, and he welcomed her frequent phone calls and visits.

From the first day he moved into the Village, McKay was struck positively by the friendliness of the residents and employees. "The other people who live here are just like I am. I never had trouble making friends with them," he said. "And the people who work here, they are my friends, too. When I first arrived, they were all calling me, 'Mr.

Christopher Taylor, grandson of a Village employee, visits Clyde the dog and his goat friends at the Village.

McKay.' I said, 'Now, I'll tell you about you calling me Mr. McKay. That makes me think I'm old!' So one of the workers here said to me, 'What do other folks call you?' I told her, 'Well, some of them call me Herbert, and some of them call me Herb, and some of them called me Hub.'" Then, with a mischievous twinkle in his eye, Herbert McKay finished his story: "I told this worker here at the nursing home, 'Now you can pick any one of those names you want to call me. The only thing I ask is that you please don't call me late for breakfast!'"

A coal miner back when he was in his 20s, McKay got a strong dose of coal dust early in life. By the time World War II broke out in the early 1940s, McKay's lungs already were so badly scared with coal dust that he was disqualified for military service. However, that didn't stop him from going forward with a career of hard labor in a difficult environment. For decades he worked for Woodward Iron Company, in the furnace area where pig iron was made.

When he was interviewed for this book in May 2005, McKay was just a few weeks shy of his 91st birthday but had the appearance of a man considerably younger. He was accustomed to people reacting with surprise and disbelief when they heard his age.

Although the compliments pleased him, he retained his modesty. "When people tell me, 'I don't believe you are that old,' I say, 'Well, I can't argue with The Book. It's in The Book that I was born the 8th day of July in 1914.

Volunteers planting flowers at Village's first Earth Day celebration.

Since it's in The Book, that's how old I am.'"

As he spoke, he sat in a wheelchair he sometimes used, a result of chronic knee problems and two knee surgeries. However, in many ways he got good marks on his health, in fact exceptional marks for a man his age. His mind was still very quick and sharp, and his wry sense of humor was always in gear. Despite his diminished mobility, he managed to maintain an active daily schedule. He complimented the staff at the Village at Cook Springs for taking good care of his healthcare needs. He praised the activities in the Village's nursing home section for keeping him entertained.

"Oh, my friends and I are all the time going down to the dining hall here when they're having parties and stuff like that!" he said. "Why, sometimes when they're having something down in that dining hall, that big room is just full of people! We have birthday parties, holiday parties, all kinds of stuff in that dining room. Really, I like just about anything they have going around here with these activities. All of us who live here get invited to everything, and we feel like we belong to whatever is going on. I've made friends with all of those employees who work in the activities programs."

When asked to name his very favorite pastime at the Village, Herbert McKay didn't hesitate. "My favorite is playing bingo," he said. "I play bingo every chance I get — all I can play, like three nights a week."

As McKay described his family unit, he spoke of his biological family and his family at the Village at Cook Springs in the same general description.

He looked forward to his daily telephone conversations with his daughter-in-law Brenda, who had become his trusted friend. "Although Brenda is my daughter-in-law, she really seems more like a younger sister to me," he said. When Brenda came for her frequent visits to see her father-in-law at the Village, she often brought along another member of the family — a dog named Dolly that had been given to her by Herbert McKay.

And, when no biological family members were nearby, Herbert McKay said he still felt like he was with family. "Some of these people here at the Village seem just like kinfolks to me."

As Herbert McKay spoke about his life at the Village at Cook Springs, he made mention several times of something that fascinated him — the bigness of the Village. He was very aware that the Village had expansive sections devoted to various levels of care — the nursing home, Alzheimer's care, assisted living, independent living, rehabilitation. He liked that bigness of this institution in the rural setting that was much like a small town within itself. "Have you looked around at this place?" Herbert McKay asked, nodding his head and gesturing and opening his eyes wide in admiration. "They've got all these big rooms, all these big halls. I've been living here nearly three years now, and I still haven't gone through all of it. You know, it's a pretty good-sized little house we have here!"

Still on the Move

Maizie White Bradford had come to know what it meant to overcome health obstacles and keep going. She was still active after battling cancer,

Village activity assistant Debra McMahon converses with nursing home resident Herbert McKay.

Residents Ruth Norman and Steve Lacanski enjoy lakeside chat at the Village. (They had just finished feeding the ducks).

two strokes, diabetes, diverticulitis, vision problems, and five broken bones resulting from falls (including a broken hip and a broken leg).

"But still I'm doing about as well as a 93½-year-old gal could do!" she said with a laugh.

Despite all the health problems she had encountered, Mrs. Bradford spoke in a 2005 interview about what she *could* do instead of what she *could not* do. She outlined in detail the active lifestyle she had enjoyed in her five years of living at Springs Manor, the assisted-living section of the Village at Cook Springs.

"Why, you don't have time to be lonely here!" said Mrs. Bradford. "If you live here and you're lonely, it's your own fault!"

By way of explaining her statement, she held up a three-page document printed in large type on super-sized paper — a document that she kept close by and one that she used often. The document was a monthly listing of activities for assisted-living residents at the Village. It was packed with schedules for various social events, outings in the community, classes, crafts, and, very important to Mrs. Bradford, the devotional programs.

"You can pick whatever activities you like. You can go to a lot of activities, you can go to a few, or you can go to none. They're here for you if you want them," said Mrs. Bradford.

As she talked, Mrs. Bradford made it clear that she herself opted to participate in a lot of the activities — "not all of them, but I would say most of them." She loved the parties and the sing-along sessions. In order to accommodate this interview on this particular afternoon, Mrs. Bradford was skipping a residents' meeting she otherwise would have attended. That evening she would be playing bingo. She looked forward to the Wednesday shopping trips to a Kmart store, with transportation provided by the Village's bus. And it was just a regular part of her routine to attend daily devotional services at the Village's Springs Manor.

"There is just something going on all the time!" she said. When time came for some activity that interested her — which was often — she reached for her walker and made her way down the hallway to participate.

Outgoing Mrs. Bradford had become friends with an ever-expanding new circle of acquaintances since she had moved into the Village. "I feel like *everybody* here is my friend," she said. She had become a member of the Springs Manor Welcoming Committee, meaning that she paid visits to new residents to help them feel at home. One year she was selected as Ms. Springs Manor at the facility's annual pageant.

Myrtis Ferguson, longtime Cook Springs community resident and early-day member of nursing staff at Cook Springs Nursing Home. Mrs. Ferguson later was a nursing home resident of this same facility during its era as Village at Cook Springs. Shown in 2006 when she was crowned Ms. Village at Cook Springs.

A widow since the mid-1980s, Mrs. Bradford praised her only child, son Barry, for researching assisted-living facilities and selecting the Village as her new home. He did so after his mother's health issues reached the point she needed to stop living alone.

"My doctors had told my son that I shouldn't be living alone," she said. After surviving one health problem after another, Mrs. Bradford herself became convinced it was time to move into an assisted-living facility after she broke her leg. She said her son had worried about her and was relieved when she moved to the Village. "Yes, my son Barry told me that The Lord broke my leg for me, that I needed to move," she said with a smile.

In selecting the Village at Cook Springs for his mother, Mrs. Bradford's son chose a facility with which his and his mother's family had historical ties. Although those family connections made Mrs. Bradford even more bonded to the Village, she said those ties from the past did not drive her son's decision about the present. She said her son chose the Village at Cook Springs based on the institution's high quality in the here and now.

Mrs. Bradford's ties actually dated back to the very beginnings of the Village at Cook Springs. It was Mrs. Bradford's uncle (her mother's brother) — a visionary man named Mack Roper — who in 1950 founded the small nursing home that grew into what decades later became the Village at Cook Springs.

Village resident Becky Askew, right, does ceramics with longtime volunteer Maxine Abbott.

In addition to her family link to Mack Roper, Mrs. Bradford had a nostalgic experience from her past that gave her a special appreciation for the rich history of the Village at Cook Springs and the beautiful property that surrounded it. Back in the 1930s, young housewife-mother Maizie Bradford had accompanied her sister to Cook Springs to attend a week-long religious retreat. This retreat took place at a campground operated by the American School of Evangelism — which Mrs. Bradford's uncle, Mack Roper, later would serve as head trustee. While in Cook Springs that week in the 1930s, Mrs. Bradford and her sister were guests in a stately old hotel, the Cook's Springs Hotel, which was built in the 1880s and would be demolished in the early 1950s. In the hotel's earlier days, long before it became a part of a religious campground, it was the centerpiece for a flourishing mineral-springs resort founded by LaFayette Cooke. It was located on a tract of Cooke-owned property that later would be the site for the Village at Cook Springs. In fact, the hotel was located about a half mile from where Mrs. Bradford later would make her home in the Village's Springs Manor. As Mrs. Bradford reflected in her 2005 interview, she said she still could vividly picture her week-long religious retreat in Cook Springs 70 years previously. She could recall details of staying at the old hotel and of taking hikes on the nearby mountain trails. She said back then the scenery in the Cook Springs area was beautiful. And, she noted as she gestured toward the window in her Springs Manor suite, the scenery in rural Cook Springs still was beautiful.

To Maizie White Bradford, any community that became her home was an important community and one worthy of her support. She had held that view dating back to her childhood and to her roots in communities near the border where Jefferson and St. Clair Counties met — communities such as Whites Chapel (named for her family). After living years of her married life in the Powderly community of Birmingham, she returned to Whites Chapel as a resident before becoming a resident of the Village at Cook Springs.

She said that five years of living at the Village had made her new home very dear to her heart. She made it clear that she not only wanted the Village to contribute to her; she also wanted to contribute to the Village.

"All my life it has been important to me to serve," she said. "As long as I'm able, and I still am, I'm going to continue to serve."

No doubt her biggest contribution to the Village had been her leadership in pushing forward a chapter of the Woman's Missionary Union (WMU) at the Village's Springs Manor. That chapter had been started by a former resident of the Village, Fay Harden. Mrs. Bradford became committed to continuing and expanding what Mrs. Harden had begun.

Reared by a father who was a Baptist minister and a mother who was a leader in the Woman's Missionary Union (WMU), Mrs. Bradford had a lifelong exposure to leadership roles in spiritual undertakings. After her mother led in establishing and leading a couple of WMU chapters, Mrs. Bradford became a WMU leader herself. She spent many hours during her adult years being involved in WMU.

"Here at the Village at Cook Springs, we have a very active and very

Village's Kristal Bell Choir during performance at Galleria Riverchase Mall in Birmingham. Choir members are assisted-living residents at the Village.

At left, the much-used chapel at the Village at Cook Springs. At right, residents Louise Vernon, Opal Terrell, and Louise Hardy gather in the chapel to worship.

meaningful WMU chapter," said Mrs. Bradford. "I thoroughly enjoy getting the speakers for our WMU programs. We have good attendance at our meetings, and our residents talk about how very much they enjoy our speakers. Even though our name of course is *Woman's Missionary Union*, at our meetings at the Village we don't exclude the men who are our fellow residents. We're so proud of our programs that we want everyone here to feel welcome to attend. That means we invite the men who live here to come and enjoy our meetings, too!"

A Place for Cook Springs in Her Family's History

On many an occasion, Mary Mashburn Williams had heard a fascinating story of a difficult journey her own mother once made to Cook Springs, Alabama.

As she had listened to the story, Mrs. Williams could have no way of knowing that this community called Cook Springs that had been such a part of her family history would one day become her own home community.

That story — that connection — had given Cook Springs a special place in Mary Williams' heart long before she moved there.

After she became a resident of the Village at Cook Springs in April 2005, 86-year-old Mrs. Williams passed along the details of the journey-to-Cook-Springs saga that she had heard from the lips of her mom, Edna Seals Mashburn.

These are the details of that journey — a difficult, primitive, and exciting journey all the way from Texas to Cook Springs, Alabama:

The journey took place in 1891. At the time, Texas-born Edna Seals (Mary's mother) was 8 years old. She was still living in her native Texas with her family — her father and mother and three brothers and three sisters.

"My grandfather — my mother's father — decided that he would return to Alabama, which had been his home. My grandfather decided that he and his wife and children would go to Cook Springs, Alabama, to the home of his own father — my great-grandfather," said Mrs. Williams.

The family's transportation and the supplies for this long trip were limited, meager, falling short of the very basics.

"My mother's family loaded up their belongings onto an ox wagon and started out for Alabama. It took them six weeks to travel from Texas to Cook Springs, Alabama, to my great-grandfather's house," said Mrs. Williams.

For the father of that family, Daniel Seals, leading the trip was a daring journey not unlike some of the pioneering experiences of risk-takers such as Daniel Boone and Davy Crockett.

"You see, my grandfather actually *walked* all the way from Texas to Cook Springs, Alabama! He let the other family members ride in the ox cart. And he walked," said Mrs. Williams. "Along the way my grandfather carried his gun — whatever kind of gun he had, a muzzle-loader I guess. And as they traveled, he hunted — squirrels, rabbits, whatever — so the family could eat what he killed."

And so the Seals family traveled — slowly, laboriously. They made their way through much of Texas, on through Louisiana, through Mississippi, and finally into Alabama.

"When I think about this, I can just see those old dirt roads that my mother's family traveled on the way from Texas to Cook Springs," said Mrs. Williams. "I'll bet those roads were awful!"

In order to earn money to buy other supplies the family needed, Edna Seals' two older sisters sat in the ox wagon and crocheted items to sell.

"My aunts crocheted collars and cuffs. Those girls did beautiful crochet work," said Mrs. Williams. "As they made their way east toward Cook

Springs, the family would stop in these little towns they'd come to and sell whatever the girls had crocheted in order to buy the other things they needed to continue on with their trip."

Edna was among the younger of the seven Seals children. Her mother and dad allowed her and the two other younger children to play as they traveled. "Actually, my mother and the other two young ones walked along and played most of the time behind the ox wagon. My mother recalled to me how they played. She also told me how my grandfather really did walk the whole way!"

As Mary Williams related the story, it became a story with a two-fold message. It became a story of the special feeling she had for the community of Cook Springs, the little hamlet that her family struggled so hard to reach in the late 1800s. It also became a story of the pride that she felt for the hearty, resilient family stock from which she was descended.

That heartiness and resilience also were present in the man that Edna Seals would marry — Mrs. Williams' father, Bill Mashburn. He became a sharecropper who rented and farmed property in St. Clair County, including property near Springville. Mrs. Williams said her dad was quite successful as a farmer partly because he had known hard work all his life, dating back to his childhood in which he was reared as one of 16 children.

Bill and Edna Mashburn had 10 children of their own — with daughter Mary being the seventh-born. Young Mary and her siblings were reared with hard work as an everyday companion. "Well, if you call it hard work to start out early and work all day doing things like picking cotton and pulling corn, well, yes, my eight brothers and my sister and I did hard work," she said. "And I learned to saw with a cross-cut saw like a man. My dad said he'd rather saw with me than with one of the boys (her brothers). He said I could beat them!"

Picking cotton and sawing wood weren't the only tasks that Mary Mashburn Williams learned to perform well with her strong, fast-moving, agile hands. In her adult life, her hands became caring hands, as she worked as a licensed practical nurse in hospital, nursing home and doctor's office settings. And, in her leisure hours, her hands became talented hands, as she worked to create beautiful crafts.

As soon as Mrs. Williams moved into the Springs Manor assisted-living section of the Village at Cook Springs, the staff at the Village got her busy helping them out by using her crafts ability.

"There's no doubt that Mary has a real creative streak," said Sheryl Mulvehill, director of marketing at the Village. "Right after Mary moved in, she used her creative abilities to help us get ready for a Mother's Day tea here at the Village."

When Mary Williams moved to the Village at Cook Springs, it was new to her to live in the Cook Springs area of St. Clair County. But living in St. Clair County was far from being new. She had been born in St. Clair County. Her dad sharecropped in the county. Mrs. Williams and her late husband, Chester, had reared their two children in the county. The St. Clair community of Springville had been her home.

When Mrs. Williams decided that, due to health issues, it was time for her to move into an assisted-living facility, she moved to a facility in Jefferson County. Then she relocated at the Village at Cook Springs. "Now that I'm back in St. Clair County, I feel like I'm back home," she said.

Interviewed about five weeks after she moved into the Village, she said she already had positive early impressions. "I like it here. The place is nice. The people are nice. And remember that I was a licensed practical nurse. I know what to look for."

As Mrs. Williams spoke of her memories and current impressions in her interview, staff member Sheryl Mulvehill was nearby taking a close look at some of the crafts Mary Williams had just created. Using her talent for both designing and creating items, Mrs. Williams had taken common materials such as safety pins, wires, beads and knitting yarn and fashioned them into delicate angels, bells and baskets.

"Mary, these creations of yours are good — very, very good," said Ms. Mulvehill. "I've got to talk to you about all this talent you have. I think that you could help us in teaching crafts to other residents who live here at the Village!"

Mary Mashburn Williams just smiled. While she was pleased that Sheryl Mulvehill appreciated her work, to Mrs. Williams all that talent with her own hands just came naturally.

After all, she was a niece of those two talented girls who more than 100 years ago had sat in an ox wagon crocheting beautiful items to sell, as their family slowly made their way from Texas to Cook Springs, Alabama.

A "People-Person" Being Served by Others

The telephone never seemed to stop ringing in the Burns household during the growing-up years of Vernon Lee "Sunny" Burns, Jr., and his younger brother, Kenneth.

An outgoing, enterprising woman by the name of Monteene Burns was a key reason. In her personal life, she was the mother of Sunny and Kenneth and the wife of Vernon Lee Burns, Sr. In her professional life, she sold Avon cosmetic products and World Books — doing quite well at both.

"I mean, our phone rang off the hook most of the time!" Sunny Burns recalled, with obvious pride in his voice regarding his mother's success. "Living in the same household with our mother was like living *inside* a business.

It was typical that a lady would call Mama and say, 'Monteene, I have run out of such and such a (cosmetic) cream. I need to come over to your house and get some, right now.' Why, my mother was so accommodating that you could have called her at 1 a.m. and asked for something and she would have been just as nice as if you were calling her in the middle of the day."

Monteene Burns was equally charming as she went into the homes of her customers to sell Avon and World Books, he said. And her openness with people extended to the Burns family's home life. "In our growing-up years, our house became like a community gathering place. It didn't make any difference to Mama how many kids came!"

As Sunny Burns recalled his mother's life in a 2005 interview, he was speaking of a woman who once had met the needs of so many others. He also was speaking of a woman whose own needs later were being met by others — by the staff at the Village at Cook Springs. (When Monteene Burns died on March 20, 2006, she had lived at the Village for four years.)

A resident of either Pell City or neighboring Eden from her childhood forward, Monteene Burns began dealing with the St. Clair County public professionally as early as her teenage years, when she worked in a drugstore.

After she married, she came to know many citizens well not only through her own career but also through the very public lives of her father-in-law and her husband. Her father-in-law, Henry Lee Burns, served as mayor of Eden in its latter years of being an independent city before it was absorbed into Pell City in the 1950s. Her husband served as the last postmaster of Eden when Eden still had its own post office.

"It got to the point that it was hard to run across somebody in our community that my mother did not know," said Sunny Burns.

When Mrs. Burns moved into the Village at Cook Springs in 2002, some of those people she had known over the years became her caretakers. One employee had once lived next door to the Burns family. Another employee had a grandmother who had lived down the street from the Burns home. One staff member came up to Sunny Burns and said, "Oh, I visited in your mother's home when I was a little girl."

This familiarity at the Village was good for Monteene Burns. It also was good for Sunny and Kenneth Burns. "My brother and I re-connected with some people at the Village that we had grown up with. It was good, like a family atmosphere," he said.

In addition to employees at the Village who already knew members of the Burns household, there were also employees at the Village that the Burns family had never met. Sunny Burns said these new acquaintances also were very caring of his mother.

This caring came as no surprise to Sunny and Kenneth Burns. For they had conducted careful research into long-term-care facilities before selecting one for their mother, who already was in the early stages of Alzheimer's disease when she was admitted to the Village at age 80. Since their father has been deceased for more than 30 years, the full responsibility for making decisions on Mrs. Burns' behalf rested with her sons. Sunny Burns said he and his brother chose the Village at Cook Springs after it was recommended to them by an individual who had previous professional experience evaluating nursing homes in Alabama.

It was comforting to the Burns brothers that the Village provided varied levels of care, which could accommodate any changes that might take place in their mother's condition. In the beginning, their mother was a resident of the Alzheimer's section of the Village's assisted-living facility. Later, as her Alzheimer's symptoms became more pronounced, she became a resident of the Alzheimer's section of the Village's skilled nursing home facility.

Both Sunny and Kenneth Burns paid frequent visits to their mother at the Village. Both brothers were retired — Sunny retired as a partner in an electrical substation business and Kenneth retired from a civil service career. Both lived near the Village at Cook Springs — Sunny residing in the May's Bend community near Pell City, and Kenneth living on the lake near the town of Lincoln.

"We like the fact that the Village is clean and well-kept. We very much like that small Southern-town kind of atmosphere that it has," said Sunny Burns. "It was good that the staff were so genuinely concerned about Mama's well-being. I must tell you that it pleased me when I was rolling Mama down the hall in her wheelchair and all these people around us at the Village were calling out, 'Hey, Monteene!' "

The confidence that Sunny Burns placed in the Village carried over after his mother's death. In 2005, Burns married Sharon Meadows. In 2006, his wife's mother, Nima Titlow, made the decision to move from Maryland to Alabama, to be near her daughter. The family selected a home for Mrs. Titlow at Springs Manor, the assisted-living section of the Village at Cook Springs.

23

Employees Bound by Their Heartstrings

"Our residents at the Village at Cook Springs know in their hearts that we love them. They are aware of our love. They feel that we love them by how we relate to them and act toward them."–Charlene Tidwell, communications coordinator and marketing assistant, Village at Cook Springs

Bobbie Hobson stands in front of a group of assisted-living residents at the Village at Cook Springs. All these senior-citizen residents are members of a very special choir that makes music with bells. Ms. Hobson is their choir director.

Each of the residents is holding a bell. The bells are different colors. Some residents hold red bells; others hold bells of yellow, purple or green.

Ms. Hobson in turn is displaying to this group an array of cards of different colors — cards in colors of red, yellow, purple and green that match the residents' bells. The residents watch Ms. Hobson closely, as she shuffles and flashes the cards rapidly. When the residents see her flash the color that matches their bells, they ring their bells accordingly.

What comes out of their bell-ringing is a beautiful song — a classic song familiar to its listeners. In fact, this group has song after song in its repertoire. This is the Village's Kristal Bell Choir, a performing group much in demand for performances at events both inside and outside the Village.

This scene came out of the year 2005, when the Kristal Bell Choir already had a track record of several years of successful performances.

310

"The Kristal Bell Choir has been a big success with our residents at the Village and also with audiences out in the community who hear the choir's music. People love it!" said Ms. Hobson, staff member at the Village who serves as director of all activity programs in the Village's Springs Manor assisted-living section.

She explained that the music created by the Kristal Bell Choir has been heard at events at the Riverchase Galleria Shopping Center in Birmingham, at various programs sponsored by church and senior citizens' groups mainly in Jefferson and St. Clair Counties, and during special performances at the Village on occasions such as Easter, Christmas, and the Fourth of July.

As with any accomplished musical group, a commitment of time and energy is required to maintain the quality. "We practice regularly, every week," said Ms. Hobson. In order to participate, a Village resident does not have to know how to read music; he or she just has to be interested and also be willing to commit the time and effort.

Residents who have become members of this acclaimed bell-ringing group take pride in their performances. At any given time, the choir members usually number from around 12 to 20. Each and every member of the choir is a resident of the Village's assisted-living facility, Springs Manor.

The idea for the Kristal Bell Choir came to the Village courtesy of the First Baptist Church of Birmingham. After being introduced to the concept through the church, Ms. Hobson got in touch with the organization that had developed the bell-ringing system. The Village obtained the bells, the cards, and the rest of the system. Soon the Village's senior-citizen musicians were ringing their bells and performing.

"We have a real rewarding history of being musical in a creative way at the Village at Cook Springs," said Ms. Hobson, who has been working at the Village since the mid-1980s. "Prior to the Kristal Bell Choir, the Village had what we called the Kitchen Band. Members of that band included one of our volunteers who was an accomplished pianist. He was joined by several of our residents to make up the entire band. Our residents who played in the Kitchen Band used such basic homemade musical instruments as rub-boards and thimbles, a bass fiddle fashioned out of a washtub and strings, our own version of the cymbals and maracas, and a very interesting contraption that we called the 'stump fiddle.' Just like with our current Kristal Bell Choir, the Kitchen Band was really something!"

A Rewarding Feeling for the Staff

As Bobbie Hobson spoke of her work with the Kristal Bell Choir, her face lit up with pride and enthusiasm. It was obvious she was having fun with that choir.

The same kind of enthusiasm embraces Ms. Hobson regarding the many other activities she and her staff plan and carry out with residents.

Nursing home resident Lula York, right, gets a hug from Village communications coordinator Charlene Tidwell.

She enjoys the activities, and she feels close to the residents. Bobbie Hobson and her staff talk about the satisfaction they feel as they interact with residents. The same rewarding feeling comes, she explained, whether they are planning a devotional service with a special speaker, watching a resident take pride in making a beautiful ceramic craft, preparing to entertain the Village's residents and guests with an Earth Day celebration or Grandparents' Tea, or accompanying residents on a local shopping trip out in the community.

"We just enjoy watching the residents participate, be inspired, and enjoy

themselves," said Ms. Hobson. "That applies to the mental side, the spiritual side, and the physical side of what we do here."

On the mental-exercise side, Ms. Hobson loves teaching residents her thought-provoking classroom-sessions on concepts — ideas such as joy, hope, generosity and forgiveness. In group sessions with residents, she tosses out one of these concepts for discussion. Then the residents share their memories and opinions about what that concept means to them.

"On the physical side, I really love the SitterCize classes we have for residents," she said. This is all part of keeping the residents as active as they can be. For the SitterCize classes, each participating resident moves at whatever level he or she can manage. "Some of the residents sit in chairs or in their wheelchairs to do these SitterCizes," said Ms. Hobson. "Those residents who can stand up behind their chairs do so. The idea is to conduct exercise that they can do — to keep them moving as much as they can."

An Elderly Woman Plants A Seed

It is not uncommon to hear staff members at the Village at Cook Springs refer to their work as a calling, as part of a mission, as something that is very special to their hearts.

Such is the case with Pam Smith. She holds the same type activity-director position in the Village's skilled nursing home that Bobbie Hobson holds in the assisted-living section.

In a 2005 interview, Mrs. Smith recalled the pivotal experience in her life that set her on a rewarding career path in long-term care. That experience had occurred years before, soon after she began doing some volunteer work in a nursing home near where she lived at the time in a small southeast-Alabama town.

"On this particular day, I walked into a room in this nursing home in my role as a volunteer, just helping out," said Mrs. Smith. "There was this little elderly lady sitting there who looked up at me and connected with me. She reached up and placed her hand on my arm, obviously wanting my attention. I was more than glad to give that attention. I responded to her, and in the process I bent down and told her, 'I love you.' She just brightened up all over. She said to me, 'Kiss me.' So I bent down and kissed her on the cheek. The wonderful look that came over her face just did something for me!"

With that experience, Mrs. Smith's own life began to change.

"Something started happening to me. As I continued to volunteer, I realized that going to that nursing home to do volunteer work was becoming very, very important to me," said Mrs. Smith. "And then I had an opportunity come my way. The lady who was employed as activity director at that nursing home went on pregnancy leave, and she asked me if I would consider working in her position while she was gone. I said, 'Yes!' That was that. I knew that working with the elderly had gotten into my blood. So I continued doing it, and I still love it today."

The experience that Mrs. Smith had in that southeast-Alabama nursing home is more or less duplicated many times every day in the work that she and her staff do at the Village's nursing home. "One of the aspects of our work that's so rewarding is tailoring the nursing home's activities program to the needs of each and every one of our residents," she said. "We base what we offer each resident on what he or she *can* do, what he or she *can't* do, and what he or she *wants* to do."

Most residents in the nursing home become involved in activities, said Mrs. Smith. "Most of them seem happier when they are active and involved." However, she said for those who choose not to be involved, their privacy is respected. "It's their right to choose not to participate if they wish, and we very much respect their privacy," she said.

On a typical day, Mrs. Smith and her four activity assistants interact with about 168 residents — those in the core nursing home, plus residents in the nursing home Alzheimer's unit, and also residents of the Village's rehabilitation center.

Among these residents, there is a wide range of abilities. Some are well enough to attend many of the events planned and carried out by Mrs. Smith and her staff — ranging from sock hops and dessert socials and birthday parties, to games of bingo or dominoes, to special events such as holiday celebrations and the annual much-anticipated "queen pageant" to select and crown one of the residents as "Ms. Village at Cook Springs." Some residents are well enough to go on trips outside the Village to dine at restaurants and attend plays and Birmingham Barons baseball games. On the other hand, there are other nursing home residents whose health problems force them to be much more confined; and the Village staff members do a lot of one-on-one work for them, which includes bringing activities such as crafts right to some residents' bedsides.

A visit on Village porch. From left, licensed practical nurse (LPN) Tammy Yates, nursing home resident Carolyn Booker, and LPN Deadra Wills.

"We just treat all our residents as individuals, addressing their needs on an individual basis," said Mrs. Smith. "Let me put it this way. As staff at the Village, we treat each resident the way we would want to be treated if any of us was a resident in a nursing home."

Connecting with the Residents

Employee after employee at the Village has stories to tell and views to share about what residents mean to each of them and their lives.

When licensed practical nurse Betty Chapman thinks about her role in taking care of residents in the Village's nursing home, she looks at that care as being two-sided. One side is the physical side — making sure the residents' physical needs are met. The other is the emotional side — making sure each resident feels comfortable with her, and going that extra step to put special attention into the care she gives each resident.

"I've been working at what's now the Village for 30 years — long enough that my own mother and father now are in the same age group as many residents I take care of," said Mrs. Chapman, speaking in 2005. "To me, giving good care to our residents has become not only a way of honoring and respecting our residents but also a way of honoring and respecting my parents' entire generation."

The physical aspects of taking care of the residents are still as uppermost in Mrs. Chapman's mind as they were three decades previously when she first went to work when the Baptists were operating the facility, then known as the Baptist Home for Senior Citizens. "There are just some things that we know we must do all the time in taking care of our residents," she said. "One thing is being gentle. Always be gentle. When you're handling an older person — turning them, doing anything for them — be careful to take great care of what can be very fragile skin. Be gentle and don't damage that skin."

To Mrs. Chapman, that gentleness extends to emotional gentleness as well. Through the years at the facility now known as the Village at Cook Springs, Mrs. Chapman had had experience rendering nursing care to residents on both the day shifts and the night shifts. No matter what the shift, Mrs. Chapman said that interacting with the residents is of great importance. "You have to learn to communicate with your patients!" she said. "And how you communicate will vary from one resident to another."

She spoke, for example, of the different ways she had approached the Village's nursing home residents when she worked the night shift. If a resident was comfortably asleep, he or she tended to be contented with Mrs. Chapman's extra pat of comfort, a tucking of the covers, and perhaps a softly spoken brief greeting. But other times the residents wanted conversation, even if it was the middle of the night. Some residents were light sleepers. Others were all-out night owls. When they wanted conversation, Mrs. Chapman was glad to accommodate. "For example, in recent times one of the residents I've been caring for on the night shift is this lady who will rouse up when I come in. Now, she's ready to talk, it doesn't matter what time it is. When she rouses up, she always greets me and calls me by name. She's got my name down pat! She wants to talk, and so we talk. I really enjoy her."

Through the years, Mrs. Chapman said she has come to know a host of residents who have helped broaden her world.

Longtime employee Bobbie Hobson also holds that view. She said her life is much fuller as a result of knowing residents and their families who have made indelible marks in her life. "It's remarkable to me when I think of all the precious people at the Village who have enriched my life in the 20-plus years I've been working here!"

Ms. Hobson said that each Village resident she encounters is a fascinating person in his or her own right. She said it's not uncommon for many of these residents to retain their talents, hobbies, and special interests with great enthusiasm, up into their 80s and 90s.

"We had one man who lived here who was a puzzle whiz. I mean, could he do puzzles! He would glue those puzzles together and put them in frames — beautiful!" said Ms. Hobson.

"Then there was the interesting lady who lived here who loved to collect coins, and we called her The Lady Coin Collector.

"There was this wonderful man who played in our Kristal Bell Choir. He lived in the assisted-living part of the Village, and his wife lived in the Village's nursing home until she died. After she passed away, he was well enough that he could have gone back to their home to live. But I'm proud to say that he chose to stay on with us, to continue to live at the Village. He was great! He became a kind of spokesman for us. He was always staying upbeat and saying things like, 'Yea, Alabama!' He would make these great little speeches. He wanted to include others as well. So he encouraged everybody to introduce themselves. And he mainly just wanted to tell everyone how happy he was to be at the Village.

"And among those who have made such an impression has been this lady, over 90 years old, with a flower bed out back of the Village. Every once in a while, she and I would go out there together and weed out her flower bed."

Ms. Hobson has seen impressive creativity among the Village's residents and their family members.

"We have a residents' library here. And I'm proud that among the au-

Receptionist Glenda Wesley puts together a puzzle with Village resident Dr. Joyce Rogers, a retired physician.

thors represented in the library's materials is one of our residents, Louise Moore Sims." She pointed to one of the historical books penned by Indian-history scholar Sims — a 1997 book, *The Last Chief of Kewahatchie.*

As an example of prized words written by residents' families, Ms. Hobson noted both poetry and narrative material about the Village and its residents that was written by well-known St. Clair County author, poet, and historian Joseph L. Whitten of Odenville. His late mother-in-law had been a resident of the Village.

In the case of some residents who had passed away, precious memories are held dear by employees at the Village who miss them, said Ms. Hobson. Among memorable examples that came to her mind were Fay and L.D. Harden, a husband and wife with strong Texas ties who for a time had made their home at the Village. "I recall a period when Mr. and Mrs. Harden would walk together at the Village every day," said Ms. Hobson. "Mrs. Harden walked more than Mr. Harden. I can still just see Mr. Harden sitting there, wanting for Mrs. Harden to finish her walk." Although Mrs. Harden was beginning to have a number of health issues, she remained active enough to help start a chapter of the Woman's Missionary Union (WMU) at the Village's assisted-living facility. The Hardens' presence also contributed to the continuing beautification of the Village — through some thriving rose bushes. It was the Hardens' son who brought those rose bushes (rose bushes from Texas), when he came to pay a visit to his parents. The rose bushes were a gift to his parents; they also were a gift to the Village. "Fay and her son and I planted those rose bushes together, out there in the Village's garden," said Ms. Hobson. Despite Fay Harden's considerable health problems, her husband preceded her in death. After the death of her beloved partner in life, Fay Harden experienced a worsening of her own health problems. But she kept fighting. "I mean, Fay was a true inspiration to all of us who knew her!" said Ms. Hobson. "At one point, they called all the family in because she was dying, but she bounced back and lived three more years." Mrs. Harden lived well into her 90s. "Although Fay and L.D. Harden are gone now, we have those memories of those precious people who lived with us," said Bobbie Hobson. "Part of those memories are living through roses from Texas that continue to bloom in our garden here at the Village."

One of the employees who has come to know many of the residents and families well is Charlene Tidwell. She joined the Village's staff in the late 1990s as a receptionist and switchboard operator. Ms. Tidwell has risen through the ranks to become communications coordinator and assistant in marketing. Part of her role is supervising employees in the Village's reception and switchboard services. She also has gotten involved in special projects at the Village, including becoming the coordinator for extensive decorating that was put in place at the Village during the 2005 Christmas season.

In watching the warm interaction between the employees and the residents at the Village, Ms. Tidwell said it occurs to her that it is all about genuine love — not just *talking* about love, but *showing* love.

"When I think of the love that the Village's staff members share with the elderly residents here, I think back to something I would tell my own children when they were growing up," said Ms. Tidwell. "I would say to my children, 'Do you *know* that I love you?' Always they would say, 'Yes.' Then I would add, 'But do you also *feel* that I love you? Can you actually *feel* my love for you?' And they would smile and say, 'Yes.' That's how I view the caring and love we feel and convey to the senior citizens who live here at the Village. And we have so many residents who really do understand this. Our residents at the Village at Cook Springs know in their hearts that we love them. They are aware of our love. They feel that we love them by how we relate to them and act toward them."

Finding Them a New Home

Registered nurse Angie Cobb has an opportunity to get to know the Village's residents and their family members even before the residents move into the Village.

Mrs. Cobb came to the Village in 2002 in the position of registered nurse case manager for the nursing home portion of the Village. In this role, she became a link in getting potential residents qualified and placed at the Village. She also became "the arranger" who makes sure that an incoming resident's medical and social needs are met.

In performing this job, she has come to know potential residents, their family members, and their caretakers in a variety of settings. She interacts with staff members in doctors' offices, and she deals with discharge planners and case managers in hospitals. She also visits in the homes of many potential residents.

"In this job, I have an opportunity every day to change lives for the better, to make a contribution," said Mrs. Cobb. "I will tell you that I indeed do view this as a calling."

Mrs. Cobb came to her position at the Village with experience in both hospital and public-health work. On the hospital side, she has worked as a staff nurse in neurosurgery intensive care at the University of Alabama at Birmingham (UAB). In public health, she has been a supervisor for home-health care for the Alabama State Department of Public Health — supervising public-health nursing services for patients in Etowah, Blount and St. Clair Counties.

As has been the case with so many of her co-workers, Angie Cobb said her heart quickly and deeply connected to her work at the Village at Cook Springs.

"I had been working at the Village no more than a couple of days before I became very much aware that I was going to give my heart and soul to the Village," said Mrs. Cobb. "There is just this sense of belonging at the Village. It's a sense of belonging with the residents and their family members, and it's also a sense of belonging with the staff. I do feel like I belong there at the Village. And I know a lot of other staff members at the Village who feel the same way."

One aspect of the Village that Mrs. Cobb finds especially appealing is that the facility provides various levels of care. She said the comprehensive nature of the Village campus is reassuring to families — to know that if their mother or father or another loved one needs to move from one level of care to another it can be done within the same institution. Along these lines,

Village activity assistant Rolanda Sewell takes on "clown role" to visit resident Buddy McCain.

Mrs. Cobb said it makes her feel good to be able to reassure families that if Mom or Dad develop major health problems and need to move from an assisted-living facility into a skilled nursing home, that can be done on the Village campus. Similarly, it makes her feel good to be able to explain that if Mom or Dad need rehabilitation services following an illness, a surgery, or a major event such as a stroke, there is a rehabilitation center right there on the Village campus.

Angie Cobb said it is a satisfying feeling, too, to be able to explain to families the attitude with which the Village's staff will care for their loved ones: "I can look a family member in the eye and say with confidence, 'We want you to know that if you entrust us with the care of your parent, we will be your parent's greatest advocates.'"

Seeing the Cause and Effect

From her view as the Village's marketing director, Sheryl Mulvehill sees many of the ingredients that go into the Village's personal touch. She also sees the positive impact of that personal touch on residents and families.

"Again and again I see examples of the personal interest that staff members take toward our residents and also toward their families," said Ms. Mulvehill.

She sees the personal touch with the bird-feeders. In the Village's rustic rural environment, a number of residents have placed their own bird-feeders

The Village's executive director, Glenn Brewer, left, joins resident John Fox for a walk on Village grounds.

on the grounds. These residents gain a lot of pleasure from watching the birds come to their feeders. "The residents' family members are generally the ones who make sure those feeders are stocked with bird feed," said Ms. Mulvehill. "But staff members keep an eye on the bird-feeders, too. On a number of occasions, I've heard staff members say something to the effect of, 'Oh, I'm going to go get some bird food for that feeder. That resident's family members had to go out of town unexpectedly, and they weren't able to bring the bird feed this week.'" To Ms. Mulvehill, the bird-feeder story is symbolic of how staff members seem to keep an eye even on the "extras" that are important to the residents.

She sees the personal touch with a Christmas tree in the Village's nursing home. "Oh, this is such a sweet thing," said Ms. Mulvehill. "When the staff puts up this Christmas tree each year, they hang names on the tree — the names of each resident in the nursing home. The staff members go by the tree and take the names of the residents. Then each staff member will go and get a gift for the resident whose name he or she got off the tree. The staff members select gifts for residents that are very personal — like a pair of special little socks, or something to brighten a resident's room. That way, every resident will have something special to open for Christmas."

Too, Sheryl Mulvehill sees the Village's personal touch come alive in caring conversations that staff members have with residents and their family members. "Now around here at the Village, we take an interest in our residents, and we also take an interest in their family members — I mean a genuine, heartfelt interest," said Ms. Mulvehill. "We talk to our residents and their families about important things going on in their lives. We rejoice with them over the birth of a new grandchild or great-grandchild. We sympathize with them when someone in the family is sick or has passed away. We celebrate with them when a family member has received some special recognition or reached some landmark. We listen with understanding when a resident's daughter or son is feeling blue because a child just went off to college. We feel happy with them when they have a new home or a job promotion. Those things are important to our residents and their families. They're important to the staff at the Village, too."

Ms. Mulvehill said nothing is more rewarding than to hear a resident or a family member report that Village employees have made him or her feel special. She hears that often. In her 2005 interview, she gave a recent example. She told of comments that had been made to her by a man who had moved into one of the independent-living apartments at the Village in early 2005.

"After this man had been living here for a while, he came to me one day and said, 'Sheryl, there is something I want to tell you about my experience moving into the Village.' He said that when he first moved in, someone at the Village told him, 'With us here at the Village, you will feel cared about.' He told me that prediction had come true for him. He said, 'From the time I've walked into the Village, I have known that I was not just another person. I have known that I am not just looked upon at the Village as just a number. Everybody at the Village has made me feel welcome, made me feel right at home. That applies to staff in various positions at the Village — I mean everybody. I have found that it's true that here at the Village you know you are cared about. You know you are cared about because you can feel it!'"

Firsthand Knowledge of a Legacy of Caring

Some employees at the Village have had relatives who at some point in time have been residents of the long-term-care facility now known as the Village at Cook Springs. That experience gives those employees a unique perspective that comes from having been "a family member."

It also gives these employees a personal insight into the legacy of caring at this facility that opened in 1950 and has gone through eras of being first the

Cook Springs Nursing Home, then the Baptist Home for Senior Citizens, and then the Village at Cook Springs.

Receptionist/switchboard operator Glenda Wesley is one of those employees in the "family member" category.

Mrs. Wesley can remember visiting her grandmother and her great-uncle there at the facility during the late 1950s and early 1960s. She remembers the loving care they received. She remembers employees going out of their way to support her grandmother, her great-uncle, and also family members who loved them.

"I recall so vividly the kindnesses showed to our family on the night my grandmother passed away in 1963 at what then was the Baptist Home for Senior Citizens," said Mrs. Wesley. "There was a male nurse working there at the time. He was such a kind, caring man. The day my grandmother passed away, this nurse stayed on and worked beyond his regular shift, remaining with me and our other family members during my grandmother's final hours. We so much appreciated his kindnesses. We never forgot that. Since those times, this facility that later became the Village at Cook Springs has always had a special place in my heart."

The facility still had a special place in Mrs. Wesley's heart when she decided to re-enter the work force in 2003. She had worked much of her adult life and had "retired" twice. She was fine with retirement until she faced the difficult year of 2002, when three of her family members died within less than a year — her mother, her husband, and a step-granddaughter. After coming to grips with her losses, she wanted to go back to work. It was important to her to go to work somewhere where she could serve others. When she heard there was an opening for a part-time receptionist/switchboard operator at the Village at Cook Springs, she jumped at the chance to work there.

"Oh, I love being employed at the Village," Mrs. Wesley said in a 2005 interview. "I wouldn't want to be anywhere else. Actually, I feel that I was placed here for a reason."

She said there is no doubt that learning to cope with her own losses has helped her in communicating with residents and visitors she has met at the Village's front desk where she works. Also, since her own grandmother, great-uncle, and mother all were nursing home residents, she said she can understand some of the feelings and needs that residents and their families experience. "I can't tell you how good it makes me feel to bring a smile to someone's face or to have someone come up and say, 'Glenda, thanks for talking to me. You don't know what it has meant to me.'"

Since moving from part-time to full-time employment at the Village, Mrs. Wesley has had an opportunity to be involved in some community-project work that has brought her special joy. From time to time, she has had a chance to assist fellow staff members in arranging community meetings held at the Village. Those meetings are gatherings of civic, professional, or community groups who choose to hold one of their regular meetings at the Village. These gatherings provide a two-way bonus: Citizens from various walks of life who attend these meetings have a chance to get to know the people at the Village, and the people at the Village have a chance to get to know their special visitors.

Being able to be involved in community projects is a good fit for Mrs. Wesley, who has lived in the St. Clair town of Odenville since 1955. Her late husband, Elton, adopted St. Clair as his home after moving there from Birmingham. Between Glenda and Elton Wesley, the scope of acquaintances and friends in St. Clair became quite broad. "I especially knew a lot of people from communities in St. Clair County who were in attendance at one particular meeting at the Village with which I assisted," said Mrs. Wesley. "I was excited that there was such an excellent turnout at this meeting. Also, once the meeting was over I heard people from various parts of St. Clair County talking about how very impressed they were with our facility."

Mrs. Wesley said it gives her pride to see people out in the community realize the specialness of the Village. "When I heard so many positive comments about the Village from people attending this meeting, I could really understand why they were so impressed with the Village. There's just something unique about the Village at Cook Springs. We're like family here. There has just always been something special about this facility. That was true more than 40 years ago when my grandmother and great-uncle were residents here. It's still true today."

Putting Down Roots

When Brenda Walker came to work at the Village in 2002, she was drawn to the job because of convenience. "My home is in Odenville, in St. Clair County. And I was working in Jefferson County, out on busy Hwy. 280. For me it had been about a 45-minute drive one way, to and from work."

So she applied for a position at the Village at Cook Springs, conveniently located only a few miles and a short drive from her home in Odenville.

It was good news to Ms. Walker that she was being hired into a brand-new position — that of administrative assistant to the Village's executive director. She liked the idea of being the first in this job, of being able to be useful and helpful in a position that never before had served the Village.

Soon a lot of other things about the Village also made her glad she was there.

Ms. Walker said in a short four years the Village has become a very special place to her. Although she came to work there relatively early in her working life (when she was in her early 30s), she had been in the work force long enough to recognize and appreciate a good working situation. Ms. Walker said she loves the feelings she has experienced in her work at the Village at Cook Springs. "It's so nice to walk down the hall and see these residents smile at you and often call to you in greeting. I see so many happy residents who obviously feel so at home and who know the Village *is* their home. And I just enjoy working with employees who are close to one another, who really care about their jobs, who care about what they do for the residents. Working at the Village really is like working in a family environment. When I came here four years ago, I came partly because it was close to my home. But I had not been working here very long before I was enjoying much more than convenience. I began thinking, 'The Village at Cook Springs is the place from which I want to retire.'"

Unable to Say Goodbye

Gail Peoples came to work at the Village in 1990, stayed for six years, and then decided to change jobs. Her decision came at a time when she was going through a stressful period that included the deaths of first her father and then her grandmother. She thought making some changes in her life would help her through the troubled period.

But she found she couldn't stay away from the Village. "Oh, I missed the residents terribly," she said. "Even though I got another job, soon I was coming back to the Village to do volunteer work." She was coming back to volunteer to do some of the same things she had done in her paid position as an activity assistant at the Village. "I was volunteering to help entertain those residents I was missing!" she said with a laugh.

Within seven months after she left, Gail Peoples returned to work at the Village. She returned to the switchboard and receptionist work, which was what she did when she had first come to the Village in 1990. Then, when an opening occurred in activities in the assisted-living section, she went back to activities.

"I'm one of those people who looks on all this as a mission," she said. "When I come to work every day, I don't look at it as a job. I look at it as helping these residents to enjoy themselves and feel at home. It just brightens my life to see them happy and smiling."

A Special Love for a Special Place

The beautiful rural surroundings at the Village have become a great bonder between the employees of the Village and the residents and their families.

It pleases the employees that the residents and their family members comment often on the outdoor beauty at the Village. It pleases employees that many of the residents go for walks on the Village walking-track and spend some time fishing at the Village lake. It pleases employees that the residents like to watch the animals and enjoy riding the "Jolly Trolley" up to the Red Barn.

There can be no doubt that the surroundings of the Village are a lure to employees who come to work there. There can be no doubt that once an employee goes to work at the Village, the surroundings can give the employee an extra edge in enjoying his or her work.

Pam Smith first saw the Village when she came there to attend a seminar. At the time, she was employed in the Auburn-Opelika, Alabama, area. "When I drove onto the property at the Village, I was just taken with that country look," she said. "I love country things. When I saw the picket fence, the big red barn, the lake and all that, I thought to myself, 'Oh, I would love to work here!'" She got her wish.

Angie Cobb said the surroundings of the Village add to her upbeat feelings during every single day she works there. A native and lifelong resident of St. Clair County, Mrs. Cobb has been fascinated by her home county's beauty all her life. "Here at the Village the surroundings are just very calming," said Mrs. Cobb. "In going in and out of the Village, it's such a relaxing feeling to see the Red Barn, to look up and see the hills, to look out and see the wildflowers and the woods."

As she discusses the Village with incoming residents and their families, Mrs. Cobb discovers time and again that the Village's surroundings are a real draw. For some city-dwellers, the Village becomes like a retreat, a peaceful vacation place to call home. On the other hand, for some new residents who have grown up in the country, coming to live at the Village is like coming back home.

"We have family members who tell us that the serenity of the Village at Cook Springs is exactly what they've been looking for as a home for their parents," said Mrs. Cobb.

Employee Charlene Tidwell pointed out that this serenity exists not only on the Village property itself but also in the community of Cook Springs and in adjacent communities.

"All around beautiful Cook Springs there are these other small, delightful communities in St. Clair and neighboring counties," said Ms. Tidwell. "Cook Springs has these wonderful neighbors such as the communities of Chula Vista, Moody, Leeds, Odenville, Lincoln, Riverside, Ragland, Margaret, Springville, and Brompton. Even our bigger towns of Pell City and Ashville, our St. Clair county seats, still are small enough to have that small-town feeling. This whole area still has a closeness about it that you can just feel. You don't have to be around long before you're running into somebody you know every time you walk down a street or go into a restaurant.

"If you're driving to or from the Village, you drive through a lot of beautiful countryside, much of which is not yet heavily developed. There are routes you can take on country roads where you see a lot of trees, hills, mountains, flowers and often lakes. It's not like hustle-bustle. It's just an everyday way of life. You see people sitting on their porches talking. You see a man or woman out working in the yard. It's nothing unusual to go by and see a mom and dad sitting in the swing while their children are playing. And there still are these little special country places that make you feel so good. For instance, there's this little place not far from the Village, kind of straight up a mountain, where there's a 'flower pond' — where you can go and cut your own flowers. Every time I see the flower pond I think about my grandmother and all her rows of pretty flowers."

In the eight years Ms. Tidwell has been at the Village, working at the reception desk and later supervising the receptionists and also involved in marketing, she has spent many hours handling phone calls and personal inquires. She is more than happy to answer questions from people who call and ask about the Village and about the community of Cook Springs. "People who don't know about us will call and say things like, 'Now, how large is Cook Springs? Is the Village within the city limits of Cook Springs?' And I say, 'Oh, we *are* the city limits of Cook Springs. The Village is the biggest thing here.' I mean, although the Village is in a rural location, it's a big facility. And it seems even bigger because the community of Cook Springs is so small. When it comes to public places in the community of Cook Springs, the community has this little tiny post office, one general store, one church, a water-authority office, and one big retirement community — the Village at Cook Springs."

When one drives onto the premises of the Village at Cook Springs, he or she is entering a special world all its own, said Ms. Tidwell.

"You drive into the Village and you see our precious sign depicting a country setting. You see our picket fence. You see our big red barn. And you see the nice buildings where our residents live. I've had people say to me, 'Charlene, this doesn't really look like an institution. It doesn't look like a facility.' I say to them, 'We are not like a traditional institution. We

Village at Cook Springs, front entrance, 2006. Right, the lake at Village at Cook Springs, 2006.

are a community.' I think 'the look' of the Village captures people. Also, I know it's not long before 'the feeling' of the Village captures them. Our wonderful sign is so inviting that it might as well be saying, 'Come on in.' When I drive in and see that sign, I feel like I did when I was a little girl and I approached something that was warm and comfortable. When I approach the Village at Cook Springs, I feel like I'm coming home."

Epilogue

For more than four decades after LaFayette Cooke opened his elaborate Cook Springs mineral-springs resort in the early 1880s, that resort property was the site of one festive attraction after another.

Newspaper articles heralded special parties and balls at the Cook's Springs Hotel and its nearby Pavilion. These were merry-making occasions, complete with music and beautiful surroundings and happy guests.

More than 120 years after the opening of that famous resort — during a holiday season in the first decade of the 21st century — the spirit of celebration was still alive in Cook Springs, a little wooded hamlet tucked at the base of mountains in St. Clair County, Alabama.

In a very public way, this same tract of property in Cook Springs that once housed the mineral-springs resort still was drawing scores of visitors. Just as in the 1880s, 1890s, and early 1900s, the 21st-century visitors came to Cook Springs to enjoy a special, spectacular attraction that was the making of lasting memories.

These modern-day visitors came to see a special attraction at the Village at Cook Springs, located on part of the property once owned by LaFayette Cooke, about a half-mile from where the old Cook's Springs Hotel and Pavilion once stood.

The 21st-century attraction was a widely known December holiday display at the Village. During the month of December 2005, the Village's quaint setting was transformed into a holiday winter wonderland of lights and

creative decorations — many of the decorations handmade by the Village's staff, in some instances with the help of family members or friends. The spectacular decorations spread out over the spacious property at the Village, treating visitors to one holiday scene after another.

As had been true with the Cook's Springs Hotel events dating back to the 1880s, news media notices in 2005 heralded the Village's holiday celebration as an attraction worthy of visitors investing time and effort and traveling miles to see. In fact, an article in *The Birmingham News* listed the Village's 2005 display as being among leading holiday attractions that area residents would especially enjoy seeing. And visitors responded favorably to the newspaper's tip.

The unveiling for this 2005 winter wonderland came with the "turning-on-the-lights" ceremony in early December, followed by tours of the decorations. Among the first to tour were some elderly residents who made their home at the Village at Cook Springs — residents from the Village's nursing home and assisted-living facility.

Some of the decorations were whimsical, while others were much more serious. Along the front and sides of the Village, visitors saw a holiday-spirited

Snoopy and his airplane, an endearing version of a now-famous train called "The Polar Express," a traditional gingerbread house, a North Pole scene, a nativity scene, and row after row of colorful garland and lights along the fences on the perimeter of the property. A favorite among the decorations was a stunning display of lights and decorations at the Red Barn, which had been a treasured landmark on the Village property ever since it was built in the 1990s. And, if one ventured inside the buildings of the Village, he or she was treated to even more colorful decorations. This included the Village's exquisitely decorated courtyard, featuring delicately carved reindeer with heads and antlers that moved slowly and gracefully.

Serving as a touching centerpiece for the decorations was a large holiday tree in front of the Village — a tree that the staff had christened as The Memory Tree. Each of the ornaments on that tree was placed there by someone in memory of a special person — a family member, friend, or other loved one. As the weeks wore on in December, more and more ornaments were added to the tree. Some ornaments were placed there by residents at the Village. Some were placed by residents' family members. Others were brought by employees and/or their families. And still others were delivered by visitors who traveled from surrounding communities to see the Village lit up during the holidays, and to add their contributions to The Memory Tree. Time after time, a nostalgic scene was re-enacted in some form or another. Someone would approach the tree on foot, or a vehicle would pull up to the tree and sometimes several people would get out. A beautiful ornament would appear. Someone would attach it to the tree. Each time an additional ornament was put in place, memories rose to the surface. Sometimes the eyes of an ornament-hanger would mist with tears. Too, many nostalgic smiles were seen, as happy memories came back of loved ones being honored by these special ornaments.

And, topping off the Village's spectacular array of decorations was a lighted star big enough to be seen from nearby Interstate 20.

This spirit at the Village that is so apparent to the public at Christmas is reflective of the Village's spirit all year-round, said Carol Moseley Knight, executive director of the Village from 1990 until 1998 and then, effective in

2006, vice president for senior housing for Noland Health Services.

"When we think about Christmas, we tend to think about things that remind us of 'home.' Keep in mind that the Village at Cook Springs generates that warmth and love that we all think about when we think of 'home,'" said Mrs. Knight.

Mrs. Knight said that at Christmas, as is true all year-round, the Village goes that extra mile to create a homey feeling and to give personal attention. She recalled an example that stuck out in her memories: "I remember a Christmas-time back when I was executive director of the Village when we were having this particularly memorable Christmas open house. One of the features was that Santa Claus paid us a visit for this occasion. The staff members brought their children and grandchildren, and we had children from our residents' families, and also children from out in various communities around the Village. Now, let me tell you that for this open house at the Village, Santa had really done his research! Santa knew the names of all our staff, even knew the shifts they worked. Too, Santa knew our residents and their families! And Santa knew so much about the communities near the Village and the people who lived in those communities. One by one, the children got on Santa's knee to tell him what they wanted for Christmas. As Santa spoke with the children, he would refer to their parents or grandparents by name. These children were so impressed that Santa was familiar with their relatives and their world and was making them feel at home at the Village at Cook Springs. Oh, that was such a delightful, meaningful experience."

By December 2005, it had been more than a half-century since the aging Cook's Springs Hotel had been demolished, taking its place as a part of the history of yesteryear. Thus it had been many years since a train had stopped near the entrance of that imposing resort hotel to deliver starry-eyed hotel guests whose eyes opened wide in awe at what they saw.

Still, at Christmas-time and at other times of the year as well, a steady stream of cars, vans and trucks from various communities were arriving at Cook Springs. The drivers were turning off Cook Springs Road at the quaint sign with wording that signaled this was the Village at Cook Springs.

It was the kind of trend that LaFayette Cooke wanted as far back as the 19th century. He loved this beautiful place called Cook Springs — where his dad had been one of the early pioneering residents, where he and his dad both had operated resort facilities. LaFayette Cooke wanted to share Cook Springs with others. His dream was for Cook Springs to be the site of very special institutions that would attract and serve others, to expose more people to the beautiful world of Cook Springs. In the 21st century, with the help of the Village at Cook Springs, the dreams of LaFayette Cooke still are coming true.

Bibliography

Books:

Allen, Lee N., *Born for Missions: Birmingham Baptist Association 1833–1983*. Birmingham, Alabama: Birmingham Baptist Association, 1984.

Crow, Mattie Lou Teague, *The History of St. Clair County*. Huntsville, Alabama: Strode Publishers, 1973.

St. Clair County Heritage Book Committee, *The Heritage of St. Clair County, Alabama*. Clanton, Alabama: Heritage Publishing Consultants, Inc., 1998.

Stewart, Daniel, and Rubye Sisson and Joseph Whitten. *Sparkling Waters: A History of Cook Springs in St. Clair County, Alabama*. Odenville, Alabama: St. Clair Historical Society, 1996.

Sulzby, James F., Jr., *Historic Alabama Hotels and Resorts*. Tuscaloosa, Alabama: University of Alabama Press, 1960.

Genealogical Compilations:

Carreker, John Russell, *Franklin Marion Polk (1829–1922): Farmer, Soldier and Pioneer*. A genealogical compilation by the grandson of subject, 2004.

Libraries and Archives:

Alabama Department of Archives & History
Smithsonian Institution Archives
Tennessee State Library and Archives

Newspaper Archives:

Alabama Baptist, The
Birmingham News, The

Birmingham Post-Herald
Pell City Observer
Pell City News, The
Southern Aegis
St. Clair News-Aegis
St. Clair Observer, The

Newsletters published by the Village at Cook Springs:

The Village Press
Village Life

Acknowledgments

ppreciation goes out to all individuals who shared their memories for this book and to staff members of various institutions who went out of their way to be of assistance.

A special thanks is expressed to representatives of the Ashville Museum & Archives, the Pell City Library, and the St. Clair Historical Society.

For professional services in designing the exterior and interior of the book, a thank you goes to NewSouth Books in Montgomery, Alabama.

Appreciation is expressed to Charlene Tidwell and Brenda Walker of the Village at Cook Springs staff for coordinating the procurement and identification of photographs. A thank you goes to Susan Cole and Lynn Edge for their services in proofreading.

Many of those who contributed information for this history of the Village at Cook Springs actually lived some of the history, and/or their relatives and friends before them lived some of the history. There also are those connected to both the past and the present; they have lived some of the past history of the Village at Cook Springs, and they continue to be a part of history-making events at the Village today.

Thank you all for your interest, for your assistance, and for sharing your precious memories.

About the Author

Anita Smith is a writer of books and articles about health, lifestyle, and history. A former medical editor of *The Birmingham News*, Ms. Smith in recent years has operated a Birmingham-based writing company, Anita Smith and Company, Inc.

Her first book was the story of the late Alabama Governor Lurleen B. Wallace and her battle against cancer. Among her other books are a history of Carraway Health System, a history of the School of Nursing at the University of Alabama at Birmingham, a guidebook on women's health issues (co-written with 13 obstetrics and gynecology specialists), and a book about senior citizens that emphasizes positive aging.

One of Ms. Smith's prior book projects has a connection to this book. That project, published in 1986, was a two-volume set of books entitled *The Lloyd Noland Story*. Those books traced the innovative programs founded by internationally known public health and industrial medicine pioneer Lloyd Noland, M.D. Programs founded by Dr. Noland formed the roots for Noland Health Services, Inc., which operates the Village at Cook Springs that is spotlighted in this book.

Ms. Smith resides in Birmingham with her husband, Jim Lunsford.

Author Anita Smith, shown at 2006 Ms. Springs Manor Pageant at the Village at Cook Springs. Ms. Smith was one of the judges for the pageant. Photo by Joe Paul Abbott.

Index

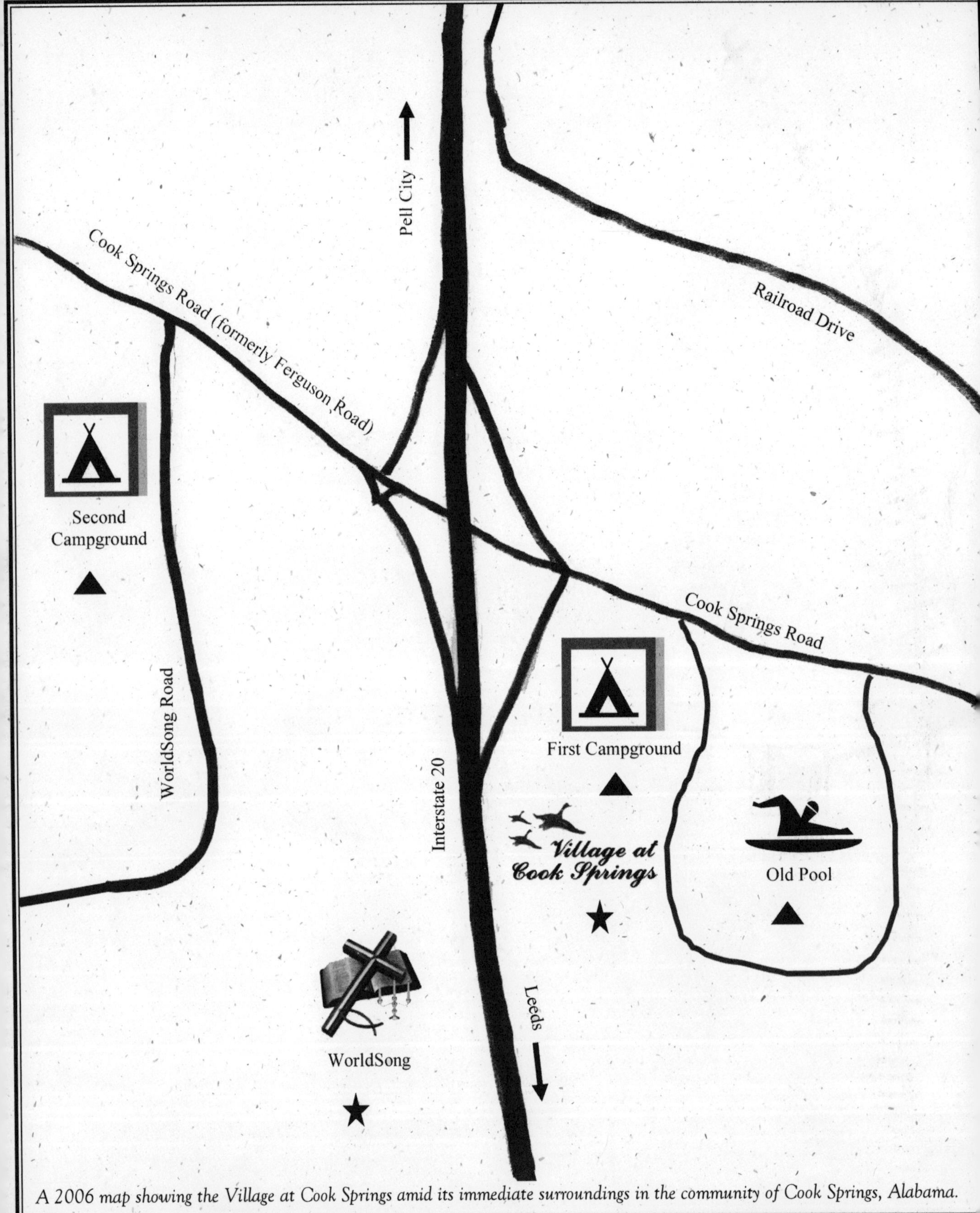

A 2006 map showing the Village at Cook Springs amid its immediate surroundings in the community of Cook Springs, Alabama.